MW00680486

A Postmodern
Nationalist

For Pedro,

To many years of friendship
and collaboration

Um abraço amigo

Phillip

29 December 2004

A Postmodern Nationalist

Truth, Orality, and Gender
in the Work of Mia Couto

Phillip Rothwell

Lewisburg
Bucknell University Press

©2004 by Rosemont Publishing & Printing Corp.

All rights reserved. Authorization to photocopy items for internal or personal use, or the internal or personal use of specific clients, is granted by the copyright owner, provided that a base fee of $10.00, plus eight cents per page, per copy is paid directly to the Copyright Clearance Center, 222 Rosewood Drive, Danvers, Massachusetts 01923.[0-8387–5585–2/04 $10.00 + 8¢ pp, pc.]

Associated University Presses
2010 Eastpark Boulevard
Cranbury, NJ 08512

The paper used in this publication meets the requirements of the American National Standard for Permanence of Paper for Printed Library Materials Z39.48–1984.

Library of Congress Cataloging-in-Publication Data

Rothwell, Phillip, 1972-
A Postmodern nationalist : truth, orality, and gender in the work of
Mia Couto / Phillip Rothwell.
    p. cm.
Includes bibliographical references and index.
ISBN 0-8387-5585-2 (alk. paper)
1. Couto, Mia, 1955—Criticism and interpretation. 2. Couto, Mia,
1955—Political and social views. 3. Mozambique—History—Revolution,
1964-1975. 4. Mozambique—History—Independence and Civil War,
1975-1994. I. Title.
PQ9939.C68Z86 2004
869.3'42—dc22

                                                    2003023400

PRINTED IN THE UNITED STATES OF AMERICA

For my Chinchanito
"because trochaic footings always outrank the postcolony"

Contents

Preface and Acknowledgments

THIS WORK BEGAN LIFE AS A DOCTORAL THESIS UNDERTAKEN WITH GENEROUS support from Trinity College, Cambridge, for which I am grateful. Subsequently, it has undergone profound changes, triggered principally by my rereading of Mia Couto's work. The nature of Couto's texts invites a constant reinterpretation of what we understand by and in them, so that the book you are about to read should be taken as an opening into the world he creates, not a conclusive reading that stakes any kind of definitive or immobilizing claim over it.

Many people have helped me during the completion of this book, and while any errors or shortcomings are entirely my own, I would like to express my deep gratitude to them for their intellectual generosity. First and foremost, I would like to thank Manucha Lisboa for her help and support, and for triggering my interest in lusophone studies. I owe my interest in Mia Couto to Fernanda Angius, who made me feel at home in Mozambique by reading his short stories to me, reclaiming her oral primacy over his written text. Others who have assisted me with perceptive comments at various stages during the production of this manuscript include Helder Macedo, Paul Julian Smith, David Brookshaw, Hilary Owen, Claire Williams, Phyllis Peres, and Ana Mariella Bacigalupo. Margarida Ribeiro has been a source of inspiration and profound knowledge, and her attention to detail and rigorous reading added enormously to the final product. Without Angelique Chrisafis, I would not know how to write. I am grateful to her and to Margo Persin for their encouragement and support. Mary Gossy has been an invaluable font of encyclopedic knowledge at crucial moments. Last and certainly not least, I must express immense gratitude to Yeon-Soo Kim for her powerful and generously shared critical acumen.

Abbreviations of Works Cited

THE CONVENTIONS USED IN THIS BOOK ARE THOSE OF THE CHICAGO MANUAL of Style (Fourteenth Edition). Where possible, I have used David Brookshaw's published translations of Mia Couto's work, and am grateful to him for his permission so to do. In the cases where no translation is available, I provide a translation and cite the original text in brackets. In the cases where I discuss a particular linguistic aspect of Couto's writing, I cite the original work, and am grateful to Caminho publishers in Lisbon for their permission so to do. The following abbreviations, used throughout this book, refer to the editions listed below.

Original Works by Mia Couto:

C	*Cronicando* (Lisboa: Caminho, 1991)
CDNT	*Contos do Nascer da Terra* (Lisboa: Caminho, 1997)
CHER	*Cada Homem É uma Raça* (Lisboa: Caminho, 1990)
EA	*Estórias Abensonhadas* (Lisboa: Caminho, 1994)
MMQ	*Mar Me Quer* (Lisboa: Caminho, 2000)
NBNE	*Na Berma de Nenhuma Estrada* (Lisboa: Caminho, 2001)
TS	*Terra Sonâmbula* (Lisboa: Caminho, 1992)
UVF	*O Ultimo Voo do Flamingo* (Lisboa: Caminho, 2000)
V	*A Varanda do Frangipani* (Lisboa: Caminho, 1996)
VA	*Vozes Anoitecidas* (Lisboa: Caminho, 1987)
VZ	*Vinte e Zinco* (Lisboa: Caminho, 1999)

Translations by David Brookshaw:

EMIR	*Every Man Is a Race* (Oxford: Heinemann, 1994)
UF	*Under the Frangipani* (London: Serpent's Tale, 2001)
VMN	*Voices Made Night* (Oxford: Heinemann, 1990)

A Postmodern
Nationalist

1

Introduction:
A Postmodern Nationalist

IN A WORLD WHERE THE EXECUTIVES OF MULTINATIONAL CORPORATIONS AND aid-agency officials often wield more influence than government ministers over supposedly sovereign states, nationalism and an assertion of national identity is an increasingly weak refuge for those wishing to oppose the inexorable trend toward globalization. Yet it remains, along with religious fundamentalism, one of the principal counterbalances to unfettered neoliberal capitalism in an age that has rejected the socialist experiment. For good or for bad, nationalism invariably operates by putting up barriers to distinguish between the national group and the foreign, making it the perfect ideological opponent to globalization, once class struggle is excluded from the equation. This is due to globalization's overriding desire to facilitate the free movement of capital across frontiers. Globalization wants to dissolve the border, which, as a range of critics have pointed out, culturally allies it with the postmodern project since postmodernism recognizes no boundary and rejects the primacy of binary demarcations.[1]

Postmodernism was used as a term to describe the cultural counterpart of neoliberalism by artists and critics based in New York in the 1960s.[2] A decade later, European commentators began to theorize the term as an attack on the dialectic mode of progression underpinning the philosophies of modernity. In many ways, like poststructuralism, postmodernism as a theory was born through the disaffection of left-wing intellectuals who suffered the disappointment of the uprisings of 1968. The failure of the student and workers' movements to rupture the structures of the state led formerly Marxist-leaning thinkers like Jean-François Lyotard to wholeheartedly celebrate an apolitical culture of consumption that, ironically, would lead to a profound undermin-

15

ing in the structures and sovereignty of individual nation-states, replacing them with the transnational sovereignty of the global market.

Postmodernism, as a political theory, not only targets Marxism's belief in historical progression, but also nationalism's need for a frontier. Lyotard warns in his 1979 treatise, *La Condition Postmoderne,* that the economic system producing postmodern cultural and epistemological practice is "imperiling the stability of the State through new forms of the circulation of capital."[3] In his 1993 *Moralités Postmodernes,* he asserts that "postmodern politics are managerial strategies" designed not with "the aim of delegitimizing the adversary but of constraining it, according to the rules, to negotiate its integration into the system."[4] In this new, all-powerful assimilative system, "national frontiers are mere abstractions."[5]

Gerry Smyth expresses concerns about the "dissolution of the border" as a standard practice in the discourse of what he terms "the postal triumvirate currently dominating the academic intellectual scene," namely poststructuralism, postcolonialism and postmodernism.[6] He problematizes the three related movements' tendency to claim to resist Grand Narratives through hybridity and the rejection of boundaries, since this allies them with the most potent Grand Narrative of our day, what Michael Hardt and Antonio Negri term "Empire." For Negri and Hardt, "Empire" is the moment through which our increasingly globalized world is passing, characterized by a lack of boundaries, a decline in the power of the nation-state accompanied by a rise in the influence of faceless capital, and the postmodern overlap between economics, politics and culture. In fact, postmodernism's attack on the dialectic boundaries of race or gender, while once seen as part of liberation struggles must now be understood to serve this new "Empire." Indeed, Hardt and Negri rightfully assert that "the postmodernist and postcolonialist theorists who advocate the politics of difference, fluidity, and hybridity in order to challenge the binaries of modern sovereignty have been outflanked by the strategies of power."[7] For all are welcome within the boundaries of Empire, "regardless of race, creed, color, gender, sexual orientation."[8] But that very setting aside of difference results in "taking away the potential of the various constituent subjectivities" and is, in effect, a strategy of imposing ignorance to subjugate the individual into accepting the need for global consumption.[9] We all become global subjects, who celebrate an indistinct amalgam of diversity and difference, cross frontiers, and consume.

Given the apparent opposition between nationalism's need for a border, and postmodernism's dissolution of all frontiers, is such a thing as a postmodern nationalist possible in the cultural field? Mia Couto's literary trajectory, as I will discuss in this book, clearly shows that it is. It is one of the central contradictions that straddle his literary personality and, in part, explains the extraordinary success of his work.

Born in Beira, the principal city of the Mozambican province of Sofala, in 1955, António Emílio Leite Couto—more commonly known as Mia Couto—claims that he was once considered the least able among his siblings: the one who promised little. Now the most famous contemporary Mozambican writer, whose work has been translated into eight European languages, he has become the representative of an incipient African national culture for a predominantly Western audience. As David Brookshaw puts it, he has become "an interpreter" of his nation "for the outside world."[10] There are clearly problems associated with this status, not least of which is the reduction of a complex culture to the voice of a single man. A similar elevation has befallen Sembene Ousmane in Senegal, and Ngugi wa Thiong'o in Kenya. Critical responses to their work render their names synonymous with the literary output of their respective countries and eclipse or erase other national writers from the consciousness of a global readership. The case of Mia Couto is further problematized by his racial origin. He is a white writer in a black space. His cultural heritage is unquestionably that of the former colonial power; the ghosts of Portugal's great writers haunt his literary education. Furthermore, his potential readership and thus his intended audience are predominantly external to Mozambique.

Couto's parents arrived in Mozambique in 1953. His father worked for the railways, but soon established himself as a poet and journalist in the then Portuguese colony. For the first two decades of Mia Couto's life, Mozambique was ruled by a regime in Lisbon, known as the *Estado Novo,* or New State, that oppressed its own people as well as those of its colonies. In 1971, Couto went to the capital of Mozambique, then known as Lourenço Marques—later to be renamed Maputo. There, he began a university degree in medicine—a course he left early in 1974 to become a newspaper editor. Couto was conscious from an early age of the iniquity of the political system under which he lived. He was not just an antifascist—like many liberal-minded Portuguese in the colony—he was actively anticolonial, supporting the Frelimo independence movement that opposed the colonial regime.[11] This explains the ease with which he assumed a new nationality after Mozambican independence. While many in the Portuguese community left after 1975, the year the nation gained independence, for a variety of complex reasons—not least of which was a sense of insecurity—Couto embraced Mozambican citizenship. He became the head of the Mozambican News Agency in 1978. In 1985, he returned to university, this time to complete a degree in biology. Subsequently, he has established a national reputation for his research and work in the field of ecology. Internationally, his reputation has been cemented as an outstanding writer who is often read to give voice to his young nation.

He is, without doubt, the most prolific writer from Mozambique at the current time. His books invariably hit the best-seller lists around the luso-phone world on publication. In part, his global success is due to a lucky break early in his literary career, when his first book of short stories was republished by one of Portugal's leading publishing houses, Caminho. In fact, the first book released in his name was a collection of poetry titled *Raiz de Orvalho* [Root of Dew], in 1983, which focuses on structuring and explaining per-sonal subjectivities.[12] It does not deal much with national identity and, inter-estingly, as Fernanda Angius has pointed out, there is little evidence of the lexical games that would become the hallmark of his later work.[13] In 1986, he published *Vozes Anoitecidas* [Voices Made Night], which Caminho re-launched in Lisbon the following year, and which David Brookshaw trans-lated into English in 1990.[14] The collection won the Mozambican Writers Association National Prize for Literature in 1991, and quickly established Couto as a writer who plays with the limits of the Portuguese language. The tone of most of the stories in the collection is quite pessimistic, and reflects the dire political situation through which the newly independent nation of Mozambique labored at the time. As I shall argue later, Couto's project then was to dissolve the frontier between the unconscious and conscious realms the country's civil conflict had blocked.

Couto's second and third collections of short stories, *Cada Homem É Uma Raça* [Every Man Is a Race] and *Cronicando* [Chronicling] continued to establish his reputation as a writer who poetically recast the Portuguese lan-guage, coloring it with the hue of Mozambique, a perfect lusophone example of what Salman Rushdie describes as the empire writing back to the center with a vengeance, or what Homi Bhabha discusses as the menace of mimicry.[15] Critics of Couto's work made sweeping claims for his primary sta-tus as a renovator of the Portuguese language.[16] Their principal concern seems to be to establish that Couto serves what Portugal's most important mod-ernist poet, Fernando Pessoa, famously terms the "língua-pátria," or the lan-guage-as-homeland. As we shall discuss later, there are a range of problems associated with the politics of the Portuguese language and, at the same time, with any desire on the part of Mozambique to reclaim a language other than Portuguese.

For the purpose of the present discussion, Couto's supposed employment as an agent of the Portuguese language-as-homeland, however postcolonially critics may position him, always hints at the emergence of Hardt and Negri's concept of "Empire." Indeed, Pessoa envisages the replacement of direct political and economic colonialism with an empire based on culture.[17] By pushing a transnational lusophone identity, and claiming that Couto crosses the boundaries of the Portuguese language, in the process enriching that global identity, critics are turning the author into a postmodern, frontier-bashing, commodity, which assures the importance of their own critical discourses and detracts from Couto's role as a forger of a distinct Mozambican identity. Paradoxically, Couto is then fetishized as the mediator of his nation's culture "to the outside world."

By concentrating on his role as a linguistic renovator, many critics of Couto's work have hitherto failed to realize how the author diegetically plays with the concepts behind postmodernism, principally the dissolution of binary frontiers, to critique the various political systems that have been grafted onto his nation from the outside. As one of my readings of his first novel, *Terra Sonâmbula* [Sleepwalking Land], (1992) will show, Couto profoundly interrogates the distinction between orality and the script and, in the process, destabilizes both the Platonic and Hegelian competing traditions of Western orthodoxy.[18] Furthermore, I will suggest that Couto foregrounds the letter as an obvious, yet often overlooked, example of orality infiltrating what Michel de Certeau terms the "scriptural economy."[19] In his blurring of the distinction between orality and the script, Couto forms a strategic alliance with Derrida's brand of poststructuralism, but on his own terms because, as my readings of Couto's texts will show, his project gainsays the apolitical nature of poststructuralism and impels his characters to dream alternative realities.

Couto's 1996 collection of short stories, *Estórias Abensonhadas,* is his work that assaults the gender frontier most acutely.[20] Its title is a pun that fuses the Portuguese words for dreamt and blessed into an epithet attached to the term for stories. By rendering patent what Judith Butler has shown to be the performative quality of gender, Couto destabilizes the patriarchal model of colonialism and interrogates the praxis of scientific socialism that affected Mozambican society at distinct periods during its history.[21] Couto's use of gender play is not merely a case of celebrating diversity. Specifically, he attaches the disruption of gender normativity to a parallel collapse in the basis for racism, or to moments of profound change in the nation's psyche.

Also in 1996, Couto published his second novel, *A Varanda do Frangipani,* which David Brookshaw translated in 2001 as *Under the Frangipani.*[22] It provides a clear example of Couto's challenge to the concept of a unitary truth. He ruptures the central premise of all but postmodern ideologies that depend on the search for a locatable truth. In the process, he fashions a syn-

cretistic identity for his nation that both rests on and refutes a return to ancestral values.

Couto's subsequent collections of short stories, *Contos do Nascer da Terra*
[Tales from the Birth of the Earth] (1997) and *Na Berma de Nenhuma
Estrada* [At the Side of No Road] (2001), and his 1998 novella published as
part of the Lisbon Expo, *Mar Me Quer,* the title of which is a pun I will discuss later, repeat and refine many of his earlier concerns that question the
primacy of the frontiers we inherit, and seek to restore his nation's right to
dream.[23] Throughout his work, he has felt the need to assert his own identity
as a "being from the border" [um ser de fronteira], something he attributes to
his complicated position as white born in Africa, who can only describe his
Africanness along "European lines" [linhas europeias].[24] At the same time, his
complex identity extends to cover the nation he chose at the end of the colonial era as his own, if only because of the way in which he is read outside
Mozambique, as an "interpreter" of that nation's identity.

His powerful 1999 novel, *Vinte e Zinco,* the punning title of which I will
also discuss later, attacks both the assumptions of colonialism, and those
who would replace it by reversing the Manichean order.[25] His novel provides
an instance of the techniques of postmodernism being deployed in what
Hardt and Negri term a "liberatory" strategy. They point out that postmodernism is only effective as such a strategy "in a context where power poses hierarchy exclusively through essential identities, binary divisions, and stable
oppositions," and furthermore, "the structures and logics of power in the
contemporary world are entirely immune to the "liberatory" weapons of the
postmodernist politics of difference."[26] Hardt and Negri's assertion is valid,
as is Couto's use of postmodern techniques to oppose colonialism and scientific socialism. However, a radical change of tact by Couto can be observed
in his 2000 novel, *O Último Voo do Flamingo* [The Flamingo's Last Flight],
which is a devastating critique of the principal agents of "Empire" in
Mozambique today, namely the United Nations and the plethora of NGOs
who have created a culture of dependency and assured the neocolonization
of the young nation.[27] Couto's fourth novel represents a significant departure
from his previous work, as he focuses his attention toward Mozambique's recent loss of sovereignty as it becomes integrated into the power structures of
global capitalism. Up until that novel, Couto had used the strategies of postmodernism to critique the colonial and Marxist paradigms foisted on
Mozambique from the outside. Following the adoption of free-market policies by the Frelimo government, and the country's effective invasion by the
forces of the United Nations that we will discuss, Couto identified the polit-

ical allies of the postmodern project, the forces of "Empire," as the principal agents that are robbing his nation of its cultural values and its independent identity. Postmodernism has become the only remaining Grand Narrative worth critiquing.

Throughout this study, I will draw on aspects of Mozambican political and cultural history, when they help to illuminate Couto's writing. In order to understand why Couto's dissolution of frontiers prevalent in most of his work is so radical, the historical interventions of Europe in Mozambique must be read as a series of impositions of rigidity. The Mozambican nation is, to a considerable extent, a product of European colonial interference in Africa. The Portuguese arrived at the end of the fifteenth century and ruled erratically for the next five hundred years. The nation's frontiers were effectively decided shortly after the Berlin Conference of the colonial powers called in 1884. At the time, Portugal realized that if it wanted to be a serious player on the imperial stage, it would have to administer its colonial house differently, and reluctantly accepted the doctrine of "effective occupation" over "historical precedence" as the determinant of colonial possession. This led to Portugal adopting an enormous charter system in Mozambique, through which it aspired to govern its large South East African territory. Foreign-owned private companies were given jurisdiction over large regions in return for payments and the promise to administer those areas in the name of the metropolis. The system was prone to abuses, and failed to stimulate much development in the zones where it operated. However, it did clearly define frontiers of jurisdiction, and imposed a racial hierarchy. By the time António de Oliveira Salazar rose to power as the de facto dictator of Portugal in 1928, the seeds of discontent had already been sown in many parts of Mozambique, seeds that would later lead to the war for independence.

Salazar, who never set foot in Africa, replaced the charter system with a racist bureaucracy underpinned by a colonial code (1930) and a new constitution (1933). His system was highly regimental, and based on the belief that intransigent categorization fostered order and harmony. There was a separate set of laws for Africans, who could apply to become "assimilated" as Portuguese citizens by passing a series of demeaning tests that many white Portuguese would themselves have failed. Very few blacks attained the status. Many, particularly from the south of the country, were exported as labor to neighboring countries, as a means of bolstering Lisbon's gold reserves.

Portugal's response to the trend identified in the British Prime Minister Harold Macmillan's "Winds of Change" speech was the replacement of the word colony by the term "overseas province." In the aftermath of the Second World War and with the creation of the United Nations, direct colonialism was no longer in vogue, and international pressure against direct colonial practice grew alongside increasing tensions and demands for independence from within African colonies. Independence movements became prominent across the continent, and the largest colonial power in Africa, Britain, made plans to exit on the most beneficial terms possible for itself. In Mozambique, anticolonial sentiment was also growing, and in 1962 Eduardo Mondlane, a United Nations employee with an American wife, founded Frelimo, a movement committed to independence.

Salazar's intransigence was unabated by the outbreak of war in the African colonies. Indeed, his reaction was to increase his patriotic rhetoric and send thousands of Portuguese conscripts to their deaths. Frelimo launched its campaign from Tanzania, and made some inroads into the north of Mozambique. In 1969, Eduardo Mondlane was assassinated in Dar-es-Salam. His successor as leader of the movement was the head of the military wing, Samora Machel. Both men were from the south of Mozambique, as is the current president of the country, Joaquim Chissano. This has often led to the charge that Frelimo is a movement dominated by a relatively sparsely populated area of Mozambique.

Salazar had ended what had hitherto been an isolationist stance on the international stage by joining NATO in 1949. The Azores were of strategic importance to the alliance whose membership were less vocal in their criticism of Portugal's continued colonialism than their rhetoric on the defense of freedom dictated it should be. Frelimo viewed NATO's silence and the logistic support some of its membership furnished to Portugal with increasing dismay and naturally, in the era of the Cold War, turned to the communist bloc for moral and practical support in its struggle for independence. The extent to which Eduardo Mondlane intended Frelimo to lean toward scientific socialism is a moot point. His successor, however, viewed Marxist Leninism as the only appropriate path for his movement and his nation to follow.

The liberation struggles in the African colonies drained Portugal's human and economic resources. Elements in the military were increasingly discontent with the political establishment's hard-line, all-sacrificing attitude. Salazar's incapacitation in 1968 heralded the undelivered promise of Marcello Caetano's leadership. Essentially, he continued Salazar's colonial policy, and insisted on the rigorous prosecution of the war in Africa. The result of this policy was the Carnation Revolution that swept his regime from power on 25 April 1974 in a bloodless cue organized by war-weary sections of the military. Postrevolutionary Portugal relinquished its claims to the colonies, and initiated talks for the independence of its African territories. A little over a year later, on 25 June 1975, Samora Machel became the first president of the Republic of Mozambique.

The early years of the Frelimo government were characterized by optimism, massive investment in the health and education sectors, and the overarching presence of the president. A large proportion of the Portuguese community that had settled in Mozambique and, given the appropriate assurances, may have stayed, fled with their expertise in fear for their lives. In retrospect, Samora Machel's presidency was a disaster for his country. Although justifiably a heroic figure, with a clear and equitable vision of what he wanted his nation to become, Machel's disregard for the exigencies of international politics and local traditions, and his ruthless obstinacy in dealing with unsavory opponents were factors that led to the rise of Renamo and plunged Mozambique into a particularly vicious civil war. The government vehemently discouraged any show of tribal identity, adopting Portuguese as the language of national unity. Additionally, whole communities that had lived for centuries in rural backwaters were compulsorily relocated to farming villages "for their own good." In fact, nearly two million Mozambicans were affected by this policy, which was uncomfortably similar to a tactic used by the Portuguese colonial regime in its dying days to maintain control over the rural population.[28] Frelimo explained villagization as a tool to prevent loss of life in the event of the cyclical flooding that occurs in parts of the country, and as a more efficient way of producing food for the needs of the proletariat. Unfortunately, it rode roughshod over local customs, and was a new way in which European ideologies targeted indigenous practice, and were inflexibly applied.

During the early years of the Frelimo government, two of Mozambique's neighbors, Rhodesia and South Africa, maintained racist systems of governance. The new government of Mozambique, which had benefited from the practical support of Tanzania during its war for liberation, gave its full support to groups opposing the racist administrations of its neighbors. At the same time, Machel dealt savagely with his own political opponents, particularly those he deemed to be corrupt or to exploit tribal tensions. There is evidence that some elements in the Rhodesian secret services decided to destabilize the Mozambican government by facilitating the creation of an opposition movement, constituted by disaffected Mozambicans. Thus was born what would later become Renamo. With the overthrow of Ian Smith's regime and the birth of Zimbabwe in 1980, South Africa became Renamo's principal backer, and fomented a low intensity armed conflict that worsened through the decade, and was replete with horrific atrocities attributed to the rebel movement. The nation's resources were severely drained, and many of its people terrorized. The optimism of the early years ceded to a seemingly intractable armed conflict, a needless loss of life, and the country's bankruptcy. A huge number of people were internally displaced by the war, or became refugees in neighboring countries, unsettling the whole region. At one point, over 10 percent of Malawi's population was constituted by Mozambican refugees.

In 1986, Samora Machel was killed in a mysterious plane crash. His death, though tragic, in some ways removed one of the main obstacles to a negotiated settlement to the civil war. His successor was the far more diplomatic Joaquim Chissano, who had previously served his country as a polyglot foreign minister. It took another six years before peace accords were finally signed, and two years later, in 1994, Mozambique became a much-flaunted UN success story, as the international agency oversaw the first multiparty elections in the nation's history, and the election of Joaquim Chissano to serve as the president of the newly pluralistic republic. A very surprising aspect of those elections, and also the subsequent elections five years later, was the high level of support enjoyed by Renamo and its leader Afonso Dhlakama. The impression the outside world received of the rebel movement was always tainted by the horrific atrocities it perpetrated. There was an implicit assumption in many of the commentaries about Renamo that the group was a terrorist organization that was externally inspired and devoid of popular support within Mozambique. Yet the election results demonstrated astoundingly high levels of support for Renamo particularly in the more densely populated provinces of the north and central regions. These results revealed, among other things, dissatisfaction with the Frelimo government, and also the complex identity of the Mozambican nation. Not every Mozambican had subscribed to Frelimo's utopia.

Mozambique is an ethnically diverse country. Within its frontiers, a range of religions, from Islam to Catholicism, is practiced and a myriad of languages spoken. Estimates of the degree of coverage of the national language vary widely, but the official census statistics from the 1990s assert that at most 40 percent of the population has any knowledge of Portuguese, and less than 7 percent consider it to be their mother tongue. Yet, as both Russell Hamilton and Benedict Anderson have pointed out, Portuguese is the language through which Mozambique is imagined.[29] Couto has been instrumental in the creation of that imagination. As we will discuss in this book, his writing is often read to capture the oral nature of Mozambique. This rather romantic view of Couto's agenda turns him into a very safe example of

"Mozambicanness" that lusophone intellectuals outside Africa can admire. Critiques based entirely on the reinvigoration of the Portuguese language interrogate very little and comfortably situate Couto in Fernando Pessoa's language-as-homeland. In such a space, Mozambique becomes mediated through a European filter: a language that even today, over two decades after the aggressive promotion of Portuguese by the Frelimo government, is not spoken by the majority of the Mozambican people.

In reality, Couto is much more radical than many critics have hitherto realized. He undoubtedly contributes to the creation of a Mozambican national imaginary, particularly for consumption outside Mozambique. But as a white with Portuguese heritage, he chooses to subvert and exploit European paradigms in order to fashion a complexity analogous to that of his nation. His texts challenge the monism of the early years of the Frelimo regime as much as they rebuke colonialism. The resulting identity is one that floats, defying fixation and allowing for a multiplicity of reinterpretations and reinscriptions. Couto's radicalism resides in his ability to transform a European heritage into an identity that respects diversity and exiles dogma. His technique strategically exploits and distorts, and leads to the most compelling and idiosyncratic depiction of his nation. He avoids an Afro-atavism, which given his contradictory status as a white writer in a black nation could never go beyond the exoticization of indigenous myths. Yet he skillfully uses such myths to debunk Western certainties, as my readings of such stories as "O Dia em que Explodiu Mabata-bata" and "Lenda de Namarói" will demonstrate. His central preoccupation is never to leave a duality intact. Whether it be the distinction between truth and falsehood, writing and orality, the conscious and unconscious, or the polar genders—all of which we will discuss—Couto disavows demarcation, the founding premise of the Platonic universe and Aristotelian categorization. The deliquescence of boundaries in his work proscribes interdiction, and is based on his belief that "anything is possible" [pode tudo].[30]

While Couto's critical acclaim privileges him among his nation's authors, he is not the first, nor the only Mozambican writer. Patrick Chabal regards three writers, Rui de Noronha (1909–1943), João Dias (1926–1949) and Augusto de Conrado (b. 1904) as the precursors of Mozambican literature.[31] Noronha, whose posthumously published sonnets are more important as a political statement than for their literary quality was a mulatto of African and Indian origins. Conrado was a black who published poetry in the 1930s and 1940s, and Dias, the author of the collection of short stories *Godido e Outros*

Contos [Godido and Other Stories] (1952), is considered by Chabal to be "Mozambique's first African modern prose writer."[32] The other famous black Mozambican prose writer from the preindependence period is Luís Bernardo Honwana (b. 1942), a postindependence Minister of Culture, whose *Nós Matámos o Cão Tinhoso* (1964) [We Killed the Mangy Dog] lays bear the iniquities of colonial racism.

For many years, poetry was the principal genre employed by Mozambican writers. During the independence struggle, a brand of militant verse predominated, often written by Frelimo cadres such as Marcelino dos Santos (b. 1929) and Armando Guebuza (b. 1935). Like the work of Noronha, their verse was more important for the political statement it makes than for its literary virtuosity. However, at least one poet from this period, José Craveirinha (1922–2003), is an exception to the rule. Both in terms of quality and quantity, Craveirinha towers over his contemporaries. The winner of the most prestigious literary prize for lusophone literature, the "Prémio Camões," Craveirinha's poetry was, prior to independence, politically militant and steeped in social realism. A mulatto, he foregrounds the syncretistic nature of Mozambican culture, adulterating his Portuguese verse with hues from the Ronga language of his mother. More recently, his work has revealed a profoundly lyrical quality and demonstrates an ability to fashion the Portuguese language shared by Mia Couto.

The classification of a writer as Mozambican, particularly when their racial and cultural heritage is that of Europe, has, at various points in the nation's postindependence era, been steeped in controversy. The most famous example is the debate surrounding Rui Knopfli's (1932–1997) inclusion in the Mozambican literary canon. His departure from Mozambique prior to independence, and his refusal to subscribe to Frelimo's vision for his country of birth, led other writers whose work is included in the canon such as Rui Nogar (b. 1933) and Orlando Mendes (1916–1990) to question whether he is a Mozambican poet.[33] The debate surrounding the nationality of his writing is stale, and riddled with racial hypocrisy since no one suggests, for example, that Noémia de Sousa (1926–2002) was anything but Mozambican, despite the fact that she wrote much less, and also left Mozambique. However, her skin-pigmentation was darker. The interesting part of the Knopfli debate is the manner in which a writer's nationality can be determined by his or her critical readership, particularly when Mia Couto's meteoric rise, despite his racial origins, to the status of the national writer of Mozambique is considered. In many ways, writers are captives of their readers. However hard Couto may wish to be read as an individual, his work is increasingly understood as an interpretation of Mozambique "for the outside world."

Despite the controversy surrounding Knopfli, he was an important influence on several postindependence Mozambican writers, including Couto, and, pertinently, given my own argument regarding Couto's work, Francisco Noa situates Knopfli as a postmodern poet.[34] In the postindependence era, the short story has become the principal genre employed by Mozambican writers. Nelson Saúte's recent anthology of Mozambican short stories includes work by thirty-four writers, a testament to the popularity of the genre.[35] The most important contemporary prose writers include Ungulani Ba Ka Khosa (b. 1957), whose *Ualalapi* (1987) critiques structures of power through a portrayal of the downfall of Gungunhana, an African emperor defeated by the Portuguese, and Lília Momplé (b. 1935), whose literary trajectory has developed from an interrogation of colonialism into a damning portrayal of post-independence corruption.[36] Paulina Chiziane (b. 1955) and Suleiman Cassamo (b. 1962) both share the same publisher as Couto, Caminho, a great advantage in the dissemination of their work, which is simultaneously problematic for its neocolonial overtones, since an agency in the former metropolis still mediates a product from the former colony and, in large part, determines its success or failure.[37]

Couto is a prose writer who began his literary life as a poet. His poetic affinity to language has never deserted him, and the innovative quality of his writing is a constant delight. However, the time has arrived to extend the debate about his writing beyond the question of language. As I will show in this book, the issues his work raises are too radical to be ignored in often-repeated assertions about his style. In the next chapter, I will locate Couto as a postmodern abolitionist of philosophical truth. Drawing on Nietzsche, I demonstrate how one of Couto's novels reevaluates the moral charge of falsehood, and posits the fictionalization of history as an essential component of any quest for the truth.

In the third chapter, I will give some historical background surrounding the political charge of orthography and literacy in Mozambique. This will serve as the basis for reading one of Couto's texts that raises these issues, and gainsays the possibility of returning to a solidly grounded African past.

In the fourth chapter, I interrogate the notion of orality in Couto's writing. I venture to suggest that Couto's treatment of the distinction between the written and the oral aligns him with the poststructural project, but from a politicized perspective.

In the fifth chapter, I link together the varied and multiple interpretations of the sea and water, from universal and lusophone culture, as a way of understanding Couto's depiction of the breach between the conscious and unconscious realms. The colonial and neocolonial resonance of the sea, together with the primordial and oneiric aspect of water, infiltrate Couto's writing, and allow him to traverse the frontier between harsh reality and the necessary imagination of a better future.

In the sixth chapter, I turn my attention to the gender frontier. I suggest that Couto uses a rupturing in gender orthodoxy to undermine patriarchal and racist assumptions that operate through the imposition of rigid and arbitrary binaries.

In the final chapter, I demonstrate how Couto's later writing has begun to savage the agents of "Empire," and the postmodern project itself. Throughout this book, I argue that Couto has always demonstrated an awareness of Portuguese and, more generally, Western influence on his work. Rather than recusing such influence, he understands and then distorts it. He disrupts the paradigms of Western orthodoxy as he fashions a Mozambican identity by turning European epistemology into a raw, repackageable material. Couto's propensity to dissolve boundaries will become apparent, particularly those frontiers that enforce the demarcations of Western tradition. The resultant identity he writes is premised on fluidity, and challenges the rigidity of the systems, both colonial and Marxist, imported from Europe that have dominated Mozambique for most of its history. In the later phase of his writing, his disavowal of the postmodern project, through an attack on the International Community's invasion of Mozambican sovereignty, logically completes the postmodern and nationalist strands in his work. He can justifiably be termed a postmodern nationalist.

2

Li(v)es, Li(v)es, Li(v)es:
The Link Between Truth and Death
in Mia Couto

THE SEARCH FOR A UNIFYING AND UNITARY TRUTH WAS THE PREOCCUPATION of diverse Western philosophical schools from the time of Plato until Nietzsche laid the groundwork for the postmodern era. Precisely what the truth is can never be known, if it is understood to mean the point at which all falsehood ceases. The more one interrogates the notion, the less probable its realization becomes. Yet this abstract concept forms the basis for a range of religions, epistemologies and political systems, and underpinned colonial ideologies that held their hierarchies to be self-evidently correct and just. In postindependence Mozambique, the dogma of the Frelimo government—based on a rhetorical fusion of scientific socialism and unifying nationalism—presupposed a totalizing truth that could logically account for all actions and situations in morally charged binary terms, and which sought to banish the multiple perspectives on reality that Mozambique's complex, cultural syncretism offers.

The relativization of a unified truth surfaced in the modern era through the work of Nietzsche and the poststructuralism that his writing triggered. Poststructuralism, the ally of postmodernism in the field of the philosophy of language, sought to remove the central tenet of religious, political, and epistemological systems by foregrounding the obfuscating influence of language—what Derrida terms its play. In a lusophone context, Fernando Pessoa, Portugal's most important twentieth-century poet, read at his most radical, questions the singularity of truth through the fabrication of his heteronyms, a multiplicity of personalities under whose signatures he wrote. Pessoa often self-consciously uses language to hide and fragment rather than to clarify and unify. One of his most famous poems, "Autopsicografia" [Autopsychography], begins with the declaration, "the poet is a faker" [o poeta é um fingidor], and then plays with the concept of poetry, for which we can understand language, falsifying to such a degree that the distinction between what is true and false ceases to operate.[1]

Mia Couto draws on, and further radicalizes aspects of this Pessoan tradition, as a means of fashioning a national identity that is more appropriate to the reality of Mozambique than the models of colonialism and socialism previously offered. He privileges linguistic innovation and word play in such a way that meaning can never be absolute in his texts. Instead, it is always subject to multiple interpretations and shifting perspectives. His idiosyncratic articulation of the former colonial language denies the possibility of any fixation—the *sine qua non* of systems driven by an uncompromising belief in truth. Moreover, Couto's challenge to the concept of truth contaminates his writing at a diegetic level, as can be seen in *A Varanda do Frangipani,* his second novel, in which the author demonstrates the instabilities inherent in the search for truth, and the aporia implicit in seeking to immobilize its constant transmogrifications.

Truth masquerades under a variety of names, the most prevalent of which in Western culture has been god. But, as Nietzsche shows, once the inviolability of the divine is breached, a whole range of binary concepts begins to disintegrate. Even in the self-proclaimed atheistic model of scientific socialism under which postindependence Mozambique labored, dogma occupied that sanctified space that rescinds free thought and attempts to reduce the number of possible explanations for any phenomenon to a unified truth. As David Brookshaw observes, there was a marked shift in the literary portrayal of "truth" in 1990s lusophone Africa. In the period following independence, the cultural output of the former colonies "was dominated by the ideological convictions of the new revolutionary regimes."[2] "Truth," he continues, "was therefore unitary rather than 'federal,' as was the utopian nation state in formation, whose identity and history literature sought to evoke." However, by the beginning of the last decade of the twentieth century, "the weakness of a superimposed unitary view of reality" had been recognized by the continent's foremost lusophone authors, including Mia Couto.[3] Their work reflected a more complex reality in which heterogeneity reigned supreme and the notion of a dogmatic, single, and absolute truth became fragmented. This fragmentation offers very unstable grounds for the creation of a fixed identity, turning the Mozambique Couto culturally inscribes into an identity-in-progress that can never be definitively rendered without destroying its essence.

Couto's relativistic treatment of truth follows Nietzsche's paradigm that inextricably associates the concept with death. "Could it be possible!" asks the German philosopher's character Zarathustra in a tone of marked incredulity, "this old saint has not yet heard in his forest that *God is dead!*"[4] Zarathustra's disbelief is provoked not by divine mortality, and hence the abolition of the central bulwark of truth, but by the fact that someone still exists who places blind faith in an abstract thought "that makes all that is straight crooked and all that stands giddy."[5] Shortly after this encounter, the demise of the deity claims its first logical casualty, Lucifer's scalp, as Zarathustra meets a sinner being dragged down to Hades. He tells the fallen man, "all you have spoken of does not exist: there is no Devil and no Hell."[6] What remains after these related disavowals is a state of constant flux in which "unchanging good and evil does not exist."[7] The assurance of these fixed polar opposites is thus forfeited at the altar of relativity. This sacrifice has consequences beyond the ontotheological since it is extrapolated by Nietzsche to disclose the fallacy of every morally static binary. Values are subject to variation since "all that is intransitory—that is but an image."[8] The removal of truth's privilege allows for identity to become a flux.

The search for the truth, which is a standard philosophical preoccupation mirrored in theological practice, hinges on the recognition and immediate banishment of falsehood, thus depending for its meaning, exclusively and excludingly, on the concept of what it is not. But this very concept of falsehood, feeding as it does into what is established to be its opposite, is never erased and always impinges on the domain of the truth, through reference and reversals. Today's truth is believed to be false tomorrow. In fact, for Nietzsche, the excluded concept becomes the more real, or at least the more life-giving, because his project is, in part, "to recognize untruth as a condition of life."[9] So, while death is associated with the location of an inflexible truth and a fantasized god, life is linked to lies, which is precisely the lesson that Couto offers in *A Varanda do Frangipani* [Under the Frangipani].

Published in 1996 after the first multiparty elections in Mozambique's history had taken place, *A Varanda do Frangipani* is at some levels a reflection on what the civil war had done to the nation. The war was fought in the name of ideological truths, at least that is the rhetoric that both sides used to sanction their actions. Renamo claimed to be fighting in the name of democracy, while Frelimo in the name of socialism. In the words of Marta, the mulatto nurse, "the war's to blame for everything . . . We start saying: 'before the war, after the war.' War swallows up the dead and devours its survivors" (*UF,* 123). War—the bringer of death—overwrites Christ—the deity-bringer of life—as the fixed reference point around which time is measured. Death and the deity are thus conceptually linked. In fact, death is the center, or rather, the cycle of the novel. The story begins with the line "I am the dead man" and ends "from now on, my slumber will be deeper than death itself" (150). The plot centers on the investigation of a death, by someone who the reader is told has only six days to live. But Couto's definition of death is far from definitive and, as will now be discussed, is inextricably linked to the concept of truth. For every truth revealed, a false nature is in due course rendered patent. If truth is an end, then it is The End, for life relies on lies.

The plot is set in a remote old people's home whose director, Vasto Excelêncio, has died in mysterious circumstances. Izidine Naíta is sent from Maputo to investigate—so the reader assumes. Without his knowledge, the spirit of Ermelindo Mucanga, a dead carpenter buried under a frangipani tree in the grounds of the home, enters his body and becomes one of the many prisms through which the narrative is related. The manner in which this occurrence is presented—as if it were nothing out of the ordinary—is stylistically reminiscent of magical realism, a form Couto often emulates.[10] Pertinently, given my argument that Couto uses postmodern tropes in his writing, magical realism, according to Wendy Faris, is "an important component of postmodernism."[11] In many respects, the two trends have fed into each other, while often retaining a demarcation based on the geographical provenance of the works to which they refer. As Theo D'Haen points out, over the periods in which postmodernism and magical realism gained their present meanings, they were terms applied respectively to texts from the North and the South.[12] The reason I cast Couto primarily as a postmodernist rather than an exponent of magical realism is due to his obsession for blurring frontiers, the overriding characteristic assigned to postmodernism.

In *A Varanda do Frangipani*, Couto forces truth to relinquish its boundaries. The various residents of the home all claim to have murdered Vasto, an apparently unpopular and brutal mulatto. Izidine's mission is to establish the truth, an enterprise whose premises are constantly undermined by a counter-discourse, which assails the novel, and which, grounding itself on the Liar's Paradox—that if everything is false, so is this statement—attests to an order of things in which all truths are shifting illusions. As Carmen Ribeiro Secco has pointed out, the trajectory of *A Varanda do Frangipani* subverts the traditional detective novel genre since Couto replaces the establishment of a truth with the dominance of a carefully crafted tissue of lies.[13] The old people left in the home lie on a boundary between truth and falsehood, life and death, past and future, and age and youth—literally so, in the character of Navaia Caetano who "grew old the moment he was born" (*UF*, 22). They ostensibly lament the loss of "the last surviving roots that might have prevented us be-coming like . . . people without history, people who live by imitation" (54). Yet, by their actions, they preclude the possibility of a fixed history in the conventional meaning of the word because they uproot all certainties. For them, history is not a series of objective facts that can be related by impartial repetition, it is a set of shifting perspectives and stories that must never be al-lowed to end. The storyteller is organically linked to the tale. Indeed, the book in which Izidine writes down all the testimonies of the old people, forming the body of the text, will rot alongside the remains of Mucanga, the principal narrator.

The case of Navaia, the *criança-velha,* or elderly child, parallels this pro-cess. Should the story he tells ever reach an end, it would be his end. His only way of avoiding death is to lie—continually to create a new truth. He tells Izidine, "I'm forbidden to tell my own story. When I finish my tale, I shall be dead" (22). In the Portuguese original, Couto plays with the fact that the same word, "história," connotes the concept of story and history (*V,* 28). In fact, for Couto, history is just another story. The *criança-velha's* survival tech-nique is thus grounded on making sure that histories are always "made up" (*UF,* 23) [inventadas (*V,* 29)].

The fallacy of a fixed truth becomes apparent at several levels within the novel. If truth re-lies on tradition, the loss of a truth presupposes the ques-tioning of the tradition that has enabled that truth. A process of rigorous de-racination unsettles the text at the level of the thematic, syntactic, and semantic, but it is a process that is always marked by being grounded on the tradition it relativizes. Couto's hallmark use of linguistic tropes has already been much discussed by critics.[14] Once again, in *A Varanda do Frangipani,* the destabilization of language through neologisms, syntax distortions, and the use of code-switching is present—an endeixis of flux in meaning, which challenges the concept of a correct form. Couto's creative manipulation of the Portuguese language exploits its roots while questioning the totality of their primacy. As he takes individual words apart and reconstructs them in novel ways, he demonstrates the structural instabilities that allow language to communicate something but never a single thing. At the same time, he shows the extent to which he needs those roots in order to construct his chal-lenge to the very same roots. Without his affinity for the Portuguese language and its literary traditions, his rupturing of it would not work.

At a diegetic level, there is a case to be made for an afro-atavistic reading of *A Varanda do Frangipani,* which would sustain that Couto favors a return to an African past. As we shall see later when we discuss the role of the United Nations in Mozambique, Couto in part reclaims an African past in his novel published in 2000, *O Último Voo do Flamingo*. But *A Varanda do Frangipani* makes clear such a reclaiming is always mired in ambiguity, and never stable grounds for defining identity. At one level, the nation is presented lamentably as being in the process of forfeiting its foundations. In the words of Marta, the country has suffered "a coup against the past" (*UF,* 99), becoming a mere imitation that lacks authenticity. The old people are perceived to be a threat to Izidine since they remind him of his roots; Marta goads the investigator, accusing him of being afraid of the residents who "are the past you are trampling on deep inside your head. These old people remind you of where you come from" (73). Izidine has lost his roots through a European education that "curtailed his knowledge of the culture, of the languages, of the little things that shape a people's soul" (38). The inspector has become acculturated into the paradigms of the West that despise as underdeveloped the mores of traditional Mozambique. He suppresses his links to those traditions deep within his unconscious but, there, they will assert their right to exist.

A similar, negative suppression of cultural roots occurs to Mucanga, the spirit inside Izidine's body. After his death, he is buried far from his ancestral home, something that prevents him becoming one of the "well and truly dead" (2). He remains anchorless, in a state of perpetual flux that facilitates the rewriting of his history over his dead body by others, most noticeably by the revolutionaries who falsely elevate him to the status of a hero. But, a trace of what he was is always left on the palimpsest and comes to light with each rereading of the novel, as we will discuss shortly. Marta is also presented as having lost her African roots through the erasure of her family's African names, and the assumption of a Portuguese name. The losses involving Izidine, Mucanga, and Marta are not deemed to be progress but rather are a cause for concern since the characters have become estranged from their own histories.

In contrast, a more positive light is shed on the relinquishing of roots by the other character in the text associated with cultural loss, Domingos Mourão—the Portuguese settler whose wife left with their child at independence. Not only will he be buried far from his ancestors, losing a reassuring link with the past, he is also beginning to lose his language, his culture, and his historic sense of identity. "Forgive me my Portuguese, I don't know what language I talk any more, my grammar is all muddy, the color of this soil. And it's not just my talk that's changed. It's my thinking too, inspector" (42). While his linguistic loss may be lamentable and, in some ways, represents the former colony's menacing, cultural appropriation of a space earlier occupied by the colonizer in a manner outlined by Homi Bhabha, it soon becomes apparent that Mourão's sense of loss is more than compensated for by his acceptance in the new nation that becomes his too.[15] His renaming as Sidimingo [Xidimingo in the original] does not carry the negative connotation associated with the imposition of a Portuguese name on Marta since it is presented as the gaining of a culture. He comes to belong to Mozambique; the roots of the newly independent country come to belong to him. As Nhonhoso tells him, "you, Sidimingo, belong to Mozambique, this country is yours. Without a shadow of doubt" (43).

All of this seems to substantiate an afro-atavistic reading of text. The loss of African roots is a detrimental step; the loss of a Portuguese heritage almost seems desirable. Yet, if it were that simple, Couto could be accused of a binary reversal, of demonizing the Portuguese elements of Mozambican culture while sanctifying the African. But it is not that simple, principally because of Couto's complicated characterizations of Mourão-Sidimingo, and of the person in the novel most entrenched in African tradition, Nãozinha—a name Brookshaw translates as Little Miss No.

While Domingos Mourão celebrates his Mozambican identity, he always retains within himself an aspect that desires a return to his former continent. In fact, the frangipani tree forms a link with his past since it reminds him of autumn and the changing seasons of Europe. Therefore, the title of the book in some ways points to the shadow European heritage always casts over the identity of the new African nation. The tree itself is a complex symbol used by Mourão ostensibly to explain his existence in simple terms to the detective. In fact, Mourão explains that in the era of Vasco da Gama, the fifteenth-century Portuguese maritime explorer who discovered the all-important sea-route to India, there was "an old black man who wandered along the beaches picking up flotsam and jetsam. He collected the remains of shipwrecks and buried them. It so happened that one of the wooden planks he stuck in the ground grew roots and came back to life as a tree" (42). The tree thus dates back to the arrival of the Portuguese in East Africa and indicates their desire to take roots on the continent. At the same time, it points to a shipwreck and to the tainted glory of the Portuguese mastery of the seas, since many such an occurrence was the direct result of the avaricious overloading of ships, as we will discuss later. Furthermore, the tree highlights Portugal's role in transporting flora around the world since the plant itself is indigenous to the Americas.[16] The role of the Portuguese as pioneers in the realm of global technology transfer emphasizes their mythological status as a people perpetually in maritime transit, looking to extend their horizons over the sea, never able yet always longing to return to their Iberian home.

As the world Mourão loves begins to wither, his desire for a return to the past intensifies. He declares, "the Mozambique I loved is dying. It'll never come back. All that's left is this little patch of ground where I seek the shade of the sea. My nation is this terrace" (44). In the Portuguese, Couto uses the word "varanda" (*V,* 50) echoing the other component of the book's original title. The veranda is the location of the frangipani, the place where the tree casts its shadow; symbolically it is the nation. The tree represents both Africa and nostalgia for Europe, while being American in provenance, from the continent where Portugal had another Empire. Mourão's new nation is a combination of all these places. The syncretism of its traditions, even postindependence, will always include that European imperial component.

Nãozinha, whose existence and magical powers are intricately linked to the African traditions of Mozambique, declares herself to be a fraud, and thus calls into question the validity of returning to the purity of that so-called African tradition. She confesses that her "powers are born out of a lie" (76). This disclosure which she makes to Izidine is not the first time that she denies being a true witch. Earlier, she had claimed to Navaia that she had no magical power at all. In fact, denial is written all over Nãozinha's name, containing, as it does, the Portuguese word for "no." The difference in the later denial is that she no longer disclaims her power, she merely establishes that there is no truth behind it—a point she later repeats to Ernestina, Vasto's wife. So, Nãozinha's power is not denied but the notion of a fixed root to her power is. Consequently, a desired return to that fixed root is, in fact, a utopian gesture to something that does not exist in truth but only in falsehood.

The character of Izidine personifies the search for truth. Apparently, the whole purpose of his presence in the old people's home is to establish the truth of what happened to Vasto. As the text unfolds, the link between the truth and death becomes clearer. Izidine's search for the truth behind the corruption in Maputo has led to a plan to eliminate him, and Nãozinha, whose existence is premised on lies, reveals the plot to the policeman. As Izidine comes to realize the variety of truths which shuffle around the text—the arms trade, the plot to kill him, the loss of his cultural roots, the abandonment of the elderly—he desires a fixed reference point; he wants his African roots back, a process that mirrors Mourão's nostalgic desire for Portugal. But, like his Portuguese counterpart, Izidine's need to reclaim roots can never be satisfied. Every action he performs to demonstrate knowledge of traditions is thrown back in his face by the old people who equate true tradition with perpetual creativity, something Izidine has lost through the acceptance of the truth-table logic underpinning his Western education. Even when he tries to impress the old people by revealing his knowledge of their tradition of eating

lizards, their response is laughingly to tell him, "it's not we who eat the creatures. It's they who eat us" (94)—the reverse of what is ostensibly happening.
Truth, as it is conceived within the old people's epistemological system, is
nothing but a perspective and, as such, constantly shifts. The more Izidine
seeks to stabilize his reality by imposing a unity in truth, the more split his
personality becomes. But it is not a dichotomous split, as Nhonhoso tells
him in an explanation that denies the comfort of binary opposites, "you are
neither good nor bad. You just don't exist" (95). The interstitial space in
which Izidine moves forces him to doubt himself as he loses fixed polar categories. In the universe Couto creates, no absolute opposite, premised on an
inalterable truth, is permissible. Yet the more this is revealed to Izidine, the
more he wants a fixed root, and a sense of belonging to a definitive, well-de-
marcated category. He is even prepared to undergo circumcision, a permanent branding, "for acceptance into the family, the community of elders"
(95). However, the old people will not perform this initiation rite on him.
They prefer instead to dress him in women's clothes, an act that can be read
not only to be symbolic of a change in an initiation ceremony, but also to
destabilize gender assignment by parodying sartorial forms, as we will discuss
later. Izidine is denied the permanence of circumcision and becomes the object of a carnival, characterized by the transitoriness of his attire. At this point
his personality becomes most split—straddling the boundary between
woman and man, young and old, alive and dead. For the first time in the
text, he will cease to be consciously inhabited by Mucanga when, dressed as a
woman, he makes love to Marta. His self-repossession as the spirit leaves his
body is the result of being able to relinquish demarcations and finally to cede
to a flux in his own self-definition. He no longer views the world in absolute
terms, and begins to approximate the tradition of perpetual creativity es-
poused by the old people.

The only absolute Couto temporarily allows in the novel is a god who is
far from present and who is blind to the lies which allow for the continuation
of life. In the words of Navaia, the clouds in the sky are "like these cataracts
in my eyes: mists that prevent God from getting a glimpse of us. That's why
we are free to tell lies" (18). Such a god is really a dead god, the god based on
a truth that cannot see ubiquitous falsehood, Zarathustra's deity. Paradoxically, that god is also the god of falsehood, given Couto's particular choice of
words. Once god is removed from the scene/seen, the old people are, in fact,
liberated from lying because the author uses the phrase "livres de mentir" (*V,*
26), which literally translates "free from lying" although the context strongly
implies "free to tell lies." Couto's pun serves to kill what, for him, is the
biggest lie of all: one, true god.

Couto parallels the problem of a lack of absolute truth/god by denying the reader the comfort of an omniscient narrative voice. Every event in the text is distilled through a series of prisms. Alternate chapters appear to be the spoken—or, in the case of Ernestina, the written—voice of different characters. Izidine, who is joined with and distinct from Mucanga, always mediates their words through his notebook, which is then spoken to the reader by Mucanga, through the written word of the novel's text. A further perspective is added when the witnesses cite the words of other characters in the narrative. All these perspectives distance the reader from the reality of what happened, reflecting language's innate distancing of the speaker from the truth.

A key trope deployed by Couto to undermine access to an attainable truth is his play with the link between signified and signifier, terms used here in the Saussurian sense of the concept and acoustic signal that constitute each morpheme. Couto, at times, distorts the unity between the two and, in the process, foregrounds the obfuscating function inherent in any language system. The most obvious example is his treatment of the narrative's location—the "fortaleza," or fortress, at São Nicolau—which is both a signifier that changes signifieds and a signified that changes signifiers. The "fortaleza," which Ana Mafalda Leite reads as an enclosure that symbolically represents the nation's dying tradition, has had its significance rewritten many times, changing from a fortress to a prison to an asylum to a refuge.[17] It appears to be a shell with a shifting content. At the same time, it is a content with a variable shell, a signified whose signifier can vary too. Izidine's first glimpse of the fortress, from the helicopter that brings him to São Nicolau, leads him to refer to it as a "fraqueleza" (*V,* 22), a pun that transmutes the Portuguese word for strong (forte) into the Portuguese word for weakness. In line with Nietzsche's disavowal of absolute binaries, Couto is suggesting that before anything can be what it is, it contains what it is not. There is a disruption in the isomorphism between what signifies and what is signified. The "fraqueleza" is not just another term. It adds to the concept of the "fortaleza" by detracting from it, by making it into the opposite of what we conceive it to be. Couto implies how the thing is seen—the fortress is glimpsed from far away—determines what it is. He privileges the phenomenal over the noumenal, perspective over "truth."

Several of the characters in the novel can be read as parallels to the shifting nature of the link between signifier and signified. Clearly, the dual nature of the protagonist Izindine/Mucanga undermines the possibility of a fixed link between a stable concept of the characters and their names. Mucanga's personality flows into and out of that of Izidine. Additionally, the same name refers to changed essences at different points in the narrative. In fact, the

essence of each character is rarely constant since each rereading is informed
and distorted by previous readings of the tale. For example, a second reading
never allows Mucanga to return to the blank space over which political authorities seek to rewrite his history. The lack of any written record of his existence, to which he initially refers, is altered by the unfolding of the text.
The text itself becomes a written history into which his existence is inscribed.
As the story evolves, Mucanga reveals things about himself that render him
the antithesis of the hero into which the Frelimo authorities wish posthumously to turn him. He feels no bond of brotherhood with the revolutionaries who fought the Portuguese who educated him. Indeed, all he feels is the
fissure between the signifier and the signified—a split rooted in an education
that distorted the link between what he was and what he could say.

> The ones they called my "brothers" weren't related to me in any way. They
> were guerrilla fighters, revolutionaries. They were fighting the rule of the Por-
> tuguese. My heart wasn't in such conflicts. I had only ever been to a Catholic
> mission school. They had structured my ways, balancing patience with expec-
> tations. They educated me in a language that wasn't my mother tongue. I
> lived under the eternal burden of being unable to match words with ideas.
> (116–17)

The loss of language suffered by Mucanga mirrors Mourão's linguistic de-
nationalization. Mourão now speaks a Portuguese tainted by Mozambique, a
linguistics code that is far removed and removes him from the former
metropolis. Mucanga, like Izidine whose body and mind he occupies, is not
able to communicate fluently in his mother tongue either and, as a result,
feels perpetually incapable of linking signifiers to signifieds. Mucanga's linguistic loss is a consequence of the educational policies of the colonial
regime. In constrast, Izidine's process of language loss is related to the policies
of the postindependence era, in which Frelimo discouraged the use of local
languages and, ironically, did more to propagate Portuguese than the former
colonial administration. His European education has severed him from his
mother tongue. He is no longer able to speak as an African. Even the Portuguese that he speaks points to a realm of meaning different from that on
which the residents of the old people's home ground the same linguistic code.
The signifiers might be the same but what they signify is not. Marta tries to
explain this to him.

> "You just don't speak their language."
> "I don't speak their language? But we always speak in Portuguese!"
> "But they speak another language, another Portuguese." (71)

For the old people, the same linguistic code points to a reality different from that of Izidine. The same signifiers become attached to different signifieds. In this way, the old people challenge the premises of unitary meaning, and destabilize the possibility of relating one truth.

The black body of Izidine mirrors this skewed network of signification. The external representation of blackness points to a Fanonian inner whiteness.[18] He might think that he is black, he might appear to be black, but the old people recognize in his body the soul of a white. It takes a white who has assumed the soul of an African, Mourão/Xidimingo, to point this out to Izidine: "these black friends of mine will never tell you what really happened. For them, you're a *mezungo*, a white man like myself" (49).

Mourão's possession of two names (Mourão/Xidimingo) replicates the process of two signifiers pointing to one signified. This replication signals one body caught between two cultures, which, in turn, points to one shell containing two essences, or rather one signifier that is linked to two signifieds. He at once belongs and does not. He is two people, and he is one person. Not only does the way he speaks Portuguese challenge the "purity" of the language, constantly breaching the conventional associations between the signified and the signifier, the duplicity and cultural ambiguity of his names reflects a paradoxical jarring of linguistic convention. At the same time, his characterization mirrors the complexity of his new nation's cultural heritage, and the continuous process whereby Mozambique's identity is progressively fashioned. Mourão's identity, like that of Mozambique, is a play of reinterpretations that blocks the possibility of definitive fixture because no single signifier is ever permanently attached to a single signified. Couto's rejection of an isomorphism between the two components of the sign is effectively a poststructural continuation of his challenge to the possibility of a unitary and absolute truth. He exaggerates the limitations of language, its inability to fix meaning, to kill the fantasy of being able to capture truth given those limitations. But these very limitations are what allow him to float meaning, and provoke multiple interpretations. By accepting the abolition of truth, and by following Nietzsche's recognition of "untruth as a condition of life," Couto proffers a new beginning for Mozambican identity that leaves behind the truths that have cost it dear—the unquestionable ideologies of colonialism, and scientific socialism. Furthermore, his rejection of definitive truth crosses continental frontiers. It both gainsays the crux of dominant Western ideologies and precludes a return to so-called authentic African origins. The result is an implied national identity that is and, as a condition of its existence, always should be, organic and changing. Such an identity eschews binary structures and oversees the dissolution of the absolute. The characters of *A*

Varanda do Frangipani utopically symbolize a postwar Mozambican nation in which the fundamental premise of dogma is banished, and identity is never conclusively grounded. As much through Izidine, who has lost his link to Africa, as through Mourão, who has become separated from Portugal, Couto sets his characters adrift, and forces them to assume new identities that respect and reinterpret traditions but never fossilize them. Once a tradition is set in stone, it becomes a truth, and is thus dead. And as we shall see in relation to the absurd orthographical atavism we will discuss in the next chapter, reclaiming a true, or "authentic" tradition, is an activity that is fraught with contradictions.

3

Righting Wrongs for Writing Rongas: The Politics of Literacy and Orthography

In an article published in 1995 in Mozambique's weekly independent newspaper *Savana*, Francisco Rodolfo made a series of interesting observations in regard to the country's official literacy rates. Drawing on his experience in both rural and urban areas of Mozambique over the years following independence, he claimed that government statistics considerably underestimated the percentage of the population who could read and write. The inaccuracy in the figures was, according to the journalist, the result of a bias inherited from the former European colonial power. The Frelimo government, like the Portuguese administration that it replaced, refused to categorize as literate those who had a reading knowledge of African languages but who, by a quirk of history related to the language policies followed by certain religious missionaries, never learned literacy skills in Portuguese. According to Rodolfo, official statistics in the 1990s only took into account those who are fluent in European languages, neglecting the substantial proportion of the older population who can read and write in African languages but who have little or no knowledge of the former colonial tongue. This was a phenomenon particular to the regions that fell under the influence of Protestant Churches during the colonial era. The Catholic Church had fiercely promulgated the use of Portuguese in the schools it controlled, in compliance with a Missionary Agreement annexed to a Concordat the Vatican had signed with Salazar in 1940. This Concordat, which for many years rendered Catholicism politically coterminous with the fascist state, attempted, in part, to restrict the influence of Protestantism in the Portuguese colonies by giving preferential treatment to the Roman Church in the education sector. The Catholic system conducted its classes in Portuguese. Previous international agreements, most noticeably those following the Berlin Congress of 1884–85, had guaranteed religious freedom in the African colonies, at the insistence of the British who saw the educational zeal of the Protestant Missionaries as a key component in increasing their own sphere of influence and in augmenting the reach of the capitalist ideology to which they subscribed. By the time of the Concordat, Protestant Missions were firmly established in several regions of Mozambique. Their relatively small number never reflected the enormous influence they would wield in the history of Mozambican independence; they were the main educators of the founder of Frelimo, Eduardo Mondlane.

Mondlane was born in 1920 in Manjacaze, to a clan that were the traditional rulers of the Chope, a relatively small ethnic group from the south of Mozambique, who were often despised by the larger Shangaan group for a perceived cooperation with the Portuguese.[1] He was educated in Portugal, South Africa and the US, where he completed a doctorate in anthropology and married a white American, Janet. His educational opportunities were principally the result of the scholarships and encouragement of Calvinist Swiss missionaries. He maintained strong ties to the US throughout his leadership of the independence movement, including a close relationship with the Kennedy administration, to the extent that he was accused of being "an American stooge."[2] His assassination on 3 February 1969, in Oyster Bay, Tanzania, was blamed by Frelimo on the Portuguese secret service, but there were also rumors that his death was the result of a power struggle within the movement itself.[3] The presidency of Frelimo was assumed by a triumvirate constituted by Samora Machel, Marcelino dos Santos, a committed communist mulatto, and the Reverend Uria Simango, a Ndau from the central region of Mozambique.

Machel had been the ruthless head of the armed wing of the movement. Educated in a Catholicism he vehemently rejected and a trained nurse, he was determined to veer the movement toward Marxist Leninism, and quickly moved against the more conservative Simango. Simango published a paper in November 1969 that was extremely critical of the brutal tactics employed by the movement to maintain discipline among its own adherents. He demanded the resignation of Machel and Dos Santos, and called for them to be put on trial for the many executions of Frelimo members. Convinced that he had the support of the military wing, he threatened to resign if his demands were not met. They were not, and in his absence, Simango was expelled from the movement at a meeting of the Central Committee held in May 1970. Machel claimed the presidency of Frelimo and dominated Mozambican politics until his untimely and suspicious death in a plane crash in 1986. Dos Santos, a man loathed by Mondlane, became vice-president. Simango was later captured, interned, and then secretly executed in October 1979, an execution ordered by Frelimo to prevent him being used as a figurehead by the then emergent rebel movement Renamo. For many years, the Frelimo government did not acknowledge the extrajudicial killing of its former member, and even led his relatives to believe that he was still alive.[4]

The whole episode of the succession to Mondlane highlights the deep divisions that raged within Frelimo at the time. Samora Machel shifted the movement's ideological compass far to the left, embracing the Soviet Bloc as natural allies, while turning the movement into a totalitarian regime far from the party created by Mondlane. Mondlane owed ideology and cultural understanding to the Protestant Missionaries that had trained him.[5] Despite coming from a family that was not Christian, he entered the Swiss Missionary School in Maússe through family contacts. His mother was adamant that he needed to learn how to operate in "the world of the white man" [mundo do homem branco].[6] The missionary education sector where he found his intellectual niche had, from the nineteenth century onward, been driven by the desire to bring the "Buku"—translations into indigenous languages of the Bible—to the speakers of those languages. That book had served as both a literacy aid, and a tool of conversion. The strategies employed by the Protestants differed greatly from their Catholic counterparts. The former nurtured a national consciousness in Mozambique, while the latter faithfully served Portuguese colonialism. One of the legacies that the Protestant Missionaries left to the postindependence era, beyond the education of Frelimo's first ideologue, was the level of officially unrecognized literacy to which Rodolfo referred in his article.

Rodolfo claims that in the Maxixe region, "there are a lot of now elderly people who can't speak Portuguese, but who read and write perfectly well in Guitonga" [há muita gente já idosa que não fala o português, mas lê e escreve perfeitamente o guitonga].[7] Other examples that he cites include districts of the northern province of Niassa where he used to be stationed and where he participated in meetings to which local people "would bring their reports written in Swahili or Makua" [traziam o seu relatório escrito em suaíli e macua]. To demonstrate the extent to which literacy in African languages stretches over the whole of Mozambique, Rodolfo gives the example of the Maputo-based "mamanas rongas" who during religious services "often put their glasses on—due to their age—and open their hymn books, and then their bibles, reading them in fluent Ronga" [põem amiúde os óculos—devido à idade—e abrem os seus livros de cânticos e, eventualmente, bíblias, lendo-os em ronga fluente]. He ends his description with the immediately rebutted rhetorical question, "could it be possible that they are illiterate? I think not!" [dir-me-ão que são iletradas? Pensamos que não!]. Once the alphabet was introduced to African languages in Mozambique, so were the notion of illiteracy and a perceived link between ignorance and the inability to write. Strangely, the retrenched association of Europe with writing was not lost even after independence when literacy in many African languages was still not officially recognized. Hence Rodolfo's vigorous defense of those literate in Ronga, Guitonga, Swahili, and Makua who had been mistakenly classified as illiterate by an administration which had inherited its former colonial masters' correlation between European languages and the written word.

Writing changes the human mindset, altering our consciousness of language. In literate societies, the written word becomes the law, the carrier of knowledge and authority. The Swiss missionaries, who were primarily responsible for the introduction of the alphabet into the Thonga language group of the south of Mozambique, were well aware of the power that the written language could produce. In the words of Patrick Harries, "in addition to its utility as a means of communication, writing soon acquired a crucial political significance. A monopoly of the Thonga language gave the Swiss an important competitive edge over other missions in their drive to save African souls."[8] Harries asserts, "people were impressed by reading as a means of communication, particularly when this was in an idiom with which they had some familiarity." He goes on to suggest that by introducing the alphabet to Thonga the Swiss missionaries felt that they possessed the language they transcribed. They had taken a spoken language and made it their own through writing it down. "Not only was the written Thonga language controlled by the missionaries but, in a manner that combined endearment, loyalty and possession, they almost owned it; Thonga was 'our' language with 'our' orthography."

The protestant missionaries marked the Mozambican linguistic landscape through the imposition of an orthography that was distinct from that of the official language in the colony. They were responsible for the introduction of letters alien to the Portuguese alphabet—such as K and W—into the Mozambican languages they codified and transcribed. The linguistic complexity caused by the protestant intervention in the writing systems of Mozambique proffers false foundations for any project based on linguistic atavism, a point amusingly made by Couto in one of his short stories, "África com Kapa?" [Africa with a K?], published in the collection *Cronicando*. The story is set at the immigration desk in a Brazilian airport, where a Mozambican friend of Couto's engages in an argument with a Brazilian official over how his name is written. He is adamant, "it is written with a K and a W!" [escreve-se com kapa e dabliú! (*C,* 175)]. The Brazilian does not understand. He has written the African's name "using the orthographical standards of the Portuguese language" [empregando as normas ortográficas da língua portuguesa (175)], it-self rather an ironic statement since Brazil and Portugal do not share the same rules of orthography. The Brazilian demands an explanation. The Mozambican obliges, rooting his argument in a reclaimed past that never was: "it's the African way of writing" [é a maneira africana de escrever (175)]. As a rather irate queue builds up behind him, he elaborates further that he has to "assume our African roots, respect our traditions" [assumir as nossas raízes africanas, respeitar as nossas tradições (176)]. The official appears to begin to understand, asking, "could it be that Ks are more African than Cs" [será que os kapas são mais africanos que o [sic] cês? (176)]. That is precisely the point. Couto remains silent at the side of his friend. The Brazilian is not satisfied, launching a barrage of arguments against the Mozambican: "He said that, as far as he was concerned, it was just a case of substituting the rules of Portuguese with those of English" [Dizia que, para ele, se tratava de pura transferência das normas do português para as do inglês (176)]. The argument is lost. History, as it has been written, is on the Brazilian's side. Africa's pure roots cannot be reclaimed through north European orthography. If he wants to make a political statement about his ethnicity, the Mozambican cannot do it by changing Africa into Afrika. It would be as wrong as writing Mia Couto, "MYA KOWTO" (177).

The point of the story is that a belief in authenticity is often rooted in ignorance. The Mozambican nationalist is claiming to recuperate his Africaness through a writing system that postdates the arrival of the Portuguese colonizers in Africa. Furthermore, the system was bequeathed by an ideological group (Protestants) who were the driving force behind capitalist expansion, the last ideology to colonize Mozambique, and the one under which it is likely to live for the foreseeable future.

There are a number of other interesting issues that the story raises. First, it is a Brazilian who defends a transnational lusophone identity through language. The immigration officer demands linguistic purity and derides the attempt to locate indigenous African culture in written Portuguese. His stance is to use history, like Hegel, to write out Africa.[9] He comes from a nation that has, from its inception, always treated indigenous culture with an ambivalent contempt. During the period following Brazilian independence in 1822, the Brazilian Indian was simultaneously despised and reified as the incarnation of the true Brazil, untainted by the detested Portuguese. Nineteenth-century Brazilian writers like José de Alencar attempted to introduce words from Guarani into their texts as a means of distinguishing Brazilian Portuguese from that of the former metropolis.[10] His efforts were perfunctory, and revealed more about his inability to speak the languages to which he claimed to be giving a voice than any authentic desire to protect indigenous culture. In fact, Alencar's efforts are best described using Chantal Zabus's term of "textual glottophagia."[11] He appropriates a language that he scarcely speaks for his own project of national cultural inscription. The true fate of many indigenous dialects and languages in Brazil is symbolically related in Mário de Andrade's 1928 novel *Macunaíma,* in which the sole surviving speaker of a language at the end of the tale is a parrot.[12] One of the lessons of the novel is that orality without orthography leads to linguistic extinction. However, orthography always bears the mark of a previous imperial game, as Mozambican linguistic history and Couto's "África com Kapa?" amply demonstrate.

The second issue that Couto's short story raises is related to that game of linguistic imperialism. The immigration officer condemns the nefarious interference of English in the language politics of lusophone Africa. Perceived interference from English is, to this day, one of the most sensitive issues for Portuguese speakers around the globe, and has been a particularly acute concern with regard to Mozambique since the Scramble for Africa, which carved the continent up between the competing European powers at the end of the nineteenth century. The British and Portuguese clashed in 1890 over a sub-Saharan territory that both deemed to be in their domain, in an incident that became known as the Ultimatum Crisis. The Third Marques of Salisbury, the British Prime Minister at the time, threatened to declare war on Portugal after a zealous Portuguese military officer, Serpa Pinto, took possession of the Makololo region, an area the British deemed to be their sphere of influence. Salisbury's gunboat diplomacy forced the Portuguese to cede. The Portuguese monarch was lampooned in the Lisbon press, portrayed as a poodle of the British Empire, and his government collapsed in a wave of popular discontent. The principal consequence of the Ultimatum Crisis was that it heralded the beginning of the end for the Portuguese monarchy, which never recovered from its loss of face. The republican movement gained momentum and Portugal became a republic two decades later. However, a second consequence that lingered well into the following century, and perhaps even into the twenty-first century, was a deep mistrust among many Portuguese about the intentions of the English speakers in and around Mozambique.

Portuguese intellectuals have a long tradition of emotively relating their national identity to the language they speak. From the sixteenth century, when António Ferreira, a poet and playwright, berated his fellow artists for not using Portuguese, preferring instead to express themselves in the then courtly tongue of Castile, language has always been at the heart of Portuguese national identity.[13] In that respect, the Portuguese predated the trend in the rest of continental Europe, where the ideas of the nineteenth-century

German protonationalist, Herder, were the first explicitly to link language and the political identity of a state.[14] Of course, there were always discordant voices within the Portuguese realm that avoided the use of the vernacular language, preferring Spanish and then French as the mediums of cultural expression. However, a strong tradition was established that privileged the *língua portuguesa* as the embodiment of the *pátria*. The seventeenth-century Jesuit, António Vieira, who spent much of his life in Brazil and began to write the analeptic and prophetic "History of the Future" of Portugal, placed the Portuguese language in the forefront of a new world order in which the Portuguese would reign in the name of Christ.[15] Vieira's assertions were appropriated and modified by the most influential advocate in the twentieth century of the Portuguese language as a patriotic territory, Portugal's greatest modernist poet, Fernando Pessoa. Pessoa's subsequent influence on the language debate has been tremendous, and his famous mantra "my homeland is the Portuguese language" [minha pátria é a língua portuguesa] has been repeated so often by politicians, writers, commentators and intellectuals, to the extent that it is almost a mandatory cliché at any lusophone gathering. Pessoa was a larger-than-life character, who wrote under a number of heteronyms, one of which was Bernardo Soares, to whom the phrase is attributed.[16] Born in Portugal in 1888, Pessoa spent much of his childhood in South Africa, where he wrote his first verses in English, and actually won a prestigious prize for a prose essay written in Shakespeare's tongue. He returned to Portugal as a young adult, and began the prolific creation of lusophone poetic identities, many of which were discovered after his death from alcoholic poisoning in 1935. Pessoa's legacy to the politics of his nation's language is to have made it a central pillar of Portugal's twentieth-century imperial discourse. The poet imagined an empire based on culture and language, and not on political domination. At the time he was writing, his attitude was remarkably progressive. However, in a postindependence era, his influence on the mindset of lusophone intellectuals becomes highly problematic because language, as Ngugi Wa Thiong'o points out, is one of the principal weapons of neocolonialism.[17] If the language is deemed to be the homeland, a claim is made for metropolitan jurisdiction over the literary output of a diverse set of countries that happen to use the language in the postindependence era. The repeated inflection of Pessoa's mantra thus problematizes the work of writers like Mia Couto, who are using Portuguese to fashion a Mozambican identity. Couto's case is even more complex because of the sensitivities surrounding language use in Mozambique. Due to a perceived threat that English will replace Portuguese as the national language, a threat that is implicitly acknowledged in Couto's "África com Kapa?," there is a tendency in Lisbon to overemphasize

the linguistic aspects of the Mozambican writer's work, as a means of demonstrating that the language is still alive and well in the former African colony.

The rise of linguistic paranoia among a certain set of lusophone intellectuals is a long story. On 13 November 1995, Mozambique became the first
officially lusophone country to join the Commonwealth. This, according to
the Angolan author Sousa Jamba, confirmed the fears of many Portuguese
that their language in Africa was being "overwhelmed by the advance of English."[18] Jamba himself writes in English and has his novels translated before
publishing them in Lisbon, something that further fuels the sentiment that
lusophone Africa is under siege from English. Jamba's critics point out that he
hardly knows the reality of Angola, having lived as a refugee in Mobutu's
Zaire for most of his youth, and later in exile in London.[19] There, he is often
taken as the principal popular authority on lusophone Africa, mainly through
his connection to *The Times* newspaper. Effectively, he is telling a particular
type of Englishman what he wants to hear: the English language is displacing
Portuguese in sub-Saharan Africa.

The historical relationship between Portugal and its oldest ally, England,
has often been characterized by an alliance of inequality. From the Treaty of
Methuen signed in 1703 to the Ultimatum Crisis, the British repeatedly
treated Portugal with the contempt they reserved for the inhabitants of their
own colonies. Agreements between the two sovereign nations disadvantaged
the Portuguese, and essentially serviced Britain's strategic needs. Spain was,
for considerable periods of European history, Britain's principal foe, with the
result that Britain considered an independent Portugal to be a necessary ally
on the Iberian Peninsula. With the demise of Spanish influence caused
largely by the Napoleonic Wars, Britain ceased to be concerned with maintaining the charade of a friendly relationship with Lisbon, and produced a
string of critical travel writers, politicians and commentators toward the end
of the nineteenth century, who indulged in a discourse of Portuguese-bash-
ing, particularly in relation to the territory of Mozambique. Cloaked beneath
a rhetoric that asserted Portuguese imperial incompetence and suggested that
Britain should assume control of Lisbon's colonies in the name of civilization
lurked a desire to control the Beira Corridor and the port of Delagoa Bay,
later to be renamed Lourenço Marques and, after independence, to become
the Mozambican capital, Maputo. Both areas provided convenient exit
routes, with deep natural bays, for the commodities Britain plundered from
its colonies in Southern Africa. Britain made a highly publicized, but never
enacted, "secret" deal with Germany in the run up to the First World War
that envisaged a division of the Portuguese colonies in Africa between the
two European rivals. It is hardly surprising that the intentions of the British

in the region have subsequently been suspect in Portugal. Add to that the global advance of English, and the fact that Mozambique is surrounded by officially anglophone nations, and it is easy to see why the nation's entry into one of the remnants of the British Empire fuels a degree of linguistic para-noia in Portugal.

For several years before Mozambique's entry into the Commonwealth, a debate had raged in the Lisbon press, centering on a perceived threat to Por-tuguese from English in Africa. Jorge Bacelar Gouveia summarizes the argu-ments in a 1994 article in the Portuguese newspaper *Espresso.*[20] He portrays a gloomy future for Portuguese on the continent, particularly in Mozambique. He outlines a coordinated strategy undertaken by anglophone agencies from Britain, the United States, and South Africa, through which the Portuguese language will be replaced by English in Mozambique. The strategy involves denigrating Portuguese, particularly by associating it to the colonial past. Then, according to Gouveia, these agencies heavily fund programs in indige-nous languages, as a means of downgrading the national importance of Por-tuguese. Finally, when Portuguese is at its weakest, Gouveia suggests that En-glish will be offered as a language of salvation, to reunite the nation. Gouveia's portrayal is melodramatic. His arguments do, however, find a resonance among some used in francophone Africa, where funding for local languages is often seen as a steppingstone to replace French with English.[21] Regardless of the validity of what he says, Gouveia embodies an intellectual trend that sees the English language as a major threat to the rights of a transnational lu-sophone sovereignty. The picture he depicts is underscored by Fernando Pes-soa's belief in a *língua* as *pátria,* itself a troubling neocolonial equation since it implies that anything written in the Portuguese language immediately be-comes the property of a lusophone community historically centered in the metropolis. Indeed, a problematic aspect of the reception of Mia Couto's work is the manner in which most critics privilege his "innovative" or "re-generating" use of Portuguese, and often neglect other aspects of his texts. First and foremost, Couto is deemed to do service to the *língua portuguesa.*

The debate surrounding the continued use of Portuguese in Mozam-bique, and in Africa in general, is one that resurfaces frequently in Lisbon's academic circles. The copious amount of articles and books published on the subject attests to an obsession that is not shared in the former colonies them-selves. One of the ironies of the Mozambican experience is the considerably greater support that the Frelimo government gave in the first decade of its administration to the former colonial tongue relative to the efforts of the Portuguese colonizers during the previous five centuries. Postindependence, Portuguese was the only language permissible in the education sector, and became the idiom through which the Mozambican nation imagined itself. Given the linguistic complexity of the country, with thirteen distinct African languages spoken within its borders, Frelimo determined that the most effective way of forging a national identity was through the adoption of the colonizer's tongue. Any other option would, in the opinion of Samora Machel and his coterie, have led to tribalism and the accentuation of detrimental divisions. During the era of the *Estado Novo*, over which Salazar and then Marcello Caetano presided and which ran for over four decades, the Portuguese government indulged in a rhetorical discourse that claimed a linguistically unified transcontinental lusophone family. The reality of the colonial regime's policies was that it did little to promote the use of Portuguese outside the white settler community and among a relatively small group of blacks living in urban areas. The available statistics vary widely as to the precise coverage of the Portuguese language at independence, and their reliability is questionable. However, what is beyond dispute is that Frelimo sharply increased the number of Mozambicans who spoke and wrote in Portuguese and, in the early years of its administration, strongly discouraged the use of indigenous languages in the interests of national unity, which goes some way to explain their reticence in acknowledging the phenomenon of writing Rongas.

More recently, and particularly following the death of Samora Machel, Frelimo has adopted a more tolerant position in regard to linguistic diversity. The fifth article of the nation's 1990 constitution foresaw an increasing role for local languages in the education sector. If this role is fulfilled, then these languages will quickly acquire more readers and writers, as textbooks are produced in a diverse range of indigenous languages for use in the elementary education sector. In many ways, the debate about the future use of the Portuguese language in Mozambique is stale and conducted with far more vigor in Lisbon than in Maputo. Concern over the demise of Camões's tongue in Africa stems from a sense of national insecurity among an academic elite in Portugal, and seems to be premised on a belief that language survival is a zero-sum game. In reality, people are capable of mastering more than one tongue—of using different languages in different contexts. Portuguese is in a stronger position today in Mozambique than it ever has been. The real debate is if a particular mindset can survive as the nation transforms from a predominantly oral culture into a modern, literate society. The duality between the written and the spoken has underpinned Western philosophical debates from Plato onward. The Platonic side of the argument has always distrusted the benefits of the script. In contrast, the Hegelian tradition has elevated writing to the supreme embodiment of civilization. Against the backdrop of this centuries-old dispute between misographs and graphophiles, Couto, as we shall see in the next chapter, positions himself as a postmodernist who rejects the validity of both sides of the argument. He melts the demarcation between the written and the spoken, not only by providing a space in his texts for the oral hues of his nation, as many have commented, but, more interestingly, by robbing the script of the characteristics traditionally assigned to it by both sides of the Western epistemological debate. His treatment of the theme of writing operates as a process whereby the attributes of the written word are colonized and transformed by the interference of the spoken voice.

4
De-Scribing the Text:
Orality's Infiltration of the Written Source

IN THE OPENING LINES OF THE SHORT STORY "O CABRITO QUE VENCEU O *Boeing*" [The Kid-goat Who Defeated the *Boeing*], Couto characterizes writing as a self-generating product: "Ladies and gentlemen, pay no heed to the witnesses: there were none. This piece of writing arose from nothing, with no testimony nor any substance. If any law befits it, it is just the authority to invent" [ignorem, senhores, as testemunhas: nenhuma não houve. Este escrito saiu do nada, sem depoimento nem substância. Se alguma lei nele cabe é apenas a permissão do invento (*C*, 149)]. Writing is the source, inventing in the absence of a referent. This is a portrayal of the script that runs counter to the opinions of both the philosophical defenders and detractors of writing. In it, writing becomes an entity associated with genesis and invention but not with progress. There is nothing before it on which to build or with which to contrast. The lines sum up succinctly Couto's attitude to writing. It is always something that is meant to interact with the reader; it fixes nothing, testifying to no truth, and it authorizes multiple interpretations.

In contrast to Plato, Saussure, and Lévi-Strauss who variously condemn writing for being dead and distanced from a presumed purity of the spoken voice, Couto's treatment of the script often renders the written an organic entity. At the same time, it becomes something fluid, a challenge to Hegel and David Diringer's approval of the writing system as a mechanism through which progress is enabled because records are fixed.[1] Essentially, Couto refuses to situate himself on either side of the polarized debate about the moral charge of writing, instead preferring to undermine the basic premises on which both sides of the argument agree. For Couto, writing, as we shall see in this chapter, is something that transcends limitations: it creates life and is subject to change. Through his portrayal of writing, Couto is at his most poststructural, but in a very idiosyncratic manner. While Derrida critiques, in *Of Grammatology,* logocentrism—the privileging of a presumed presence of the spoken voice over the writing system—by asserting that the mechanisms of the spoken voice follow those of its written counterpart, Couto reverses the concatenation of the critique.[2] For him, writing acquires the attributes of orality. This is a crucial distinction and one that is grounded on the particular historical moment through which his nation is passing. The postindependence literacy drives, although hindered by the horrific conflict, achieved impressive results. Mozambique, for the first time in its history, is turning into a nation where the population beyond urban elites can read and write. One result of this transition is, according to Walter Ong, a demotion of the status afforded to the spoken voice. For him, speech, in literate societies, becomes an adjunct of writing, and literate people lose the ability to "sense what the spoken word actually is."[3] Couto, in repeated displays of highly literate linguistic virtuosity, attempts to recuperate the residue of orality in his texts. Given his personal privileged position as the product of a literary tradition, he could never truly grasp what it means to be from an oral culture, nor is that his project. Instead, his writing provides what Niyi Afolabi terms "a bridge between tradition and modernity, Portugal and Mozambique, orality and the written word."[4] At the same time, his diegetic treatment of writing serves as an affront to Western expectations. Writing never behaves as it is supposed to.

Orality has become a very fashionable shibboleth in postcolonial studies, following on from poststructuralism, particularly as a binary counterpart to the written word. However, the term is rarely defined in its own right, and seems to have become a universal category that is essentially invariable between the cultures and social classes to which it is applied. At the same time, literate critics patronizingly assign the designation to predominantly illiterate societies as a means of explaining a particular brand of literature, or a particular cultural mindset that orders time and space in a manner different from the Western paradigm. Clearly, orality is related to the spoken voice, and may be understood as a tradition of transmitting cultural knowledge through acoustic repetition. As such, it is a tradition that affects all cultures: the first stories a child learns are heard, not read in silence. Furthermore, the Western literary canon may have been written down, but it began life as the repeatedly inflected poetry of performers in Ancient Greece and then the troubadours, and these beginnings remain imprinted on what has followed.

The repeated use of orality as a marker of national identity often applied to Africa suggests that the processes of cultural inscription related to the continent's new nation-states diverge significantly from the model that Benedict

Anderson outlines in the case of Europe. For him, print capitalism was essential to the forging of European national identities.[5] This has not been the case for most of Africa, and the dilemma facing many African writers is how to forge a national identity that is inclusive in a medium (writing) that still excludes many Africans. Bringing orality to bear on the script has provided part of the answer, and is a tactic that Couto has refined in a way that avoids being patronizing because he never relinquishes his personal position as a writer who belongs to a very literate lusophone tradition. In fact, he has added a new dimension to the relationship between orality and national literature because he never compromises his extremely literate writing skills, but recenters the voice. His strategy takes the attributes of one medium and gives them to the other. His repeated use of letters as a narrative trope demonstrates this tactic. Letters, in all traditions, bring the voice to bear on the written text. The spoken word is filled with emotion and subjectivity; it is a performance that places a person at the center. Writing, in both Hegelian and Platonic logic, objectifies and distances. Letters as a genre, however, bring subjectivities back to the forefront, and almost act like the spoken voice, in placing a person back at the center. It is hardly surprising, then, that Couto should use letters in so many of his narratives. They bring the voice into the script. They render explicit what Michel de Certeau views as a necessary tendency followed by orality: "orality insinuates itself . . . into the network . . . of a scriptural economy."[6]

Certeau critiques what he terms as the "modern mythical practice" of writing, and suggests that, through it, "the oral" is linked to "that which does not contribute to progress" while "the scriptural" is "that which separates itself from the magical world of voices and tradition."[7] In essence, he is challenging Hegel's hierarchy, a challenge Couto takes up too, by ensuring that his scriptural economy is always invaded by the voice. As Maria Lúcia Lepecki astutely observes, Couto's work is a constant play between writing an orality and narrating a script.[8]

Couto's style has variously been described as renovating, recreating, and revitalizing the language in which he writes. His texts are seen to bring life to, and bring to life, the Portuguese tongue and, as Jared Banks has pointed out, the critical reception to Couto's work has tended to focus on his use of language.[9] It has become an often-repeated belief that Couto's writing is grounded on the spoken language of Mozambique. David Brookshaw was among the first to note that Couto's writing is "inspired by the oral narrative, and elaborated in a literary language derived from the way Mozambicans speak Portuguese."[10] João Louro similarly claims that the principal base for Couto's writing is "the richness present in the orality inherent in the speech of the Mozambican people" [a riqueza existente na oralidade inerente ao falar do povo moçambicano].[11] Orlando de Albuquerque and José Ferraz Motta argue that Couto captures the spoken language of Mozambique with "a masterly spontaneity and fidelity" [uma espontaneidade e fidelidade magistrais].[12] Such assertions reveal a tendency toward reductionism on the subject of how Mozambicans speak Portuguese. Indeed, Gerald Moser recounts the opinion of a Mozambican friend that, for many intellectuals, "Maputo is Mozambique, Mozambique is Maputo. Nothing good can come from the provinces!" [Maputo é Moçambique, Moçambique é Maputo. Nada de bom pode surgir da província!].[13] This comment echoes the nineteenth-century Portuguese author Eça de Queirós's allegation that a country is little more than its capital.[14] As the most accessible point for many academics, particularly during the civil war that followed independence in 1975 and lasted until 1992, Maputo was taken to represent the whole of Mozambique. Characteristics of the urban, cosmopolitan capital with a relatively well developed formal education sector and a high degree of fluency in Portuguese were adduced in evidence to support claims covering a largely rural, ethnically diverse country.

Patrick Chabal and José Ornelas have made much of the cultural diversity of Mozambique, and thus avoid the charge of homogenizing the country. Ornelas argues that Couto's work, viewed in its totality, "is characterized by a hybridity generated through the intersection of the voice and the script" [caracteriza-se por um hibridismo gerado pela intersecção da voz e da letra].[15] There is a spoken source for the written text. However, Ornelas's interpretation of Couto's work foregrounds the intervention of the tropes of the written text on the spoken voice. Couto changes the language that he hears, rendering it more complex through very literary devices, and this process mirrors the complexity of Mozambican society. Of course, no society is anything other than complex, so Ornelas's argument could be redeployed to assert that Couto has created the ultimate "universal" text, an accolade the writer himself carefully sidesteps. For example, Nelson Saúte, interviewing Couto, attempted to link the local character of what Couto writes, to its universal appeal. Couto replied, "Quasimodo used to say that being from a particular place and from a particular time is the secret behind writing with universal appeal. Someone once said that the world begins in our village. But I don't know to what degree I've been able to paint a picture of my village" [Quasimodo dizia que ser de um lugar e de um tempo é que faz o segredo da escrita universal. Alguém disse que o mundo começa na nossa aldeia. Mas eu não sei até que ponto fui capaz de fazer o retrato da minha aldeia].[16] Couto does not allow himself to fall into the trap of claiming that he represents anything other than himself. At the same time, he is prepared, implicitly at least, to accept that the appeal of what he writes is partly due to the Mozambican local flavor that his world readership happily assigns to his texts.

For Chabal, writing in 1996, because of its historical complexity and its nature as a poorly integrated colonial construct, "Mozambique is not yet a country in any meaningful sense of the word."[17] Largely devoid of the social and cultural attributes of the modern nation-state, "Mozambique is itself part reality and part fiction," a type of nonentity which exists.[18] The logic of Chabal's argument is that cultural attributes are essential to the creation of a nation, and for Mozambique to become a reality more fiction is required. The (non)country is at a phase of cultural inscription; the nation is in the process of being written. Chabal describes Couto's project in the author's first novel, *Terra Sonâmbula,* which we will discuss in depth later in this chapter, as seeking to "contribute to the construction of a 'national' culture." The importance of this enterprise, in Chabal's opinion, is that "it is culture, the word, which transforms the land called Mozambique into a coherent entity. So that Mia Couto has written in this book a 'text' in which the inhabitants of Mozambique might one day recognize themselves as Mozambicans."[19] The *logos* is to be the means by which the nation will be defined. Yet Chabal's interpretation of Couto's role in this defining process attributes the characteristics of the *logos* to the script. The spoken word may be seen to permeate Couto's work, but the written word gives the nation meaning by fixing it through his texts. Couto attempts to construct something that "binds the oral and the written." His style is "eminently oral, both in language and in structure" and "text and dialogue straddle each other creatively and combine to produce an orality which the written language in turn seeks to accommodate."[20] The spoken word of Mozambique, as complicated as that geographical entity is, constitutes the life-blood of Couto's written texts to the minds of Chabal, Brookshaw, Louro, and many other critics. While these critics render the spoken word a natural source for the written, they do not concomitantly devalorize the script, as Plato, Saussure and Lévi-Strauss do. Indeed, Chabal concludes that Couto, like José Craveirinha, who is considered to be the greatest twentieth-century Mozambican poet, is able to "craft an original literary text drawing on the oral African tradition *only* because he is privileged enough to come to the oral tradition from the perspective of a solid and wide ranging universal literary culture."[21] Chabal views the technology of writing as a necessary and positive force in the construction of a national identity—a useful tool which, in the case of Couto's Mozambique, captures the spirit of an oral culture. As we shall now see, in Couto, the oral also infiltrates and undermines the preserve of the written, insinuating itself into the "scriptural economy."

"A LIÇÃO DO APRENDIZ":
A PLAY ON PRESENCE

Epistles make appearances on many occasions in Couto's texts. Letters, in literate traditions, serve many purposes. They carry the voice afar, and act as
permanent records. They become the property of the receiver, while remaining the emotional asset of the remitter. A letter writer relinquishes legal ownership of his or her words once the missive is sent. Letters also render patent
a subjectivity in the script, and are the written manifestation closest to the
spoken voice. Letters may serve as introductions and, in such instances, the
written precedes the spoken; the bearer of the letter remains silent until the
receiver has absorbed the contents of the note.

The opening line of the short story "A Lição do Aprendiz" [The Appren-
tice's Lesson] is "he introduced himself with a letter in his hand" [apresentou-
se com uma carta na mão (C, 73)]. Before we learn of anything else, we know
of the existence of an epistle. Before anyone speaks, the written is given
precedence. Before anyone is identified, the letter comes into play. The tale is
centered on the relationship between the barber Lázaro and Antoninho
whom the war has orphaned. Lázaro's cousin, Ezequiel, has sent the young
boy with the intention that the barber should look after him. Antoninho
soon reveals himself to be technically skilful but refuses to profit personally,
preferring to return to his rural home, which he deems to be in need of his
ability.

While the letter remains in play, the child remains voiceless. He replies to
Lázaro's questions using various parts of his body, "doing without his voice"
[dispensando a voz (73)]. His actions run counter to Walter Ong's assertion
that only spoken words and not the written text "engage the body" since the
contents of the letter are clarified and supplemented by the movement of the
child's body: "he nodded his head"; "it was his shoulders which replied" [ace-
nou com a cabeça; foram os ombros que responderam (C, 73)]. Ong, a Jesuit
whose books have variously attempted to reaffirm the Platonic supremacy of
the spoken voice and condemned writing for its lack of presence and its close
association with death, asserts that, in opposition to written words, "spoken
words are always modifications of a total, existential situation, which always
engages the body."[22] Yet spoken words are absent from the orphan. In contrast, the text of the letter and its bodily accompaniment—for the child's
presence is the point of the missive—say it all. The letter substitutes the oral
domain. Antoninho remains taciturn until the very end of the story when his
actions—what he does with his body—will speak louder than his words.

Lázaro is left to decode the meaning the letter brought into his life. We are told that the barber, who has momentarily doubted Antoninho's honesty, is left to ponder his own image in the mirror the young orphan has fixed for him, "as if there was in his nephew's absence a lesson that he could gradually decipher" [como se houvesse na ausência do sobrinho uma lição que ele lentamente decifrasse (*C*, 76)]. The barber has judged the boy by the self-interested and less than honest standards to which he subscribes. The orphan has gone. All that is left is a letter, which now marks the child's absence rather than introducing his presence, and a repaired mirror through which Lázaro can see himself more clearly. It is at the point that presence flickers into absence that the text of Lázaro's life takes meaning, for it is only then that the barber understands the significance of a destitute orphan who can retain hope, integrity and a sense of duty to his community in the midst of immense suffering. Lázaro, whose name marks him as someone who will be resurrected, is brought back to meaningful life by the boy's example.

Couto, in this story, plays with the concepts of presence and absence, and their relationship to the written and the spoken. Western tradition has generally ascribed presence to the spoken voice and absence to the written text. Couto reverses the correlation, by rendering spoken words sparse and by allying the epistle to Antoninho's body, in the process subverting one of Plato's main complaints against writing. Plato objects to writing's tendency to symbolize a lack because written words are meant to mark absences.[23] But for Couto, the letter introduces, and is linked to, a bodily presence—something even more tangible than the spoken voice. It is only at the end of the story that the written reverts to a marker of absence, and at that point, the child's former presence as an illuminating influence on the cynical barber acquires its meaning.

"A CARTA":
ORALITY OVER LITERACY

Presence and absence are also crucial concepts with which Couto plays in "A Carta" [The Letter]. The narrative tells the story of Mamã Cacilde, an old woman who possesses one letter her son, a conscripted soldier who is now absented from her life, has sent to her. She cannot read it herself for she is illiterate so the narrator does that for her, repeatedly. Initially, he is true to the harsh and loveless text but, as time passes, he changes it into a warmer missive.

As in "A Lição do Aprendiz," the absent writer of the letter is called Ezequiel. Ezequiel is the name of the Old Testament prophet who was struck dumb by Yahweh and became his mouthpiece, able to speak only the words of the Lord. In one of his visions, Yahweh gives him a scroll, with writing on both sides, and makes him eat it before going on to speak to the House of Israel.[24] A complex relationship is thus established between the script and speech: the written word is consumed and transformed into the spoken voice, a voice devoid of human volition. The voice is informed by the digested text, which it internalizes. This mirrors the religious practice of chanting psalms or learning other biblical texts by heart, a process through which the primacy of the written is complicated by the requirement of the voice to bring life to the text. In "A Carta," the relationship between the script and speech is as complex since the written text is effectively consumed by the spoken voice. The difference is that the authority of the author is not respected and human will very much intervenes in the realm of the creator, the "original" author of the letter.

Ezequiel was also the Prophet of Exile, writing his text at a time when the Jewish people were absent from their homeland. Absence thus marks the text of the prophet, and similarly, the Ezequiels of Couto's tales are characterized through texts that mark their absences. They may be the sources of the letters but the letters themselves, once they have left the hands of their writers, take on an independent existence. Indeed, in the case of "A Carta," the epistle literally takes on a life of its own.

Ezequiel in "A Carta" dies as a consequence of war, with the result that the absent source of the letter no longer has life. Yet the letter constantly attaches itself to the organic. When it is first introduced to the tale, it is described in the Portuguese text as "dobrado em mil sujidades" (*C*, 13)—"folded in filth a thousand times over" (*EMIR*, 89). Prior to the letter's appearance in the text, Mamã Cacilda is introduced: "A velha dobrou as pernas como se dobrasse os séculos" (*C*, 13)—"The old woman bent her legs as if she was bending the centuries" (*EMIR*, 89). Derivatives of the Portuguese verb "dobrar," which Brookshaw translates as both "to fold" and "to bend," link the letter to the life of the old woman, to her longevity ("centuries") and to her body ("legs").

Over time, the letter becomes more than merely representative of the son: "Now, with the passing of time, the bit of paper was the only proof of her Ezequiel. It was as if her son only complied with existence through that ever more faded handwriting" (*EMIR*, 89). His existence, in absence, depends on the letter, but for the wrong reasons. It is not because of the script's ability to assure perpetuity since his handwriting will fade. Rather, it is because of orality's interference with the script as the attributes of the voice permit constant recreation. By the latter stage of the tale, he becomes the letter as Mamã

Cacilda asks the narrator, "Have you come to read me my son?" (91). The letter is no longer a written text, it is a living being that takes on a character of its own, replacing the source (Ezequiel) that it supplements.

The apparently permanent writing on the page becomes more and more "faded" as it is subjected to the rigors of the spoken voice. The script becomes the passive object that is changed by the activity of the voice. The letter becomes an orally over-written palimpsest and the permanence of writing is lost.

The loss of scriptural permanence signaled in Couto's text ruptures one of the pillars of the Hegelian Grand Narrative. Henry Louis Gates places Hegel in a paradigm that covers Decartes and Vico, and that associates the operation of reason, and history itself, on the repeatability of the written sign, a quality dependent on writing's fixture.[25] Spoken words are lost the moment they are uttered. History, according to Hegel, is only able to progress once it is written down.[26] Similarly, but from an epistemological standpoint, Diringer asserts, "writing gives permanence to man's knowledge."[27] Once writing is allowed to mutate, Hegel's concept of history, and Diringer's perception of knowledge construction are undermined.

The story that Couto relates, overshadowed by the reality of a civil war and a Frelimo dogma that broke the tradition of respect for elders, becomes a game of ambiguities in which the power writing has (to privilege literates over illiterates)—one of Lévi-Strauss's principal complaints against it—becomes less than certain.[28] In this way, Couto successfully distorts both flanks of the moral debate about the nature of writing, and offers an alternative in which an illiterate woman demonstrates a status superior to the literate narrator and a more profound knowledge than him through the effect she has on a sample of writing. The alphabetic letters that make up the missive in "A Carta" change their characteristics as the tale progresses. They mature and come to open up infinite possibilities. Initially, when the narrator is true to the epistle's text, "the letters were uneven, like school children breaking out of line" (*EMIR,* 89). The value of each letter is not fixed. They are dubious and variable, and have yet to grow up and fulfill their potential. The illiterate Mamã Cacilda redefines their never-ending potential for playful multiplicity rather than finite meaning when she insists that "letters are the same as stars: though few, they are infinite" (90). By linking the technology of writing to the stars, she establishes an equivalence between a source—stars are the source of light and heat—and what traditionally is deemed to represent a source—writing is supposed to represent the voice. Once the narrator is told this, despite his condescending attitude toward the "poor mother without any schooling" (90), he turns the letters into the source. They no longer represent Ezequiel; they recreate him and, in the process, turn him into a source of emotional light and heat, which in reality he was not. The letters are the starting point for the transformation that will be mediated through the voice of the narrator. The narrator's voice comes to represent the written source—a source that changes and is changed by each reading since "at each reading, a new letter emerged from the old missive" (90).

One day, the narrator is required to inform Mamã Cacilda of the death of Ezequiel. He does not manage to fulfill this duty but instead ends up "reading" the organic letter once more. Prior to performing this task for the last time, the narrator claims in the Portuguese text that "atravessei a escrita, ao avesso da verdade" (C, 15). This phrase, like so many others in Couto's work, is rich in possible meanings. Brookshaw translates it as "I set off across the writing, in the opposite direction of truth" (EMIR, 91). "Atravessar" can, and usually does, carry the connotation of traversing, of crossing, of going over. So, "atravessar a escrita" communicates the notion of crossing over the writing, as if the writing were a path. But it is a path leading elsewhere since "atravessar a rua" would in most cases not imply that one were following the road. Rather, it often connotes crossing over the road, to the other side of the street. The street is leading elsewhere. The road-crosser meets the street, is changed by the experience of meeting the street, but is not led by the street. By analogy, the writing changes the reader but does not lead him or her.

"Atravessar" can also mean to hinder, to block, to thwart. In some contexts, it can mean to pierce through or to perforate. The phrase "atravessar a escrita" is haunted by these other possibilities. The writing could be being thwarted by the narrator. Or it could be that he perforates the page, piercing through the written fact to reach the other side of the truth. In both these cases the writing is not left unchanged by the experience. Its permanence and impenetrability are called into question.

"Avesso" is certainly used to mean "contrary" or "opposite." However, in the phrase "ao avesso" the connotation of being "inside out" is often signified. As such, it would not necessarily mean that it was the "opposite" since a shirt worn inside out is still essentially the same shirt. Considered in this way, "ao avesso da verdade" does not intrinsically change the truth. What alters is the perspective from which the truth is viewed. This change in perspective is linked to the intervention of a written letter on an oral culture.

"A Carta" is a tale in which traditional views of writing—as something unchanging and unchangeable—are not wholly reversed since there is from the beginning until the end of the story a fading letter inscribed with Ezequiel's handwriting. As he himself evanesces into a distant memory, his inscription metaphorically wilts on the page. The linked etiolations symbolize the death of the author, even before Ezequiel is killed. With each reading of his letter, another nail is hammered into the coffin of authorial intention. Both the body of his text and the text of his body become rewritten through the intervention of oral culture since it is the perspective of the illiterate Mamã Cacilda that induces the narrator to allow the written word to change.

Literate culture and orality may thus be seen to interplay in the text of the tale, invading each other's territory. Both are changed by their mutual interaction. Just at the moment when it appears that the narrator—the representative of literacy who is seduced by the techniques of orality—has successfully and compassionately deceived Mamã Cacilda—the representative of oral culture who esteems the written letter—Mamã Cacilda tries to deceive the narrator. She consigns the letter to flames, at once ending both its organic life and, permanently, the permanence of its writing.

The importance of this story is that it privileges the techniques of orality through the medium of a written text. The arrogance and dominance of literate culture is taught a lesson by a woman it mistakes to be ignorant because she cannot read. She shows the narrator, and the reader, that all texts vary each time they are read. As in so many other stories by Couto, a woman teaches a man a lesson he barely understands. The ultimate fate of the letter, its incineration, is an epistolary demise repeated in another of Couto's short stories, "A Princesa Russa."

"A PRINCESA RUSSA": A PLAY ON ABSENCE

Letters consigned to flames do not necessarily cede their influence in Couto's texts. Indeed, they can continue to exist in Couto's realm of magic possibilities. In fact, in "A Princesa Russa" [The Russian Princess], letters burned before they can be posted provoke replies. The story involves a Russian couple, Nádia and Iúri, who come to Mozambique to prospect for gold, and is narrated by Duarte Fortin, an *assimilado*, who serves them. Assimilados were Africans who were deemed by the colonial Portuguese to be acculturated in European mores. As a consequence, they ceased to be classed as natives, and in principle, this conferred the privileges of Portuguese citizenship on them. In practice, their skin pigmentation was never, during the colonial era, forgotten. The concept of the assimilado became a prominent feature of Portuguese colonial rhetoric after the Berlin Conference of 1884–85, which carved Africa up between the European powers. Up until that point, all inhabitants of Mozambique were technically deemed to be equal under the law, a vestige of the enlightened dictatorship of one of Portugal's strongest and most controversial rulers, the Marques de Pombal. Pombal, who ruled in the name of D. José, used the opportunity of the great Lisbon earthquake of 1755 to move ruthlessly against his opponents and to bring Portugal into the Age of Enlightenment.[29] In effect, the antidiscriminatory legislation he enacted was often ignored in the colonies, and the range of racist laws passed in the aftermath of Europe's division of Africa merely reflected common practice. In 1899, António Ennes, a Portuguese High Commissioner in Mozambique, introduced a Colonial Labor Law in the Lisbon Parliament that classified Africans as "indígenas" and was principally a mechanism through which forced labor was relegitimized after slavery had been officially abolished in the colonies.[30] A practice developed whereby an African could apply to the local administrator of his area for a certificate that would reclassify him as *civilisado,* or civilized. In theory, this meant that he enjoyed all the same rights and protections as a white. The term was replaced by assimilado in 1954, when Salazar revised his colonial labor legislation, and formalized the expectations required to achieve this status.[31] It was finally abolished in 1961 as international pressure mounted on the Portuguese colonial regime. Very few Africans achieved the status that required, among other things, the demonstration of a proficient command of speaking and reading the Portuguese language.[32]

In Couto's tale, an assimilado takes center stage, controlling a narration in the form of a confession. The confession is told to a priest who, given the vocative structure of the tale, is the reader. Fortin's voice is the written text. The priest's ear is the reader's eye. Through the events of the tale, Fortin becomes close to Nádia who is more or less imprisoned by her husband. She becomes ill and, one day, asks Fortin to post a letter for her that was "a matter of the greatest secrecy, no one should ever suspect" (*EMIR,* 45). Secrecy already pervades the tale at other levels since Fortin and his reader/priest are morally constrained by the sacred bond—effectively an unspoken contract—which restricts both human parties in the Sacrament of Reconciliation to perpetual silence with regard to the penitent's revelations inside the confines of the confessional. Given the structure of the text, this oral and therefore fleeting confession becomes an eternal, written narrative since the reader of the tale is the priest in the confessional box. Thus, at an extradiegetic level, secrecy operates as a bond between reader and narrator. Within the narrative, the secrecy surrounding Nádia's letter also functions as a bond, further linking Fortin to his employer's wife. The symbol of this union is something written. Its significance, however, is only gained in the physical act of hand-ing it over since it can mean nothing else to Fortin as he cannot read it: it is in Russian.

The written letter also symbolizes the trust that Nádia places in Fortin, when she asks him to post it and to remain silent about what he is doing for her. She had previously confessed to him that the only love of her life was a man called Anton, who lived in Russia. The reader presumes that the letter is destined for this lover. It was the first of many letters.

The more Nádia writes, the more ill she becomes. Her handwriting reflects her emotional state, and is an instance of physicality invading the scriptural economy: "the letters on the envelope shook with her fever" (46). The heat, which characterizes her script, signals in advance the fate of each letter. Similarly, Fortin's explanation for his betrayal of Nádia's trust also signposts the letters' destiny. Immediately prior to confessing he burned all the letters she gave him to post, he claims, in the Portuguese text, that it was the fear of being caught with the proof "ardendo em plena mão" (*CHER,* 82) [burning in his hands] that led him to feed them to the kitchen stove. The written word is related to heat and to fire before the reader/priest learns that it is actually burned. Hell and writing are linked. In contrast, absolution and the spoken voice are tied together by the confessional setting of the tale. However, these moral charges are far from fixed. Fortin ends his confession acknowledging that he will probably end up in hell; absolution will have no effect and the spoken word will fail to heal. But it will be a hell inscribed with Nádia's footprints and therefore, because she is there, more akin to his idea of heaven.

Furthermore, it appears that at least one of the letters escapes from hell since, one day, Nádia claims that Anton has sent her a reply. She shows Fortin the physical proof although the assimilado doubts its provenance. She might have written the letter to herself. In any case, she believes in the letter, and insists on going to meet Anton at the train station. At this point in the tale, Fortin begins to fantasize about Nádia in her vulnerable state. He imagines that he is Anton. He, who has attempted to destroy the letters that created Anton, wishes to become the source of the reply (Anton), creator and created, written to and spoken of by Nádia. That very reply is now fantasized by both Fortin and Nádia, as is its nonexistent, dead author. Since the letter is both a fiction—with its intangible author—and a reality—as it physically exists—it serves to fuse both presence and absence. Moreover, Fortin wishes to give presence to the absent man of the dreams of the woman of his dreams. As he later confesses to his reader/priest, "opposites are the most alike" (*EMIR,* 48). Presence fuses with absence. Anton, for Nádia, becomes Fortin and then Iúri when he appears at the train station. The spoken collapses into the written and vice versa since the confession is an oral testimony read by the priest. The feminine combines with the masculine as Nádia becomes a part of Fortin, while never belonging to him. He describes himself as "a widower of a wife I never had," and claims that the footprints he leaves on the ground are a combination of hers and his (50).

The letters in "A Princesa Russa" bring Anton, the present/absent author, to life for Nádia, as well as serving to bring meaning into the life of Fortin through the bond to Nádia they represent for him. Once again, as in "A Lição do Aprendiz," a play between presence and absence results in a new meaning, the tangibility of which flees immobilization. Additionally, Couto ruptures religious expectations in the tale, since Fortin essentially seeks to be forgiven for not sinning. His desire for Nádia had been constrained by his training as an assimilado, upholding the patriarchal order of Iúri by destroying the evidence of his wife's longing for another. He betrays his Russian princess and prevents her emancipation; because of his actions, her letters of desperation never reach their destination. But like so many other characters in Couto's work, that does not stop her dreaming a different reality into existence. The power of the written text as Couto constructs it resides in its ability to create a new reality that transcends the existence of those it allows to dream.

"O Coração do Menino e o Menino do Coração": The Life-giving Letter

While the letters in "A Princesa Russa" bring Anton to life for Nádia but result in her own death, the letters in "O Coração do Menino e o Menino do Coração" [The Heart of the Boy and the Boy of the Heart] bring life back to the young child protagonist, at least when they are recognized for what they are. The young boy of the story remains nameless throughout, as does the disease from which he suffers which renders his speech unintelligible to other human beings. The doctors are more interested in defining the child's affliction than in curing him.

The narrator of the story claims, "there is nothing more frightening than not understanding as human the voice of another human being" [não há medo maior que não se entenda humana a voz de outra humana pessoa (*CDNT,* 241)]. The child's inability to speak appears to render him less than human. Yet he exhibits a skill that, although unrecognized until after his death, in Diringer's logic, makes him even more human than the skill of speech. Diringer, like Hegel before him, established a clear hierarchy in which writing was "more peculiar to man than speech."[33] To be human, for the historian of the script, means to write. And that is precisely what the child does, writing letters copiously. In the hospital, "the child held in his hand, hanging like a petal, a letter that he himself had edited. He would have liked to have given this little paper, which his inability had filled with small letters, to the doctor. With inattentive tenderness, his mother took the paper from his fingers and threw it in the bin" [o menino levava em sua mão, descaída como pétala, uma carta que ele mesmo redigira. Queria ter dado ao doutor esse papelinho que sua inabilidade enchera de letrinha. Com desatenta ternura, a mãe lhe tirou o papel dos dedos e o lançou no latão (242)]. The letter is linked, through its association with a petal, to nature. Writing is a natural part of the child, even if intelligible speech is not. The child's mother has just been patronized by the doctor, a man of letters, whose only concern is to categorize the disease and fix it permanently in the realm of nomenclature. But the mother has seen through the lack of concern the doctor had for her son. The medical profession, as he represents it, is more concerned with the progress of its own discourse than with the welfare of "those simple little people" [essa gentinha simples (242)]. As the mother leaves with her son, she absent-mindedly disregards the letter the child has written as "another one of those tons of letters that the daft little boy pretended to write to his passionate young cousin" [outra dessas tantíssimas cartas que o tontinho fingia escrever para sua apaixonada priminha (242)], thus marking the technology of writing as one which involves pretence. Furthermore, writing, rather than his inability to speak, is what designates the child as daft, or even stupid, since the Portuguese word Couto uses is "tontinho." In this way, she combines two strands of the Platonic argument against writing—its falsehood and its stupidity. No matter what question is put to it, writing will always inanely repeat itself. As Plato asserts, "written words: you might think that they spoke as if they had some thought in their heads, but if you ever ask them about any of the things they say out of a desire to learn, they point to just one thing, the same each time."[34]

However, the key role of writing in the story runs counter to the Platonic view because writing gives the author life after death; it gives him a presence even in absence. The child dies and his body becomes an object of medical science. Then one day the cousin to whom the letters were addressed discovers them. As she reads them and is touched by their beauty, the boy comes back to life. The written text resurrects the author through its interaction with the reader. In fact, the child is perfected by being reread. Prior to his death he has a defect in his feet, which leads his grandmother to conclude, "this child is going to follow a path inwardly to himself" [este menino vai caminhar para dentro dele mesmo (241)]. After his body has regrown, his feet become "divergent, like he who comes to search for people from other stories, outside of himself" [divergentes, como quem viesse para procurar, fora de si, gente de outras estórias (243)]. Through his text, he is able to do something that his nature had prevented him from doing. He can communicate with others. The reading of his texts changes his nature and is a process of exchange. He lives on through the permanence of the written and through the permanent change in the interpretation by his reader of what he has written. At the same time, he uses letters to achieve an orality denied to his voice and, through them, reclaims a subjectivity.

In this story, Couto ruptures a variety of orders and orthodoxies. First, the Platonic image of writing is seemingly endorsed, only to be undermined by its ability to bestow life. Second, the medical establishment is savagely critiqued for its inhumanity and patronizing nature. The doctor is only interested in naming and the progress of his own research. Yet his discourse is based on writing, and the child whom he disregards and then dissects is the embodiment of a written text. In fact, the doctor paradoxically dissects his own discourse through the boy, who, in turn, uses letters to achieve orality. Finally, Couto offers his familiar opinion that the written text can leave the page and assume an organic existence that is transformative and transforming. Words can lead the way to a new reality even in those that have been denied a voice, as is the case of the child in the story, and of much of the Mozambican population. Through words, and the verbalization of dreams, a new order can, in Couto's world, be brought to life. An interesting aspect of Couto's use of letters is the way in which they allow marginalized voices, such as Mamã Cacilde, Antoninho, and the young boy, to become the center of a text.

"As Cartas" and "Dois Corações, Uma Caligrafia": Writing Unfaithfully

Letters have repeatedly surfaced as a narrative trope in Couto's work from his collection *Cronicando* that published as an anthology many of the stories that had appeared between 1987 and 1988 in Maputo's *Notícias* to his 2001 collection *Na Berma de Nenhuma Estrada*. "A Carta" and "A Lição do Aprendiz," both from *Cronicando,* share a preoccupation with equating meaning to a play between absence and presence. Both are also set against the backdrop of the civil war. In many respects, "A Princesa Russa" from the 1990 collection

Cada Homem É Uma Raça repeats the use of an epistolary text as a means of playing with the demarcation between presence and absence. In 1997, five years after the Mozambican peace accords and three years after the first multiparty elections in the nation's history that effectively marked the end of the conflict, Couto published *Contos do Nascer da Terra* of which "O Coração do Menino e o Menino do Coração" is a part. In it, letters become a device that symbolizes the overcoming of death. The author's priorities had changed. Meaning no longer had to be reestablished in the postconflict situation. The main source of death had been overcome, and a different portrayal of letters reflected the new reality. By the time Couto published *Na Berma de Nenhuma Estrada,* he was using letters to undermine the possibility of a univocal truth, but once again through play with meaning dependent on the interaction between presence and absence. In many respects, the tales that deploy letters in Couto's 2001 collection repeat the lesson of *A Varanda do Frangipani* that no single truth is possible or desirable, but from the less fraught position of a society that had successfully recovered from the conflict and had adopted a pluralist, democratic model. Democracy, as it has come to function in Mozambique and most of the rest of the postmodern world, tends toward a bland lethargy in which globalization confines political choice to a matter of different faces propounding essentially the same free-market policies. After two multiparty elections, radical ideology has disappeared from the Mozambican political landscape, replaced by a discussion of who can manage the economy more efficiently and with less corruption. In this new climate, the concept of a fixed ideologically distinct truth has vanished. Ideological dogma that was, in no small part, responsible for a failure to resolve the armed conflict more quickly, has given way to a political apathy, symbolized in the 20 percent drop in turn-out between the elections of 1994 and those of 1999.[35] In this new era of apathetic pluralism, Couto uses humor to reflect his society's rejection of definitive truths. Letters enter the foray, as shifters of truth in two short stories, "As Cartas" [The Letters] and "Dois Corações, Uma Caligrafia" [Two Hearts, One Caligraphy]. As the confusion related to their writers' identities grows, new truths emerge.

"As Cartas" and "Dois Corações, Uma Caligrafia" focus on women, and reorder the moral charge associated with adultery. Adulterous acts, as they are revealed, bring women together in a unity that excludes the men they share. Letters that stereotypically form a trail leading to the discovery of adultery by the injured party are redeployed as a mechanism through which the women in the stories come together, and bypass the men. The traditional compulsion to blame women in adulterous situations, prevalent in Western literary tradition, finds an equivalent in the praxis of a Mozambican society that severely restricts expression of female sexuality as an undesirable vice while lauding male promiscuity as the embodiment of virility.[36] However, in these stories, Couto once again puts women in the narrative driving seat and subverts the paradigms of orthodoxy.

"As Cartas" is the story of a set of mysterious letters that circulate among the women of Mutarara, imploring them to have an affair with Marcelo, who has been transferred there without his wife, Nurima. At the beginning of the tale, Couto declares, "waiting is a web, people create presences with the materials of absence" [a espera é uma tecedura, a gente cria presenças com materiais de ausência (*NBNE*, 85)]. The implication is that the wife is left with a void that her husband formerly occupied and must somehow fill it. Before reading the remainder of the story, the possibility that Nurima will be unfaithful, replacing her absent husband with present lovers, is suggested, particularly since the sentence prior to the one just cited describes her as "sozinhando-se" (85), one of Couto's neologisms that connotes "becoming lonely." The reader is then told that Nurima's fingers "desinventavam dias" (85), another neologism, the pragmatic meaning of which will only become apparent at the end of the story. At this stage of the narrative, it semantically means that her fingers "uninvented days." The subsequent sentence that the wife was "habituada, não habitada" (85) could be read as a play on words that asserts that she was used to her condition, but not in a (presumed-to-be celibate) nun's habit. This interpretation compounds the implication that a sexual practice, be it masturbation or adultery, provides the outlet for her loneliness. Another way of reading the pun is that the wife becomes used to her condition of not being inhabited, a metaphor for a lack of intercourse. This second reading still allows for the possibility of her own masturbation, particularly given the earlier reference to fingers being used to wile away the days. At this point, letters are introduced to the narrative, when an acquaintance, Florlinda, visits Nurima to tell her about the appearance of missives imploring the most attractive women in Mutarara to have affairs with Marcelo. Florlinda describes the letters as a threat to Nurima. The wife asks if her husband knows of their existence to which Florlinda replies that, as far as she can tell, Marcelo's life is just work and then home. The two women spend the afternoon in intimate conversation, becoming closer to each other, until night falls, and Florlinda has to leave. At the door, she promises Nurima that she will find a way to stop the letters circulating, at which point Nurima takes hold of her newly established friend's wrist as if she wanted to "confess something personal" [confessar alguma intimidade (86)]. But she does not. Several weeks pass before Florlinda returns with a plan to eliminate the letters. At that point, Nurima becomes "strangely absent" [estranhamente ausente (86)]. Absence is her defining characteristic as she confesses that she is the writer of the mystery letters. She explains that Marcelo is such a good husband that he did not deserve the "punishment of absence" [castigo de ausência (87)]. Should he have an affair, he would discover that no woman loves him as much as she does. At this point, Florlinda confesses she has, in fact, had an affair with Marcelo. Nurima's reaction is, in turn, to confess she already knew this, and that she had known it from Florlinda's first visit. As Florlinda begins to explain why she came, Nurima maternally silences her, with a heart full of gratitude. So the story ends. While the adulterous experience may have shown Marcelo how much his own wife loves him, the main effect of the adultery is to bring the two women together.

There is a constant play between presence and absence in the story, and the letters more than anything else embody this play. The process of writing them occupies the space that Marcelo leaves in Nurima's life; there is a pleasure in their textuality that substitutes an absent sex life for the abandoned wife. At the same time, they exclude Marcelo at a number of levels. First, they are not directed to him: a corruption of the expected epistolary protocol related to an absent lover. Second, they reduce him to an object traded between women. It is, after all, his wife who is calling on other females to sleep with her betrothed. Third, they create a bond between two women that need not be spoken, and that marginalizes Marcelo. Although at one level he has brought them together, they no longer need him to enjoy intimacy with each other. Nurima physically covers Florlinda's lips at the end of the story; spoken words have been superceded by their more profound understanding of each other, by the emotional orality of the letters. For Couto, the written word is the medium through which a new reality that subverts traditional constraints may be reached.

Two women are literally brought together in the text of a letter in "Dois Corações, Uma Caligrafia." The narrative is a missive sent to a philandering Adriano by his betrayed wife Zuleila. This process is complicated by the fact that Zuleila is illiterate and must rely on her young sister, Esmeraldinha, who also happens to be Adriano's discovered lover, to transcribe the angry words she directs to her unfaithful husband. Like Mamã Cacilde in "A Carta," Zuleila is a character who cannot read or write but who outwits the supposed sophistication of a representative of literate culture. As she transcribes her sister's words, Esmeraldinha surreptitiously inserts her own commentaries in constant fear that her scriptural duplicity will be discovered by the shrewd Zuleila who may not be able to read letters but who can read her sister's eyes. Zuleila's oral attack on her husband subtly undermines Esmeraldinha's affection for him as the transcriber discovers that she too has been cheated. The mention by Zuleila of a third woman with whom her husband is having an affair, Palmira, unites the two sisters against the promiscuous Adriano. The transcriber's secret interjections in the letter are replaced by a common voice of the two women against the unfaithful man. Their coalition then extends to include Palmira, with whom they intend to go to the bar and drink on Adriano's account. By the end of the letter, the sisters become Adriano's cowives, demanding that he service their needs fully, and reserve something for their newly found friend Palmira.

The humor of the story does not attenuate its powerful message. Couto uses the format of the letter to fuse the experiences of two very different women—one literate, one illiterate—and to identify a common problem from which they both suffer—their treatment at the hands of a man. The women form a common front that erases the frontier between their degree of educational attainment and foregrounds the principle cause of their restricted status in society—sexism. By the end of the tale, the frontier between the oral and the written disappears, to be replaced by another frontier that marks Mozambican society—the gender frontier that we will discuss in more detail later in this book. Yet again, Couto uses a letter to center a marginalized voice, and to allow orality's emotional subjectivities to infiltrate the "scriptural economy."

WRITING IN *A Varanda do Frangipani:* TWO ORALLY OVERWRITTEN TEXTS

A woman writes a letter that plays a crucial role in *A Varanda do Frangipani,* and once again, hierarchical distinctions between the oral and the written are called into question. In this instance, the role of the letter runs into conflict with Claude Lévi-Strauss's immense dislike of the written word. The Belgium anthropologist, who was one of the paladins of the structuralist movement, claimed that usurers and imperialists used writing as a mechanism to enslave and enforce power. He asserts that the "struggle against illiteracy is indistinguishable, at times, from the increased powers exerted over the individual citizen by the central authority" and that "the primary function of writing, as a means of communication, is to enslave other human beings."[37] The power of writing stems from its ability to delineate between individuals hierarchically, and to enforce a law against which ignorance is no longer a defense. The literate, for Lévi-Strauss, always gain the upper hand and oppress those who cannot write. His case against writing rests on a critique of the advantages exercised by those who can write and becomes less convincing as soon as literacy campaigns achieve universal coverage. However, Couto unravels Lévi-Strauss's argument from a different angle, by refusing to cede any advantage to those who write. As we have already seen, the illiterate character of Mamã Cacilde in "A Carta" is portrayed as possessing a more profound knowledge than her literate narratorial counterpart. Similarly, in *A Varanda do Frangipani,* a written text is given no more weight than its oral equivalents.

A letter constitutes the text of one chapter (the eleventh) and gives a powerful voice to the absent Ernestina. Her testimony of the events surrounding her husband's death is given as a written deposition. Her writing, to a certain extent, appears to clarify what has been going on in the old people's home. Ernestina's letter confirms Vasto's black market activities to Izidine, building on the oral intimations of Marta in the preceding chapter. Yet Couto does not give the written text the last word or any greater degree of permanence than the statements of the oral witnesses. Indeed, the letter is mediated through Marta, Vasto's mistress, who presents it to Izidine. Subsequently, she paints a very different portrait of Vasto from Ernestina's. Ernestina describes how, during the civil war, Vasto behaved without morals, confirming his brutality and his disrespect for the old people under his protection. Two chapters later, it is Marta's turn to narrate. Her evidence is oral, and she is the last witness to give her version of the events. Her portrayal of Vasto's character is more ambivalent. He is not completely evil and was capable of putting his life in danger in order to save the old people in his care. Her oral testimony overwrites and interacts with Ernestina's written evidence, destabilizing the absolute status of the written since the written text does not finish the history: it merely adds another perspective to it.

The letter has the peculiar characteristic of claiming to be purposeless. Most letters are addressed to someone. This one is not; it is destined for no one in particular and written for no particular reason. This contrasts sharply with the other written text of the novel, Izidine's teleologically marked notebook. In order to work out precisely what has happened, the detective plans to interview the old people and to write down all that they say. He wishes to structure the events and to solidify the oral evidence by "fixing down the spoken words of the elders" [fixando as falas dos mais velhos (*V,* 25)].[38] In essence, he wants to write a history—in a Hegelian understanding of the term—to make a permanent record, to force the oral voice into the permanent prison/prism of the script.

Izidine and Ernestina contrast at various levels. He is a black who has turned white. He was educated in Europe and this has alienated him from his African roots. She is a "a light-skinned lady . . . with such a Portuguese soul" (*UF,* 106), who believes in the magic powers of Nãozinha and thus privileges the spoken voice since the sorceress derives her power from the words she speaks. Yet Ernestina's medium of communication is writing. For her, the written serves to extend the oral, to allow for a multiplicity of interpretations. Her letter effectively behaves as another oral testimony, informed by and informing the other evidence in the case. For Izidine, the written fixes the oral in order to reach a single, true interpretation. So, there is a westernized African, longing for the certainty of a fixed and permanent truth, set in contrast with an africanized mulatto, who adds to the confusion through the very medium (writing) that is supposed to clarify, structure, and fix. In the malaise, neither writing nor orality can exercise advantage over the other.

Mucanga, the spirit who inhabits the detective's body, describes the fate of Izidine's notebook. He claims the notebook will rot with him in his grave and, as a consequence, animals will feed off the voices of the elderly residents. The written is seen as transient and succeeds in capturing the spoken voice but only temporarily since the voices escape as the book disintegrates into the ground. Alternatively, it could be argued, the voices are given a new lease of life precisely because they have been in the notebook since both the written text and the spoken voice in that text provide a fertile source for new life. Apparently, then, as the book decomposes, it feeds the earth—an image also used by Couto in *Terra Sonâmbula*. Simultaneously, animals derive nutrition from the voices as they are released from the written text. It appears that even at the moment when the written is in closest proximity to death, rotting in a grave, it maintains, for Couto, a life-giving and organic characteristic, entering a natural lifecycle. It also appears that writing's ability to enslave the spoken voice, so lamented by Lévi-Strauss, is denied by Couto, who allows the voices to be preserved and then to escape through the written text.

"O ESCREVIDO": DEFYING DEATH THROUGH WRITING

Couto often foregrounds the ambiguous relationship between writing and death. They are central motifs in *Terra Sonâmbula*, as we will discuss shortly. They also figure prominently in a short story from the collection *Na Berma de Nenhuma Estrada*, "O Escrevido" [The Written One]. The narrative is about Bernadinho, who is desperate to be the subject of a writer's plot. He spends his time, without success, offering himself to writers as a raw material from which they may craft their books, until one day a failing writer, Tiotanico, accepts his offer. The writer's name resonates with the ill-fated ship, and he is described as "shipwrecked in the middle of nowhere" [naufragado em nenhuma (*NBNE,* 138)]. He begins to write a plot in which Bernadinho is dead, leaving behind a distraught widow. When Bernadinho returns home, he finds his wife in tears at the death of her husband:

> That was how Bernadinho disappeared. He existed but was not there. The man was legible but only palpable between the lines. He could sense himself, and hear his own steps at night. He would call for himself but not receive any presence.

> [Foi assim o modo de desaparecimento de Bernadinho. Existia mas não havia. O homem era legível mas apenas palpável nas entrelinhas. Ele a si mesmo se sentia, escutava seus passos de noite. Chamava por ele mesmo e não recebia presença. (139)]

The demarcation between life and fiction becomes blurred. Bernadinho's existence becomes an act of writing that kills him. Once he has been written down, he becomes an absence, following the Platonic paradigm. But the ending of Couto's tale rejects the Platonic critique of the written, because the dead object of Tiotanico's narrative changes the plot, and murders the writer to prevent his widow being written out of the story. The written, once again, takes on a life of its own. Symbolically, the tale represents the death of the author, in that way reflecting the removal of Ezequiel from a position of authorial control that occurs in "A Carta." Couto is making the point that writing belongs to the reader once it has left its author's desk. He uses and then subverts the link between writing and death to authorize the abolition of authorial intent, in the process advocates a Barthesian centrality of the text.[39] That post-structural paradigm effectively renders the written a fluid mass that is refashioned with each rereading. In many ways, it reflects the traditions of orality in that each time a story is brought to life by a retelling, a new nuance or detail is added. For Couto, the same holds true for the written text.

Terra Sonâmbula:
DISTANCING DESTRUCTION THROUGH WRITING

Terra Sonâmbula [Sleepwalking Land] was Couto's first novel. Published in 1992, it was released in the same year as the peace accords were signed between Renamo and the Frelimo government. It is set in war torn Mozambique and relates the journey of an old man, Tuahir, and a young boy, Muidinga, as they travel down an abandoned road. They come across a burnt-out bus and discover a set of notebooks written by someone called Kindzu. The chapters alternate between relating events and conversations that occur between Muidinga and Tuahir, and reading the text of Kindzu's notebooks. The deconstruction of the boundary between the written and the spoken is a central theme of the book, which seeks to recuperate hope after one of the most pitiful episodes in the history of Mozambique—the armed conflict between Frelimo and Renamo.

The blame for the existence of Renamo, an acronym for *Resistência Nacional de Moçambique* [National Resistance of Mozambique] was for years laid by Samora Machel and sympathetic intellectuals in the West at the door of Rhodesia and then South Africa. The Frelimo version of Renamo's birth was that a handful of corrupt, disgruntled Mozambican bandits were trained, with the connivance of some former Portuguese colonizers, as terrorists by the racist Smith regime in the dying days of Rhodesia, as a means of destabilizing its black-ruled neighbor who actively supported Robert Mugabe's nationalist movement. With Zimbabwean independence, Renamo had to find a new foreign backer, and turned to South Africa under the Botha regime, which was much more sympathetic to interfering in its neighbor's politics than the Vorster administration it had replaced in 1978. A progressively more horrific conflict ensued that displaced, maimed and killed millions, and paralyzed the nation's economic development. In 1984, Samora Machel did the unthinkable, and signed a nonaggression pact with the Apartheid regime, which became known as the Nkomati Accord. The agreement effectively limited the Maputo government's support for the ANC, and revealed the level of desperation within the Frelimo administration, which had been unable to break Renamo militarily.

Renamo never managed to win the diplomatic war against Frelimo abroad. During the Cold War, the Unita movement (*União Nacional para a Indepedência Total de Angola* [National Union for the Total Independence of Angola]), which waged a civil war in Angola against the Marxist-leaning government of Luanda, always enjoyed a large degree of support in Western capitals. In contrast, Renamo was never given the same level of backing, despite its claim to be fighting for democracy against a communist regime. In part, Unita's prestige on the international diplomatic front, which evaporated after the fall of the Berlin Wall and once the Luanda government whole-heartedly adopted a free-market program, was rooted in the presence of Cuban troops on Angolan soil, something that riled a powerful lobby in Washington. In Mozambique, no such "occupation" took place so there was never the additional incentive particularly on the part of the USA to support the destabilization of the Mozambican government. Additionally, relations became strained between Frelimo and Moscow when the latter refused to allow its African ally to enter its economic community, Comecon, with the result that Machel aggressively began to court the West.

The Frelimo public relations machine had always been extremely efficient, and for several years, Couto himself belonged to it, as the director of the Mozambican Information Agency (AIM) from 1978. They managed to promote a great deal of goodwill from the West, even when the Mozambican government was at its most repressive, implementing policies such as the forced resettlement of peasants into villages, and the deportation of deemed-to-be undesirable elements from urban areas to rural reeducation camps that were more in line with the ideology of Mao than Marx. But most importantly, Renamo was always suspected of carrying out atrocities against civilians, something that Robert Gersony's report confirmed in 1988.[40] The little credibility that Renamo enjoyed externally quickly waned, but the war did not end. In fact, it intensified. This intensification, and also the extraordinarily high proportion of the popular vote that Renamo gained in the first multiparty elections held as part of a negotiated peace settlement in 1994, gainsaid the central premise of Frelimo's characterization of its opponent.[41] Clearly, despite the government's assertions, Renamo was not merely a foreign device devoid of any popular support within the country. Precisely what Renamo was, and where it came from, is now an object of academic argument, and not particularly relevant to the lives of most Mozambicans. The important thing is that the former terrorists/freedom fighters were transformed into a politically acceptable and viable group in a newly pluralistic state, and this transformation ended a senseless war. A point is reached in many conflicts, particularly those in which neither side appears capable of winning, when the apportioning of blame is no longer pertinent; a peaceful solution and reconciliation is a far more pressing concern. Couto's *Terra Sonâmbula* captures that particular historical moment in the story of Mozambique, written as it was, when pressure on both the government and Renamo to end the war had reached overwhelming proportions.

The novel received wide acclaim after it was published. Chabal describes it as "a turning point in the development of Mozambican literature."[42] His reading of it leads him to the conclusion that "the point of the book, as it is in oral literature, is in the voyage, in the telling of the stories." Crucially, "the act of telling, the literary journey itself, becomes part of the story and creates a cultural memory."[43] It is also an instance of writing seeking to "accommodate" oral tradition. In the process, a cultural consciousness is inscribed. A new nation, in the midst of despair, is being written. David Mestre describes the novel as an adventure story, or a tale of chivalry.[44] In some sense, the way in which the two protagonists come to reverse roles as the story develops or, at least, the way in which an initially cynical Tuahir comes to believe in the world imagined by the idealist Muidinga reflects the dynamic of Cervantes's *Don Quijote,* which parodies tales of chilvary. Niyi Afolabi suggests that the novel dramatizes "the middle passage between fantasy and reality, war and peace and other polarities such as the present and the future that capture the tragic spirit of a country coming out of a devastating civil war," a more positive reading of the novel than that of Gilberto Matusse, who claims that *Terra Sonâmbula* reflects an indifference to violence provoked by years of conflict.[45] The novel does, in fact, go beyond violence, although the national tragedy of the civil war pervades its pages. Couto offers a new reality in which clear demarcations are no longer acceptable because the Manichean order they imply has been at the heart of a failure to resolve the national conflict for so many years. He uses a blurring of the distinction between the written and the spoken, and also a blurring of the barrier between the conscious and unconscious realms we will discuss in detail in the next chapter, in order to challenge hegemonic polarities.

The novel intersperses writing with orality, and forces each to deal with the other. It is less a process of writing adopting the tactics and characteristics of orality, and more a case of the script and the voice informing and reforming each other. The specter of war pervades both strands of the novel; it is the backdrop against which everything is written, both in the text and in the notebooks. Apparently, Muidinga has been orphaned by the hostilities, while Kindzu, his counterprotagonist in the notebooks, is constantly trying to escape from and find an explanation for the war. His notebooks describe war as "a snake which uses our own teeth to bite us" [uma cobra que usa os nossos próprios dentes para nos morder (*TS,* 17)] and as an excuse "to authorize theft" [para autorizar o roubo (114)]. Death and destruction legitimize everything, by ensuring that "laws are forgotten" [as leis fossem esquecidas (114)]. The law, as Lévi-Strauss points out, relies on writing for its authority.[46] So, in a sense, the war serves to erase the written world. At another level, since the formal education sector was severely disrupted by the war, literacy was not propagated to the extent that it would have been had there been a peace. From this perspective, the conflict becomes allied to the oral world. Couto, in an interview about the novel, while being careful not to glamorize or defend the bloodshed, makes an analogous point. He asserts that "the war helped to bring to the surface dimensions of Mozambique which would probably have remained hidden if the process of constructing the nation had proceeded 'normally'" [a guerra ajudou a trazer à superfície dimensões de Moçambique que, provavelmente, ficariam escondidas se o processo de construção da nação tivesse decorrido "normalmente"].[47] In Couto's opinion, the war revealed something about the cultural essence of Mozambique that would have remained unknown had the nation followed the usual developmental paradigm imposed on other African nations, which "implies a profound lack of respect for cultural values" [implica um profundo desrespeito para com os valores culturais]. The cultural values to which he refers are usually associated with orality.

As well as running the risk of glamorizing conflict as a preserver of oral values, his argument has become poignant in retrospect because, with the end of the civil war, Mozambique has plunged whole-heartedly into the process of capitalist globalization, one of the principal effects of which is the relentless erasure of those cultural values. His novel captured a moment in history when Mozambique's acquiescence to the forces of globalization, while highly probable, was not yet totally assured. In some ways, Couto, in his statements, was fighting a rearguard action to preserve and restore traditional values, or at least have their spirit influence the future path of the nation.

In *Terra Sonâmbula*, Couto portrays writing as a mechanism to flee the effects of war. Kindzu's perception of the nature of writing—as one step removed from the present—leads the character to use the script as his creative medium of escape, an escape based on writing's ability to distance presence and to capture the painful memories of his traumatic experiences. The opening lines of the first notebook explain Kindzu's motive for writing:

> I want to tame the times, to put them in order, in line with hopes and sufferments. But my memories disobey, between the will to be nothing and the desire to rob me from the present. I light the story, I erase myself. By the end of these writings, I will once again be a shadow without a voice.

> [Quero pôr os tempos, em sua mansa ordem, conforme esperas e sofrências. Mas as lembranças desobedecem, entre a vontade de serem nada e o gosto de me roubarem do presente. Acendo a estória, me apago a mim. No fim destes escritos, serei de novo uma sombra sem voz. (15)]

In the final notebook, Kindzu reasserts his motivation for writing.

> That is what I desire: to erase myself, to lose my voice, to cease to exist. Just as well that I have written, step by step, this my journey. Written down like this, memories remain captive on the paper, well away from me.

> [É isso que desejo: me apagar, perder voz, desexistir. Ainda bem que escrevi, passo por passo, esta minha viagem. Assim escritas estas lembranças ficam presas no papel, bem longe de mim. (214)]

In using writing to put as much distance as possible between himself and the presence of a painful past, Kindzu imbues the script and the voice with the characteristics Plato assigned to them, of absence and presence. Plato disassociates memory from writing, claiming that memory is a living organism, like the voice. One of his criticisms of writing is that it gives the false impression of being a memory while, in fact, being external to it. Memory, for Kindzu, is only lost once it has been distanced from the living organism, the voice, and put into writing. While Plato views this distancing with hostility and deep suspicion, Kindzu sees it as a necessity or, at the very least, a relief, given the conflict that saturates his memory. The paradox of the novel is that the notebooks are brought back to life by and will restore a memory to Muidinga, who stumbles upon them, and reads them aloud. As *Terra Sonâmbula* reaches a conclusion in the final notebook, the distance between Kindzu and his texts is lost as he describes the actual discovery of the notebooks in a fusion of the oral and written universes: "I move closer and, shocked, I verify that . . . they are my notebooks" [me aproximo e, com sobressalto, confirmo: são os meus cadernos (218)]. The novel takes the form of a cycle, in which its end is also its beginning, and the written account of the notebooks' discovery predates the fate it describes. By structuring the novel as he does, Couto foregrounds the creative aspect of the process of writing, even when it is meant to be a descriptive account. Kindzu sought to ensure his own erasure through writing. Instead, he guarantees his own survival, and the work that he leaves symbolically fertilizes the earth onto which it falls in the closing lines of the novel, which now relate occurrences in both Kindzu's written and Muidinga's oral realms: "the letters, one by one, gradually change into grains of sand and, little by little, all my writings transform into pages of earth" [as letras, uma por uma, se vão convertendo em grãos de areia e, aos poucos, todos meus escritos se vão transformando em páginas de terra (218)]. As the story finishes, a point that also represents its beginning, the text becomes organic and gives new life. Concomitantly, it changes form and loses permanence, two further affronts to traditional depictions of the script.

The structure of *Terra Sonâmbula,* like the structure of *A Varanda do Frangipani,* is one in which every other chapter has a different narrative voice. In the case of *Terra Sonâmbula,* Kindzu's notebooks represent the written world, for they are very consciously presented as written texts, whereas the alternate chapters, which are primarily constituted by dialogue between Muidinga and Tuahir, represent an oral universe. As discussed, Kindzu writes his notebooks to rid himself of painful memories. In contrast, Muidinga has no memory and knows nothing of his past. According to Tuahir, who is very evasive on the matter, Muidinga's amnesia is due to a spell cast on him. Tuahir considers Muidinga's lack of memory as a blessing, something that clearly runs contrary to the Platonic view, and he comes to realize that Kindzu's notebooks are providing Muidinga with a new set of memories, the only advantage of which is that the young boy thinks they are false. Like Kindzu, Tuahir appears to accept a Platonic characteristic of writing, in this case, that it deceives. Also like Kindzu, characteristics disliked by Plato are, in fact, viewed by Tuahir as a positive advantage. In Kindzu's case, writing as a distancing from presence was seen as a good thing. In Tuahir's case, writing viewed as far from truth is considered to be a benefit. In both cases, writing refuses to behave as they wish it would. For Kindzu is reunited with his writing, a removal of the distance he sought to establish, and Tuahir realizes that there is a truth in the written text.

The notebooks transfer memory from the written world to the oral world, from Kindzu to Muidinga. But they also transfer memory from the oral world to the written world since they are, first and foremost, Kindzu's memories inscribed on the page. Additionally, Kindzu cedes his narrative voice in the notebooks to the beautiful Farida who orally relates the story of her lost child, Gaspar. The novel's conclusion reveals that Muidinga, from the oral domain of the chapters, is in fact Gaspar, in the written notebooks. As the tale progresses, it becomes increasingly clear that the boundary between the two worlds is evaporating. When the notebooks are first discovered, Muidinga manages to read them but he does not know how. He smiles "with the satisfaction of a conquest" [com a satisfação de uma conquista (14)]. The written world appears to be subservient to the oral as he and his voice have mastery over the written text. Orality's dominance is accentuated by Tuahir's insistence that the young boy read aloud the contents of the first notebook, which does not entirely endorse writing. Indeed, Kindzu in that first notebook tells of how his father, Taímo, who haunts him throughout the novel, disapproved of his son learning "white men's witchcraft" [feitiçarias dos brancos (25)]. Writing is an alien import, the product of the Christian missions, while orality is presented as natural and African. Yet toward the end of the novel, Taímo, for all his oral prophesies and never-ending stories, will be turned into writing, in the form of the inscription on a canoe which floats into Muidinga and Tuahir's oral domain.

After the first notebook is read, Muidinga and Tuahir's oral existence is never the same again. The child becomes obsessed by the text. There is a physicality in the written; it is something that can be touched as well as seen: "the youngster passes his hand over the notebook, as if he were touching the letters" [o jovem passa a mão pelo caderno, como se palpasse as letras (35)].

At the same time, there is initially a shortage of the spoken word in Tuahir and Muidinga's world—"conversation is also scarce, there is no wasting of words" [a conversa também é pouca, sem desperdício de palavra (36)]—and the written texts progressively take over their consciousness. As Kindzu's notebooks restore a memory to Muidinga, the tropes of orality reassert themselves. For the young boy temporarily loses the notebooks but proceeds to demonstrate how he has committed their contents to memory. He tells Tuahir, "I left the notebooks on the bus. But I've already read another notebook, a later one. I can tell you what it says, I almost know it all by heart, word for word" [deixei os cadernos lá no machimbombo. Mas eu já li outro caderno, mais à frente. Lhe posso contar o que diz, quase sei tudo de cabeça, palavra por palavra (99)]. The first thing to note is that he has corrupted the linear order of the written, having already read the next notebook ahead of time. This scriptural anachronicity is a signpost for what will happen to the novel itself in the final notebook. Secondly, Muidinga has internalized the written, like the prophet Ezequiel. Having consumed the script, it becomes his memory, not letters on a page, the opposite of Kindzu's intention. As such, it is true in the Platonic sense, and no longer a false aid to recall characterized by the external marks of the graphemes. Thirdly, and most importantly, Muidinga has changed the written through this process of incorporation because, although he knows the text very well indeed, he does not know it perfectly: "I *almost* know it all by heart" [emphasis added]. There is an uncertainty in his knowledge. The permanence and stability of the written is lost as he incorporates it. The story is now Muidinga's and not Kindzu's: the reader kills the author, and becomes the subject of the text. Orality insinuates itself into the scriptural economy.

The repeated challenges to Platonic ideals that Couto corrupts in *Terra Sonâmbula* are signposted from the novel's epigraphs. There are three citations. The first claims to be a belief of the inhabitants of a fictionalized Matimati, a realm to which the notebooks refer. The second is a saying attributed to Tuahir, the old man who looks after Muidinga and is thus grounded on the oral world of the chapters. The final citation is a quote that Couto attributes to Plato: "There are three species of men: the living, the dead, and those who walk through the sea" [há três espécies de homens: os vivos, os mortos e os que andam no mar (7)]. As we shall discuss in the next chapter, water plays a pivotal role in the novel, but what is more interesting for the moment is the role of Plato in Couto's text. In one of the most original readings of *Terra Sonâmbula* to date, Laura Cavalcante Padilha points out how Couto uses the novel's epigraphs to link the most ancient of occidental traditions with the ancestral voice of an assumed Mozambican identity.[48] In fact, the Platonic citation is false, or rather, another of Couto's invented truths, or alternative perspectives. Couto himself claims to have heard it second hand, but cannot remember the source, and none of the sophisticated Platonic databases currently available produces anything approximating the words Couto puts in Plato's mouth.[49] However, his Borges-like use of quotation merely adds another interesting dimension to Padilha's argument, because Couto is purposefully falsifying the tradition that claims a knowledge of the truth, giving it equal status with the creative orality of the Matimati, and then drawing on both traditions in order to produce a new identity in writing.

The play between the written and the oral continues throughout the novel. At one point, Tuahir requests "that the lad give voice to the notebooks" [que o miúdo dê voz aos cadernos (149)]. For Couto, the written needs the oral, in the same way that the oral needs the written in order for Muidinga to regain his past. Tuahir explains his request: "'Just as well you know how to read,' the old man comments. If it were not for the readings they would be condemned to solitude. Their daydreams now wandered over the small letters of those writings" ["Ainda bem você saber ler," comenta o velho. Não fossem as leituras eles estariam condenados à solidão. Seus devaneios caminhavam agora pelas letrinhas daqueles escritos (149)]. The process is one of mutual benefit. Without orality, the notebooks would remain silent. In turn, the written offers Muidinga and Tuahir a pathway through which they are able to dream of other possibilities. They bring life to the text and the text brings life to them. With each reading, Muidinga is profoundly changed: "On the day after the reading, his eyes flowed into other visions" [No dia seguinte à leitura, seus olhos desembocam em outras visões (109)]. His perspective on the world is altered—as Ong suggests it always is—by his interaction with the text.

The process of exchange between the written (the notebooks) and the oral (the chapters) becomes progressively more marked. Initially, it takes the form of an occurrence in the text signaling a subsequent occurrence in the notebooks. The second chapter involves an episode in which Muidinga demonstrates his ability to write by inscribing the word "AZUL" (blue) in the dirt (38). The notebook that follows this incident describes how Kindzu sets out from a place where "the sea opens up like a blue word" [o mar se abre como uma palavra azul (42)]. One word links the two worlds. A strange type of symbiosis then takes place in which both worlds come to interdepend, until in the ninth chapter, Tuahir and Muidinga become Kindzu and Taímo. What begins as a game develops into a confusion between text and reality, between the written and the oral.

> Muidinga rocks himself, quite numb. As that faking goes on he can no longer tell whether what is happening there is being taken out of the book, like a sheet torn from reality itself. He closes his eyes and sees Tuahir, or rather Taímo, bathing in a lake of liquor.

> [Muidinga se embala, entorpecido. À medida que aquele fingimento avança ele já não sabe se o que ali se está passando não está ser tirado do livro, como folha rasgada da própria realidade. Fecha os olhos e vê Tuahir, aliás Taímo, se banhando num lago de sura. (167)]

This confusion is an example of what Fionna Gonçalves terms "identity transversion," in which the characters from the two strands of the novel become profoundly interrelated and interdependent.[50] The fusion is complete as the last notebook is read. In it, a description is given of what is happening in the oral world, as it happens. The reader reads that he is reading. Furthermore, the reader discovers his identity; his memory is restored by the written text, an occurrence that counters the Platonic critique of writing as a destroyer of memory.

As well as the notebooks, the other example of writing in *Terra Sonâmbula* is letters. Once more, they are used to create new realities. Farida, a character in the notebooks whose beauty both challenges and defies language—"that woman's beauty was enough to put the name of things to flight" [a beleza daquela mulher era de fazer fugir o nome das coisas (66)]—tells Kindzu the story of Virginha's letters and he, in turn, writes it down for Muidinga to read aloud. Before considering it, it is worth noting two things.

First, Farida's voice has a peculiar quality. When she is introduced to the tale, we are told that "her voice came out without clothes, naked as if it needed no words" [sua voz saía sem vestes, nua como se dispensasse palavras (66)]. The essential quality for intelligibility of the voice, spoken words, is deemed in her to be obfuscating. Spoken words, in Farida's case, conceal rather than reveal and behave as a disguise, as if they were Saussure's written words. Ferdinand de Saussure, the Swiss linguist who provided the concepts behind structuralism, detested the written word for its tendency to "usurp" the supremacy of the spoken voice.[51] Like Plato, he assigned the spoken voice the status of the natural, and deemed the written to be a nefarious artifice that conceals the purity of the spoken. But for Couto, spoken words, in reference to Farida, are as concealing and cloak the naked truth. They are, after all, a means of representation, thus putting distance between the essence they seek to replace and the recipient of their meaning. They behave, if we accept Derrida's critique of the Platonic strand of structuralism, suspiciously like their written counterparts. Yet Farida's beauty somehow manages to overcome the block of words and to communicate at the source. Beauty, following the Platonic paradigm, is presented as a means of reaching essence. In contrast, the spoken word in reference to Farida is characterized as a mere representation, a signifier which supplements and supplants a signified, as Kindzu asserts, "the woman exchanged herself for words until it was nearly dawn" [a mulher se trocou por palavra até quase ser manhã (77)]. Once she begins to speak, words displace her. She is exchanged for the spoken voice. Couto uses the character of Farida to perform the Derridean maneuver of demonstrating that spoken words are not pure presence, as Plato and Saussure would have us believe. Like writing, they too defer meaning and depend on a process of exchange and metaphoric chains.

The second thing to note is that Virginha is rendered unstable by the way in which she is represented in writing. What is isomorphic in the oral domain becomes dimorphic in the written text, as the spelling of her name flickers randomly. She is both "Virgínia" (82, 83) and "Virginha" (82, 83). The spoken voice cannot distinguish the homophone in Portuguese. The diorism is only inscribed on the page. In the oral world, one acoustic signal represents her essence, one signifier points to one signified. As Muidinga reads the notebook aloud to Tuahir, the old man will notice no difference. But Muidinga will see a difference, as he reads the text, all of which represents an inversion of the normal paradigms of language: writing is meant to fix and standardize; the voice is open to the vagaries of accent and intonation that subtly alter the inflexibility of the script. But in this case, the voice standardizes a multiplicity of written variables. Furthermore, Virginha/Virgínia's world is grounded on the written, since she will instigate the very letters that are sent to her. However, the permanence her written world should give to her, by fixing her name, is lost. It is only in the spoken world that she is a constant, that her identity is one. On paper, two signifiers point to her signified.

Like Nádia in "A Princesa Russa," Virgínia lives imprisoned by her husband, Romão Pinto. He forbids her from participating in many activities, including reading. Also like Nádia, Virgínia wants to return to her homeland. By banning her from reading, Romão Pinto seeks to deny his wife a route to distant worlds accessible through literature and beyond his control. Virgínia exercises her right to dream, in any case, by recreating a past for herself. Initially, she treats the permanent images of her photograph collection as mutable palimpsests. Farida does not have the heart to contradict her fantasy since "the photos reconfigured brought new truths to a life made of lies" [as fotos recompostas traziam novas verdades a uma vida feita de mentiras (82)]. Subsequently, Farida becomes drawn into the process of creating new truths, out

of old li(v)es, when Virgínia tells Farida a version of her autobiography. She
explains her motives when asked by Farida.

> "Why are you telling me all this, Mamã Virgínia?"
> "Because I want you to start writing me."
> "Writing?"
> That was right. Farida was to start sending her letters, falsifying authorships,
> faking distance.

> ["Por que me conta tudo isso, Mamã Virgínia?"
> "Porque quero que me passes a escrever."
> "Escrever?"
> Era. Farida deveria enviar-lhe cartas, falseando autorias, fingindo o longe.
> (*TS*, 82–83)]

Like Kindzu, Virgínia wishes to escape the present through writing. Unlike
Kindzu, writing will not be used to distance the present but rather as a means
of filling the present with an imagined past. Writing will supplement the present, not carry it away. There is a certain degree of ambiguity in Virgínia's response to Farida's question. In most contexts "me passes a escrever"—the
Portuguese translated above as "to start writing me"—means "to start writing
to me." But "me" could be taken as a direct as well as an indirect object.
Farida might be being asked to "write me." Interestingly, American English
retains the ambiguity. Virgínia is to be written, her history and her present
are to be refashioned through the text; she becomes the letters as well as the
destination of the letters. She is the subject and object—both direct and indirect—of the writing. Writing will bring the distant, "o longe," into proximity, rather than distancing the present. The falsehood of the missives will
be forgotten even by Farida. Through the text, the past can be relived and, in
the process, rewritten in the present. Once again, a marginalized character
acquires a centrality by interacting with letters. Furthermore, it is an interaction that foregrounds the oral nature of missive texts because the letters are
used to recreate constantly new subjectivities for Virgínia, in a process that
follows the strategies of an oral storyteller and not the archetype of writing as
a mechanism used to stabilize knowledge or identity.

The other character in *Terra Sonâmbula* who makes use of letters is the
blind prostitute, Juliana Bastiana. Like Mamã Cacilda in "A Carta," Juliana is
not able to read the letters she receives. Like Virgínia, Juliana strives to bring
the past into the present. Indeed, her whole mode of being is one that will
not acknowledge temporal constraints as she mixes tenses. She is both living
in the present through the past and living in the past through the present.
The letters her supposed lover sends her every week also defy the constraints

of time. Her description of her lover, Silvério Damião, is anachronistic since he is a member of the colonial army who has recently left on a mission. She describes him as such to Kindzu who in an earlier notebook has situated the tale in postindependence Mozambique. In fact, his little brother was named after the date independence was proclaimed from Portugal (25 June 1975). So, conventional time would render Juliana's tale false. But the physical evidence of the unread letters leads her to believe in the past/present that she has recreated for herself.

Virgínia, after the death of Romão, becomes temporally disordered too. She cannot distinguish between the past and the future: "she would repeat to herself fractured sentences like 'yesterday, when I die'" [repetia, de si para si, desencostadas frases: "ontem, quando eu morrer" (171)]. Once she has created a new past for herself, through the letters that Farida inscribes for her, her whole world goes into flux. Time means nothing to her, and certainly ceases to be a linear concept. Through writing, it becomes unfixed, and provides another example of Couto's insinuation of orality into the scriptural economy since, following Hegel, writing creates linear time by fashioning history, while oral culture stereotypically only perceives a present, or rather, possesses a different concept of chronology that always brings history into the present. But Juliana and Virgínia's letters affect time in a manner not dissimilar to the oral stereotype, by skewing its linearity, furnishing another instance of how Couto renders patent the oral nature of the epistle.

In the context of a predominantly oral culture, literacy becomes a distinguishing feature. As Lévi-Strauss points out, it marks an elite that may take advantage of its privileged position.[52] Yet Couto's presentation of literate characters does not allow them to assume a greater status than those without access to writing. For example, the narrator in "A Carta" might think he has deceived Mamã Cacilda but the tale ends with the revelation that she is far more astute than the narrator would like to think. Zuleila's oral tropes in "Dois Corações, Uma Caligrafia" win over her literate sister. In *Terra Sonâmbula*, one of the characters most associated with illiteracy is Siqueleto, an apparently deranged man who captures Muidinga and Tuahir, and subjects them to random beatings. Siqueleto only releases his prisoners because Muidinga writes in the dust. The madman asks the boy what he is doing, and Tuahir claims that Muidinga has written Siqueleto's name. Immediately prior to this incident, Tuahir has given Muidinga some advice: he must never believe a man who does not know how to lie. It could be that Tuahir is lying to Siqueleto; we do not know for sure that the designs Muidinga was drawing in the dust were, in fact, Siqueleto's name. But Tuahir's intervention will save their lives because Siqueleto appears to believe him. Furthermore, he appears to believe in the power of the written word. He orders Muidinga to write his name on a tree then announces, "you can go now. The village is going to go on, now that my name is in the blood of the tree" [agora podem-se ir embora. A aldeia vai continuar, já meu nome está no sangue da árvore (75)]. The fate of Siqueleto is similar to the fate of Taímo, Kindzu's father: both end up inscribed in wood. Their names outlive them through writing, in the same way that misographs like Plato and Saussure have ironically survived through the texts that have been ascribed to them. In the case of Siqueleto, he is organically and magically transferred into the blood of the tree through the script.

It appears that the illiterate Siqueleto privileges the power of writing. However, the story that is told to him about his name being written in the dust—which could easily be blown away, hence presumably Siqueleto's need to have it written on something more durable—may or may not have a reality outside its oral version. Muidinga may or may not have been inscribing Siqueleto's name in the dust but, for the young boy, an oral tale buys him his life, although he can write. For Siqueleto, who cannot, the imperishability of a word written on wood rather than sand is the minimum necessary guarantee. Yet, despite his reverence for the written, like several characters in the novel, such as Farida who must be listened to in order to be healed, and her son, Gaspar, whose death is postponed by the telling of a tale, the oral enunciation of Siqueleto's story is key to his existence. This may be seen to signal a privileging of the spoken. Indeed, Gaspar must tell his story in order to avoid being executed at the hands of Virgínia and the many children that surround her. Like Scheherazade, a prolonged orality purchases his perpetuity since the children intend to kill him once the story ends. They want to eliminate Gaspar so that he can never repeat his tale to anybody else: "afterwards we'll kill him, no one else is ever going to cast their ears on his tale. His story remains ours alone" [depois matamos, ninguém mais vai pôr ouvidos na narração dele. Fica estória só nossa (175)]. It appears, at one level, that Gaspar's story must remain in the oral realm, leaving no record that can be repeated. But, at another level, his story cryptically points to the written domain. It acquires a tangibility; it is a possession that may be transferred and kept, more akin to a piece of paper than an acoustic signal. More subtly, it is something onto which others may "cast their ears" [pôr ouvidos], a corrupted phrase which resonates with "cast their eyes" [pôr os olhos]. The intrusive ear points to the absent eye. The auditory sense on which orality depends is underwritten by sight, on which writing relies, in relation to the effect it has on Gaspar's tale. The boundary between what is written and what is spoken is, in Couto's universe, far from impenetrable.

Siqueleto, once he has revealed his name to Tuahir and Muidinga, "presents himself with his story" [se apresenta com sua estória (72)]. He accompanies his tale rhythmically, shaking a tin, and rendering his story a very oral experience; writing could never completely capture that percussive quality. When urged to abandon the village because of rebel insurgency in the area, Siqueleto refused, stating, "I'm like the tree, I only die from lies" [eu sou como a árvore, morro só de mentira (72)]. In that statement, Siqueleto forestalls any apparent subservience to writing. Or, at the very least, he recognizes that part of the power of writing is derived from its falsehood and its ability to misrepresent. For the old man will die or, at least, will wither away, bleeding profusely. It will happen immediately after his name is inscribed into the blood of the tree. Once writing has taken over his existence, through the tree, he dies, presumably "from lies" [de mentira], as he has foretold. He dies from falsehood; he dies from being written. But the Portuguese phrase is ambiguous: "de mentira" could indicate that he does not really die at all since it may adverbially connote that the statement to which it is attached is false, providing yet another example of the semantic ambiguity that so enriches Couto's texts. In that ambiguity that casts writing as both death and falsehood, Couto proffers a creative space founded in accordance with Derrida's critique of the Platonic attitude toward the written. For writing becomes a "pharmakon" that kills but also cures.[53] Its redemptive quality lies in its ability to stimulate the imagination of another existence, where death becomes part of a natural cycle and is no longer the byproduct of a senseless war.

Throughout his work, Couto's portrayal of writing aligns him with the postmodern rejection of Grand Narratives, through the techniques of poststructuralism. The concept that writing's historical and epistemological power rests on its immutability, an idea defended by Hegel and Diringer, is replaced by a characterization of the written text as subject to change and fluidity. The permanence of writing gives way, in Couto's world, to the flexibility of interpretation as letters symbolically alter and come to life. At the same time, Couto blurs the distinction between absence and presence in many of his epistolary depictions, in direct challenge to Plato's rigid codification of the spoken voice as presence and the written as a marker of absence. Neither writing nor orality is allowed to predominate. Instead, Couto makes them complementary. Letters are central to that complementarity since they foreground how orality impinges on the scriptural economy, while centering characters from the social periphery. Writing's longstanding association with death is permissible in Couto's realm only as part of an organic chain that points to the creation of new life. In that respect, Couto goes beyond poststructuralism as he advocates a role for writing in the imagination and creation of a different reality; poststructuralism provides a mode of critiquing but is not itself a political project. Given the troubled history of his nation during much of the time he has been writing, his aim has often been to persuade fellow Mozambicans to dream of an order not based on binary distinctions such as oral and literate, good and bad. During his country's darkest hour in the 1980s and early 1990s, his call to dream a dichotomy-transcending reality into existence was at its strongest, as we shall discuss in the next chapter, which deals with Couto's attempted recuperation of a fluid link between the conscious world and the realm of the unconscious.

5

Seaing into the Unconscious:
The Role of Water in Mia Couto

TWO RECURRENT THEMES IN COUTO'S WORK, FROM HIS EARLY POEMS TO HIS more recent novels, are the role of water and the role of dreams. Often, the two are linked. In a poem written in 1979, for example, entitled "Poema da Minha Alienação" [Poem of My Alienation], which deals with the theme of transcending the Self, Couto combines the oneiric and the water cycle.[1] His dream, however challenged by the world around, will be achieved through the medium of water. As the poet sublimates into vapor, he enters a state with no beginning and no end: becoming "infinite drops" [infinitas gotas], a form capable of permeating every aspect of organic life. Twenty years later, in 1999, Couto published the novel *Vinte e Zinco,* as part of his publisher Caminho's celebration of the twenty-fifth anniversary of Lisbon's Carnation Revolution. That bloodless coup, led by cadres from Portugal's Armed Forces who were tired of the needless loss of life preserving the colonies in Africa, swept Salazar's successor, Marcello Caetano, from power on 25 April 1974. The number twenty-five thus became shorthand in Portugal for the long-overdue moment that ended the fascist reign of the *Estado Novo.* As will be discussed later in this chapter, Couto's book celebrating the end of the Salazar-Caetano era and the resultant independence of Mozambique, the title of which echoes the Portuguese word for twenty-five, foregrounds the significance of water and dreams, continuing a preoccupation that surfaces continuously from his early poems and short stories to his later novels. *Mar Me Quer,* his novella published by Caminho in 2000, repeats the pattern, as does *Terra Sonâmbula.* But, before considering the role of water and the unconscious in Couto, it is worth briefly considering the intellectual heritage from and against which he writes, for water and dreams have often been linked in national imaginaries, in general, and the lusophone imaginary, in particular.

Couto principally deploys water as an evocative gesture that rescinds the blockage in the imaginations of the people of Mozambique between a harsh reality they live and the dream of a different future they need. In essence, he uses water to restore the flow between the conscious and unconscious realms of his characters. At the same time, he draws on the powerful, cultural resonance of water, particularly the sea, to capture distinct ontological moments in Mozambique's evolution as a nation. First, the sea represents the colonization process and the ritual cleansing of past oppression, as in *Vinte e Zinco*; then, water's association with birth mirrors the birth of a new nation, as we witness in a number of Couto's short stories; finally, the sea metaphorizes the nation's decline at the hands of the forces of neocolonization, marking the influx of foreign aid and interference exemplified in the story "As Baleias de Quissico." Couto, as we shall see, alters the semantics of the sea to reflect Mozambique's political trajectory. It is something external to the nation, forming a large part of its frontier with the outside world. Simultaneously, it is deeply internal, as an intrinsic component of its troubled history, and its national unconscious. Furthermore, every time Couto mentions the sea, or draws on the symbolism of water, he enters a discourse on the deep that is both a cultural universal, as a store of human mythological and historical experience, and very particular to the experiences of lusophone Africa, as the medium which delivered the Portuguese, and inexorably linked the histories, cultures and languages of five disparate regions of the continent. Given that linkage, a brief consideration of the literary representation of the oceans in Portugal and lusophone Africa, while by no means exhaustive, will help to illuminate the cultural backdrop against which Couto writes.

Like writing, water has tended to carry a moral charge in the mythical traditions in which it occurs. For example, Plato's theory of punishment by metempsychosis reserved the aquatic milieu for "the most foolish and senseless" of all creatures since "the gods who molded their form considered these unworthy any more to breathe the pure air, because their souls were polluted with every sort of evil-doing." As a result of their misbehavior, the gods "thrust them down to inhale the muddy water of the deep;" they were assigned "the last and lowest habitation as punishment for the uttermost degree of folly."[2] The myth of divine retribution by inundation, to which Plato also refers in the *Timaeus,* recurs in numerous traditions across the globe. Examples of irritated creator gods who send floods as punishment are recounted in the Bambara mythology of Mali, in the Sumerian and Babylonian traditions, in Hinduism, among the Yao of China, the Chewong of Malaya, the Wapangwa of Tanzania and, of course, in the Judeo-Christian tradition, to mention but a few.[3]

In his book, *The Lure of the Sea,* Alain Corbin argues that Judeo-Christian attitudes toward the sea and seaside underwent a profound change between the middle of the eighteenth and the middle of the nineteenth centuries. Prior to this period, he claims, the influence of less than positive biblical images of water informed a perception of the sea as a "great abyss, a place of unfathomable mysteries, an uncharted liquid mass." The sea presented in Genesis was, according to Corbin, a "quivering expanse, which symbolized, and actually was, the unknowable, was frightful in itself."[4] Before God's initial intervention, there was nothing but chaos, and the sea came to represent the state prior to that intervention. In the words of Corbin, "the ocean was the remnant of that undifferentiated primordial substance on which form had to be imposed so that it might become a part of Creation. This realm of the unfinished, a vibrating, vague extension of chaos, symbolized the disorder that preceded civilization."[5] Corbin argues that the advent of industrialization rendered positive the sea's moral charge precisely because of its distance from civilization; it became an escape outlet of a desired return to primordiality for those locked into the excesses of the industrial age.

W. H. Auden, in *The Enchafèd Flood,* echoes Corbin's argument regarding the sea as symbolic of disorder in Judeo-Christian tradition, and extends it to suggest that, postdiluvianly, the sea always bore within itself the threat of a further flood. "The sea, in fact, is that state of barbaric vagueness and disorder out of which civilization has emerged and into which, unless saved by the effort of gods and men, it is always liable to relapse."[6] Paradoxically, the sea comes to represent a godlessness used by the gods, through floods, to reestablish their preeminence among humankind. This imbues the sea with a resurrective quality: it represents both death and subsequent rebirth. It becomes what Clyde Ford terms the world's "aqua mater."[7]

The sea has been linked to maternity as much as to death. Indeed, it is, at a symbolic level, as often a womb as a tomb. In Sumerian, for example, the word "mar" from which the Portuguese word for sea derives, meant both uterus and sea. In Japanese mythology, the word for ocean "umi" was homophonous with the verb "to give birth."[8] Aphrodite, in some versions of Greek mythology, was born from the womb of the sea.[9] Famously, Freud declares water to be a symbol of birth in dreams.[10] There are many examples in myths throughout the world of heroes being born symbolically in water. Otto Rank dedicated a monograph to an exploration of many of these myths, in which he points out that water often represents a rebirth. The child—be it Moses, or Sargon, the founder of Babylon, or Karna in Hindu tradition—is abandoned to water and reborn through it.[11] The infant escapes death at the moment he is supposed to be surrendered to it. In an early version of the

Oedipus legend, related by Rank, Laios's child is placed in a box on the sea, only to be rescued by Queen Periboa.[12] In Roman tradition, Romulus and Remus were condemned to death as babies by Amulius, and abandoned to the River Tiber. Far from becoming their grave, the river provided amniotic protection and thus ensured the birth of an empire. These examples imbue the sea with a resurrective quality; it brings what is meant to be dead back to life. By extension, when Couto draws on thalassic cultural discourses, he implicitly signals the postcolonial rebirth of the Mozambican nation.

In Portuguese mythic tradition, the tale of the lost king Dom Sebastião is intricately linked to his symbolic rebirth through his much-desired return to Portugal over the sea that carried him away. Dom Sebastião was a sixteenth-century king, who led a disastrous mission to conquer the Moors of North Africa in the name of Christendom and was slain on the battlefield of Alcácer Quibir. His death led to the Spanish takeover of the Portuguese throne in 1580 because he left no heirs. In an ironic twist, the myth arose that he would return to Portugal and liberate his nation from the nefarious clutches of the Spanish Crown when, in reality, his foolhardy and politically irresponsible actions were the direct cause of the accession to power of a Spanish king in Lisbon, since Dom Sebastião failed in his primary duty as king to secure a succession, and led a campaign in Africa that his advisers warned was doomed to failure, and that resulted in his own death. When Portugal regained its independence from Spain in 1640, the myth did not die. Instead, it was reconfigured through the centuries at the whim of political vagaries, becoming a recurrent motif in the lusophone collective unconscious that affects Portuguese literature to this day. Portugal's leaders, including Salazar, were willing to exploit the Sebastianic resonance prevalent among the Portuguese, to cast themselves as messianic figures capable of saving their people. As Miguel de Unamuno, the Spanish writer and renowned lusophile, commented, throughout the various manifestations of the myth of Dom Sebastião, the sea always serves as an ambivalent barrier that keeps the lost king out of Portugal and promises his return.[13]

The myth of Dom Sebastião combines three characteristics prevalent in the sea's depiction in the human imaginary. First, it represents death. Second, it points to a rebirth. And third, it is intricately related to dreams: in Portugal's case, the dream of an imperial glory that was to be triggered by Dom Sebastião's retarded return over the oceans. In *Water and Dreams,* Gaston Bachelard links the three strands, arguing that the human unconscious needs death to possess the meaning of a journey, as a mechanism to replace certain mortality with the reassurance of eternity. Presenting death as the crossing of a river or a trip into the sea preserves the symbolism of a voyage and draws on a maternal emblem. For Bachelard, "water carries us. Water rocks us. Water puts us to sleep. Water gives us back our mother."[14] Water is the dual symbol of birth and death. Bachelard argues further that the conquest of water becomes symbolic of the conquest over death. "No utility could justify the immense risk of setting out over the water," he asserts, continuing, "for man to run the risks implicit in navigation, powerful interests have to be present." These interests are the things "about which one dreams," "mythical interests" etched on the unconscious of a nation. "The hero of the sea," he declares, "is a hero of death" concluding, "the first sailor was the first living man who was as courageous as a dead one."[15] Bachelard is not arguing that hardheaded calculation had nothing to do with the exploration of the sea. Rather, he is claiming that more than just material interest had to be present to inspire crossing the oceans in the first instance. A powerful force lay inside humankind's unconscious. It was a force that made the deep irresistibly attractive; water was the stuff of dreams.

One of the great legacies of the Portuguese nation is the manner in which it opened up the seas to the Old World. The efforts of Prince Henry the Navigator, the fifteenth-century visionary who encouraged Portugal's voyages of discovery, made available sea routes that had previously been unconquered by Europeans. Of course, there was a dark side to the Portuguese maritime expansion. It opened the era of colonialism, and facilitated the transportation of slaves across continents. However, given Portugal's geography, as a small country with a proportionally vast seaboard, maritime exploration was inevitable.

In the canon of lusophone literature, the sea occupies center stage. The great Portuguese Renaissance poet, Luís de Camões, immortalized his nation's conquest of the oceans in his epic *Os Lusíadas* [The Lusiads] first published in 1572 in the middle of Dom Sebastião's reign, and dedicated to the ill-fated king. Camões repeatedly uses the metaphor, in his most famous poem, of the Portuguese cutting open the sea.[16] They carve new routes, which link the various parts of the globe, and lead to an exchange of knowledge and values. The sea, in *Os Lusíadas,* represents Portugal at its most assimilative. However, this noble aspect is tainted by personal interest. Individuals view the sea as the source of personal gain, ignoring the greater good. In often-cited verses from the tenth canto, Camões berates "deaf and hardened people" [gente surda e endurecida] who are characterized by their "taste for greed" [gosto da cobiça] and "baseness" [rudeza].[17] The ambivalent aspect of Portugal's mastery of the seas, which Camões portrays on several occasions in the poem, renders his epic prescient of his nation's decline. Written during and celebrating the halcyon days of Portugal's maritime expansion, it forewarns of the disaster that was to follow. As the prototext of the lusophone canon, it has provoked many literary replies, including António Quadros's *As Quybyrycas,* written in Mozambique during the dying days of colonialism by a Portuguese sympathetic to the African nation's independence.[18] Quadros's title cleverly corrupts Camões's original so that it resonates with the locale of Dom Sebastião's demise (Alcácer Quibir). Quadros also feminizes the title's gender, and proceeds to portray the negative aspects of Portugal's control of the seas: the slavery, the shipwrecks, and the suffering.

There are examples of Portuguese writers from Camões onward who characterize their nation's relationship with the sea as simultaneously empire-building and soul-destroying, or as the source of human progress tainted by pusillanimity. In the seventeenth and eighteenth centuries, a genre based on the narration of shipwrecks became popular in Portugal. The growing demand for such texts was exploited by the publisher Bernardo Gomes de Brito who, in the eighteenth century, collated a series of these accounts in what became known as the *História Trágico-marítima* [Tragic Maritime History].[19] A frequent cause of the shipwrecks was the fact that the sailors had overloaded the ships due to avarice. The result was that Portuguese souls were lost to the deep that they had made available to the world. The nobility, which their enterprise had bestowed upon them for their services to humankind, was once again tainted by a desire for personal gain. The source of Portuguese greatness, the sea, would serve as their punishment for failing to live up to that greatness.

In the nineteenth century, Almeida Garrett, the Portuguese author and politician, used the symbolism of the crossing of water to signify loss or disaster for the Portuguese. In his most famous play, *Frei Luis de Sousa* [Friar Luis de Sousa], each time water is crossed, disaster ensues.[20] The play is the story of an unwanted return from across the sea. The plot centers on the family of Manuel de Sousa, who is happily married to Madalena de Vilhena, and together they have a daughter, Maria de Noronha. Madalena has been married previously to the very noble João de Portugal, who is presumed to have died in the battle of Alcácer Quibir. The first crossing of water is Dom Sebastião's expedition to North Africa, which leads to the Spanish takeover of the Portuguese throne, and to Manuel's insistence that their family home be burnt to prevent it being used by agents of Spain. As a result of this incineration, the family has to cross the River Tejo that separates Lisbon from Almada, and move into Madalena's old home. This second crossing of water provokes a series of nightmares in Madalena; she fears an imminent disaster. The third crossing of water is when Manuel returns to Lisbon to make peace with his former enemies. During his absence, a mysterious pilgrim appears, who turns out to be João, Madalena's first husband. The plot ends with the death of Maria, whose life becomes unviable with the return of her mother's legitimate husband, a return Maria herself paradoxically longs for earlier in the play. A possible reading of this story is that Maria represents a Portugal that pines for the return of Dom Sebastião. For Garrett, the consequences of such a return would be disastrous, as are the effects of such longing. Indeed, the playwright debunks the sebastianic myth in his play, and delivers a message that the crossing of water has led the Portuguese astray, leading the nation to ignore its own internal poverty and live on the dream of an imperial endeavor that never delivered and never could deliver.

From the perspective of those who were colonized, the sea brought the Portuguese, and is consequently tainted by the blood of conflict and slavery. José de Alencar's nineteenth-century Brazilian foundation novel, *Iracema*, captures the colonizing component of the sea's role in the lusophone experience.[21] It tells the story of an indigenous Indian girl Iracema's doomed love for a colonizer, Martim. The sea brings him into her life, and he leads her to abandon and betray her tribe, before leaving her alone to return to his homeland and spouse. Iracema dies, but leaves a son, whose name, Moacir, signifies "born of my suffering." References to the sea abound in the text, often pointing to the suffering of Iracema. The sea represents the medium through which centuries of destruction were unleashed on the indigenous cultures of Brazil since it symbolizes the arrival of the Portuguese. These same Portuguese would transport slaves over to the New Continent's sugar and coffee plantations from Africa, imbuing the oceans, from an African perspective, with the negative connotation of being the medium over which the human misery inherent in the slave trade was systematically peddled. One of lusophone Africa's leading intellectuals of the twentieth century, the poet and first president of Angola, Agostinho Neto, captured the misery signified by the sea in his famous short story, "Náusea" [Nausea], first published in 1952. The narrative centers on an old man, João, who takes his young nephew to the beach, where the vision of the sea triggers a series of unpleasant memories that associate the oceans with death and, specifically, with the slave trade that had taken his grandfather to other continents, leading João to declare, "the enemy is the sea" [O inimigo é o mar].[22] Neto's depiction of the deep as hostile to Africa cedes ownership of the sea to the colonizer to the extent that it becomes a metonym for the Portuguese. Portugal's uncontested possession of the oceans, heralded and desired by Fernando Pessoa in his famous poetic celebration of Lisbon's maritime expansion *Mensagem* [Message] becomes more problematized in the work of contemporary lusophone African writers such as Pepetela and José Luandino Vieira who draw on the slave discourse of the sea. Luandino Vieira, an Angolan with whom Mia Couto has repeatedly been compared, principally on the grounds that both are innovative with the Portuguese language in which they write, declares, "tears run in the sea. Tears came by sea" [As lágrimas correm no mar. As lágrimas vieram no mar] in *Nós, Os do Makulusu* [Us, the Ones from Makulusu].[23] The tears running allude to slavery and are African tears that intertextually distort the tears of Pessoa's poem "Mar Português" [Portuguese Sea] in which the oceans are rendered saline by the weeping of Portuguese mothers, children and lovers left behind by the noble explorers who set out to conquer the sea.[24] Pepetela, another Angolan, develops the sea-slave discourse further by rendering ambiguous the culpability for the trade in a powerful maritime contemplation from his novel *A Geração da Utopia* [The Generation of Utopia]. The novel, first published in 1992, deconstructs the postindependence Angolan nation, portraying the betrayal of the idealism that had been the driving force behind the struggle for independence. Like Neto's João, Vítor, a character from *A Geração da Utopia,* deems the sea to be a hostile space: "old family echoes led to an association between the sea and death. Echoes from the times of the slave convoys that found in the sea their port of departure for the plantations and mines of Brazil. Or more recently, for their forced labor in São Tomé" [ecos antigos da família faziam associar o mar à morte. Ecos vindos dos tempos das caravanas de escravos que no mar encontravam o porto para o degredo nas plantações ou minas do Brasil. Ou mais recentemente, para os trabalhos forçados em São Tomé].[25] Having linked the sea to the slave trade, Pepetela then complicates its moral dimension by referring to the involvement of Africans in the trade—those who did the "dirty work" [trabalho sujo] capturing the slaves and selling them to the Portuguese for deportation to the New Continent—so that the sea contains both the blood of Africans and blood on the hands of Africans and the colonizing Portuguese.

In his earlier novel, *Mayombe,* written during and about the Angolan war for liberation and whose title points to the area in which it is set, Pepetela deploys the sea as a metaphor for a shared humanity that both unites and confines [o mar une, o mar estreita] and includes an internalization of the "sweat and crushed tears" of slavery and colonization [suores e lágrimas esmagados], while simultaneously representing the hope inherent in the dream of liberation.[26] Once again, Pepetela offers a complex image of the sea, celebrating the positive while acknowledging the negative, a strategy followed by his compatriot author, Manuel Rui. Rui culturally crafts the sea as a space for debunking collective memories, as in his *Memória de Mar* [Memory of the Sea], or as a space holding the dreams and hopes of the future, as in *Quem Me Dera Ser Onda* [If Only I Were a Wave].[27] In *Memória de Mar,* published in 1980, five years after Angolan independence, Manuel Rui places colonialist opponents of independence, trapped in a time warp, in a broken-down submarine sought by a postindependence Angolan expedition that itself defies the constraints of linear time. Thus, in the narrative, the sea's contents parody elements of the ocean's role in the five-century colonial domination of lusophone Africa. As Phyllis Peres points out, "the submarine is only the latest Portuguese sea vessel to embark on voyages of colonization; it lies in wait as the present-day caravel of neocolonialism."[28] *Quem Me Dera Ser Onda,* a novella that has sold over one hundred thousand copies worldwide, and which was first published in 1982, uses the sea in a way that Couto repeats later in his own work, as a store for dreams amid an unpalatable reality. The plot recounts the exploits of an emerging middle-class family in postindependence Luanda who are illegally raising a pig to slaughter. The children in the story become emotionally attached to the swine, employing a series of tactics to save its life that ultimately fail. The closing lines of the story describe the children resorting to the sheer "force of hope" [força da esperança] to save the already-lost animal, repeating a phrase used throughout the narrative "if only I were a wave" [quem me dera ser onda].[29] The waves of the ocean represent their freedom to imagine an alternative reality, an interesting reconfiguration of the maritime metaphor given the particularly gruesome toll the slave trade inflicted on the Angolan nation. Carmen Secco has commented on the ubiquity of the sea in Manuel Rui's texts, asserting, "the sea and memory are always present, in a game that reconstructs a lost nationality, corrupted by years of colonialism" [o mar e a memória estão sempre presentes, no jogo da reconstrução da nacionalidade perdida, esfacelada pelos anos de colonialismo].[30] For Secco, the colonial legacy of the sea underpins the Angolan's work.

Contemporary Mozambican authors and poets share their Angolan counterparts' tendency to metaphorize of the sea. As a nation with an extensive seaboard like its former colonial master, the sea naturally features in Mozambique's cultural output. The country's colonial legacy also colors its authors' depictions of the deep, particularly Mia Couto's, as we will discuss shortly. One of Couto's contemporaries, Ungulani Ba Ka Khosa describes the sea in his "Fábula do Futuro" [Fable of the Future] from *Orgia dos Loucos* [Orgy of the Mad] as "always open" [sempre aberto] since it "receives everyone" [a todos recebe]. For Ungulani, the sea is "democracy in nature" [a democracia na natureza].[31] His idiosyncratic portrayal of the oceans contains the notion that the sea consumes everything—all memories and ideologies, all life—and remains relatively constant. In some ways, this echoes a trend Peres identifies in Manuel Rui's work, since the sea is "a symbolic synthesis of permanence and movement."[32] In essence, Ungulani is casting the sea as a collective unconscious that includes and draws from all humanity. As such, it encompasses the scars of the colonial enterprise and the mechanisms through which to heal.

Virgílio de Lemos is probably the Mozambican poet who has, throughout his work, drawn most on the cultural discourse of the oceans. Like Fernando Pessoa, Lemos has written under a series of heteronyms, all of which fixate on the sea. Born in 1929 in the north of Mozambique, his poetry repeatedly eroticizes the deep, and renders it a depository of dreams. For Lee-Li Yang, his orientalized female heteronym, the sea is marked by a solitude provoked by the absence of loved-ones [ausência e a solidão do mar], which reflects the experiences of both the colonizers and the colonized of Mozambique.[33] Like Luandino Vieira, Lemos echoes Pessoa's depiction of the sea as a haven of Portuguese tears, shed for the absence of sons and lovers sent to conquer the oceans, and of Africans whose sons and lovers were traded away over the waves as slaves, never to return. Additionally, Lemos confers on the sea a femininity and role as an emblem of the unconscious ("the imaginary has the feminine face of the sea" [o imaginário tem o rosto feminino do mar]), a fusion that Couto repeats in his work, as we will see.[34]

Couto acknowledges a strong cultural debt to Lemos in the preface to the latter's 1999 retrospective collection of poetry. He asserts that both belong to the Indian Ocean that is not just a sea but "a web of relationships" in which "Western thought loses its hegemony" [uma teia de relações . . . o pensamento occidental perde hegemonia].[35] Couto grants to the sea, the forum of a plexiform history and emblem of the unconscious, the ability to undermine the binary certainties that underscore European tradition. As such, his treatment of the sea, and water in general, falls into his wider postmodern pattern, favoring ambiguity over definiteness, and liquidity over rigidity. His refusal to fix frontiers does not disqualify him from commenting on and depicting the clear horrors of the colonial past. However, as we shall now discuss in relation to Couto's novel, *Vinte e Zinco*, it prevents him from painting the past as a black-white dichotomy.

Vinte e Zinco:
CLEANSING THE COLONIAL LEGACY

In his novel, *Vinte e Zinco*, Couto symbolizes the Mozambican experience of Portuguese colonialism as blood on the hands of the colonizer that turns the sea red. The book's title is, in fact, a pun: it almost sounds like the Portuguese for the number twenty-five, but instead of using the word for five, Couto uses the similar-sounding word for the metal zinc. The book, as already mentioned, was written as part of the celebrations to mark the twenty-fifth anniversary of the Lisbon coup of 1974, and it makes a very strong point: twenty-five years after the Carnation Revolution, the dreams which the fall of the *Estado Novo* made possible have not yet been fully realized in Mozambique. One of the epigraphs to the book is a quote attributed to the character of Jessumina in which she asserts, "the number twenty-five is for you who live in the suburbs where houses are made of concrete. For us, poor blacks who live under wood and zinc roofs, our day is yet to come" [vinte e cinco é para vocês que vivem nos bairros de cimento. Para nós, negros pobres que vivemos na madeira e zinco, o nosso dia ainda está por vir (*VZ*, 11)]. This epigraph helps to explain the novel's title; the zinc points to the poverty of the Maputo slums. To a Portuguese ear, the number twenty-five recalls a revolution that brought colonialism to an end. But, as Couto himself has pointed out in interviews, the number twenty-five usually has a different significance in Mozambique to the one it bears in Portugal. It represents Mozambican Independence Day, 25 June 1975, a day full of hope.[36] However, as the novel title itself suggests, whatever hope the twenty-five then signified, it has not yet been fulfilled for most of the population of Mozambique who still live in conditions of considerable poverty. In the aftermath of Frelimo's conversion to market economics, discrimination on the grounds of race, against which the movement fought, has been replaced by extreme economic inequality that, while not racist in theory, disadvantages the black majority far more acutely than Mozambican whites. In the midst of this desperate economic situation, Couto published a novel that recounts the final days of colonialism from the perspective of a Portuguese settler family, and strongly supports the notion that under no circumstances should the afflicted abnegate their right to dream. This message, as we shall see in relation to Couto's early short stories, has been a constant throughout his work.

Vinte e Zinco is set over a period of twelve days, immediately before and after Lisbon's Carnation Revolution of 1974. Its central male character is Lourenço de Castro, a white Portuguese member of the hated state security service, the PIDE, who lives in Moebase with his mother, Margarida, and his aunt Irene. The PIDE (the *Policia Internacional de Defesa do Estado* or the International State Defense Police) arrived in Mozambique in 1956 and began bringing under surveillance known opponents of the Salazar regime. Within Portugal itself, Salazar relied on a variety of incarnations of the secret service to maintain his authority throughout his regime, and established a vast network of informants that successfully quashed most political opposition. In some respects, it is surprising that he took so long to send the PIDE to the colonies; only when conflict loomed did he deem it appropriate and, by then, it was too late for them to be as effective as they had been in the metropolis. In Couto's novel, Lourenço's father, Joaquim, had also served in the Portuguese State police, dying at the hands of those he was himself in the process of killing, in front of his young son. Lourenço retains the memory of his father being hurled out of a helicopter toward the sea below. Significantly, Joaquim does not reach the sea until after the April Revolution many years later, at which point the sea itself turns red, a narrative gesture that represents the cleansing of the colonial past through the medium that had brought the colonizer to Mozambique five centuries before. Lourenço is haunted by the image of his father's demise and will never again allow a fan to operate near him, as the sound acts as an objective correlative for the helicopter's rotary blades. Etched on his memory is the sight of his father struggling against the fate that had befallen him: "he saw his father being thrown out of the heli-copter. . . . But nothing fell into the sea" [viu o pai ser ejectado do he-licóptero. . . . Mas nada tombava sobre o mar (27)]. On 25 April, however, Lourenço learns of the Lisbon coup that signifies the end of the order he and his father had sought to defend. Suddenly, his life flashes before him and he hears "a thud: it is his father's body falling into the waters. All of sudden, foam emerges, but it isn't white. Rather, it's red" [um baque: é o corpo de seu pai caindo nas águas. De chofre, se levantam espumas, mas não são brancas. Antes, são vermelhas (92)]. As the sea consumes Joaquim, it obliterates him, becoming a tomb that debars the possibility of his rebirth. Couto uses the sea to hint that the cycle of colonialism is coming to an end. Joaquim's life ap-pears to have reached its end: "finally, his father was suffering his last death" [finalmente, seu pai sofria sua última morte (93)]. Yet Couto's choice of tense here introduces an ambiguity; the death he was suffering was in the imper-fect—the "suffering" itself implies a continuity, not a completed action. In many ways, the effects of colonialism can never be erased since they leave a legacy with which Mozambique must learn to live. Couto's prescription in such circumstances is to dream beyond the dichotomies that colonialism left, something the powerful female characters in this novel do by recourse to water.

As well as maternity and primordiality, particularly in Jungian theory, water represents the unconscious itself. Jung's approach to psychoanalysis is one that rests on a firm belief in the crudest binary opposites; for him, no po-sition exists "without its negation."[37] Within this set up, the sea becomes the emblematic representation of the unconscious, and an island is the metaphoric configuration of the conscious realm. His metaphor becomes most interesting when it allows for an interaction between the two parts of the human psyche. Describing a patient's dream at a seminar in 1929, Jung depicted the unconscious as an ocean sending "powerful waves with almost certain regularity into our conscious, which is like the valley that contains the bay."[38] Clearly, the boundary between the unconscious and the conscious can be crossed, and that is what happens when we dream. For Couto, the principal problem that faced Mozambique during all the years of colonialism and then civil war, and that still faces it today, is a loss of the ability to dream; a severing of the link between the conscious and the unconscious. He uses the Jungian trope of rendering the unconscious symbolically equal to water, but then ensures that water retains its principal attribute of fluidity in order to represent the restoration of that severed link.

In *Vinte e Zinco*, the female protagonists are most associated with moisture and with the ability to envisage a reality different from that imposed by their colonialist male counterparts. Through water, they enter the realm of the unconscious and dissolve the men's racial binaries. In the first chapter of the novel, the reader is informed that there are very few whites in Vila de Moebase. There are only five white men and two white women: Margarida and her apparently insane sister, Irene. This information is imparted in a manner that establishes a male-female binary, in which women are assigned the role of a shadow-like nonpresence: "women don't count. That's what they said at the Castros" [as mulheres não contam. Assim se dizia em casa dos Castros (16)]. The Castro household, in fact, has only one man, Lourenço, who, for all his rhetoric that women are not relevant, suffers from a total dependence on his mother. He constantly needs her reassurance and, in his unconscious, he desires a return to her womb, dreaming that he is regrowing an umbilical cord. Even when he awakes, the desire is so strong that he is psychotically convinced of a physiological change, claiming, "I can feel my umbilical cord growing out" [já estou a sentir o cordão umbilical a sair-me (20)]. This desire is paralleled by his father's need to reach the sea—to return to the prototype womb from which all life emerged. Neither desire will be fulfilled: the sea will eventually operate as Joaquim's (ambiguously) definitive tomb, eradicating him from human memory, while Lourenço will be abandoned by his mother and aunt at the end of the story.

A key aspect differentiating the male and female worlds in *Vinte e Zinco* is the ability of the women to transcend the boundaries set by the men. They are fluid, rendering deliquescent separations demarcated by their male counterparts. For example, Lourenço tells his mother how much he detests all blacks. His morally charged world is black and white, an outlook that his mother contests, not by reversing the binary, but by setting it aside, telling her son, "don't say that, son. Some are good, some are bad" [não diga isso, filho. Há bons, há maus (19)]. As the novel progresses, Margarida will be drawn further and further into the feminine world of water, already inhabited by her sister Irene and the black diviner Jessumina, whose status as a soothsayer was achieved through her seven-year disappearance into Lake Nkuluine. This disappearance was foretold in one of her dreams, and her stay in the lake is what confers her power to read dreams. Lourenço's mother is initially wary of the black woman and her powers, principally from fear of the unknown. She lives in the shadow of her deceased husband who had set clear limits on her life. She is only able to lay his ghost to rest after the coup when she ceases to set a place for him at the dining table, once his body is consumed by the sea.

The first major step taken by Margarida on the road to her own independence is provoked by a recurrent nightmare, in which male savagery is depicted against the backdrop of a very dry world: "the drought had punished the plain all around and green had been totally exiled. . . . There was no longer any river, nor any sea, nor any rain. There was not even a vestige of green" [seca castigara a savana em volta e o verde todo se exilara. . . . Já não havia rio, nem mar, nem chuva. Não havia nem réstia de verde (60)]. Couto also uses the image of drought to signify man's savagery in *Terra Sonâmbula,* as we will discuss later. In *Vinte e Zinco,* Margarida goes to see Jessumina for the first time following her nightmare about the drought. Like Nãozinha in *A Varanda do Frangipani,* the sorceress who dissolves nightly and sleeps in a bathtub as water, Jessumina is another woman with magic powers who is inextricably linked to water. By visiting Jessumina, Margarida is seeking to abandon the dry, binary-ridden world of men, and to ally herself with the fluidity inherent in the female realm as it is presented in Couto's universe.

Jessumina has already been visited regularly by Margarida's sister, Irene, whom other Europeans dismiss as crazy. Irene's world is one of madness, but this allows her to cross boundaries with impunity, drinking with blacks and going to the lakes: "she wasn't supposed to, but who can give orders to madness?" [Estava proibida, mas quem pode mandar em loucura? (25)]. These visits allow Irene to escape the external constraint of time; she lives for the moment. Socializing with blacks places Irene on the margins of her own society's warped morality, and so that society must categorize her as beyond reason. As Margarida flees the moral drought of the colonial world of the men around her, her sister seeks to bring moisture back into that world, challenging its authority in the process. She flaunts her visits to the lakes, provoking her nephew by returning with flasks full of water given to her by Jessumina. This water represents a challenge to colonial authority, because of its fluidity and its provenance: the product of the African land, providing a pathway for seeing into the unconscious and a means of restoring a link with the realm of the precolonial ancestors. It is destined for the eyes of the blind Tchuvisco.

Andaré Tchuvisco's name marks him as the property of the world of the wet. It contains the Portuguese word for "drizzle" [chuvisco]. He is the only man allied with moisture in the novel but, unlike the women, he has not chosen the realm of water for himself. His blindness has placed him there. Like Tiresias, the gender-ambiguous soothsayer from Greek mythology, Tchuvisco's loss of vision was caused by witnessing something he should not have seen, namely, Joaquim's predilection for raping black male prisoners. Tchuvisco's inability to see turns his eyes blue, the color most associated with the deep. His eyes become a liquid conduit through which the unconscious world is able to communicate with the conscious order. But this communication requires the intervention of women who allow for a flow from one realm to the other to take place, as can be seen in Couto's description of the day Tchuvisco foresees the dramatic political change that was about to occur. Twenty-four hours before the coup, he has a vision of a dramatic flood. The flood symbolizes the rupturing of old demarcations and, like its biblical and mythological equivalents, is a punishment triggered because of humankind's evil, in this case, the evil of colonialism: "he announces his terrible visions: the river is about to burst out of its bed, tired of its banks" [anuncia suas terríveis visões: que o rio está para se desprender do leito, cansado da margem (81)]. His declaration that the old order is about to be washed away is not understood or appreciated by those around him because they cannot see it. Then Jessumina takes a tear from Tchuvisco's eye and the interaction between the female diviner and the blind man's lachrymal fluid gives the conscious world access to the communication from the unconscious. Everyone is able to see, through the prism of the teardrop, "the flood swallowing up the entire world" [a inundação engolindo o universal mundo (85)]. Tchuvisco's vision is important because it marks the ending of a particularly sordid period in Mozambique's history, the dying days of colonialism, as a deluge that sweeps the regime aside. As in the case of Joaquim Castro's ultimate demise, water symbolizes a cleansing of the imperial legacy. Additionally, through Tchuvisco's tear, water functions as the mechanism through which a link to the unconscious realm of dreams and fantastic possibilities is reestablished, a realm readily inhabited by the women in the novel and shunned by the male colonizers.

Vinte e Zinco is an important advance in Couto's work because it explicitly tackles the ambiguities of the colonial legacy. Capturing a historical moment of revolutionary change in Mozambique, it refutes clear moral demarcations between the white settler community and the black population, choosing instead to depict the ambivalences and interactions between the two groups. Couto's portrayal of the dying colonial order is one in which dichotomies were regularly flouted, and dreams shared between races. Irene's fate in the novel—she enters the waters of the lake as the tale concludes, and is consumed by the same liquid mass that had taken her black counterpart Jessumina years before—represents that fusion of dreams. Irene's entry into the lake is an entry into the unconscious realm where a new reality must be dreamt before it is born.

Mar Me Quer:
RESTORING THE MATERNAL

Like *Vinte e Zinco, Mar Me Quer* deploys water as a mechanism for the sharing of dreams. Originally published as part of the Expo 98 exhibition in Lisbon, the novella was republished by Caminho in 2000, colorfully illustrated by João Nasi Pereira. Its plot centers on the conversations between two characters, the narrator, Zeca Perpétuo, and his older neighbor, Dona Luarmina, whom he wishes to seduce. Like Muidinga in *Terra Sonâmbula,* Luarmina's true identity is only revealed at the end of the narrative. Prior to that epiphany, we learn of her immense beauty as a young woman, and of her mixed racial heritage as the mulatto daughter of a Greek fisherman. Several of Couto's strongest characters are mulatto women. Examples include Ernestina in A *Varanda do Frangipani,* Dona Candida in "O Último Aviso do Corvo Falador," and Dona Luarmina, who are all powerful statements of the syncretism of Mozambique. They represent the combination of cultures as well as races that makes the nation such a rich tapestry of beliefs and customs. Additionally, they are part of Couto's constant preoccupation with race, doubtless the result of his own ambiguous position as a white writer in a predominantly black space. The title of one of his early collections of short stories *Cada Homem É Uma Raça* [Every Man Is a Race] renders patent his conviction that racial stereotypes occlude the individuality he so prizes. His position that each individual, in racial terms, is precisely an individual parallels Martine Rothblatt's assertion in *The Apartheid of Sex* that there are "five billion sexes," an exaggeration that challenges reductive categorizations and firmly posits identity as the preserve of the individual.[39] In *Mar Me Quer,* Luarmina's paternal racial heritage imbues her with the culture of one of Europe's earliest maritime powers, also the bedrock of much of Western mythology. As in so many of the myths of Western culture, the sea represents loss in Luarmina's tale, but also allows for the rebirth of her identity.

Maritime allusions surface ubiquitously in the novella. Luarmina's name contains the Portuguese word for moonlight [luar], something that associates her with sea tides. The title, *Mar Me Quer*, stems from Luarmina's practice of pulling petals from flowers and chanting "mar me quer, bem me quer" (*MMQ*, 16), a corruption of the Portuguese phrase for "He loves me, he loves me not" [mal me quer, bem me quer] which switches the negating adverb "mal" for the word for "sea" [mar], so that Luarmina's phrase, while resonating with the "He loves me, he loves me not" chant of the besotted, actually means "the sea loves me, it loves me a lot." As the novella's title suggests, the sea plays a central role in the tale. Couto exploits a number of its associations. It is a womb and a mother, and an infinite resource of multiple possibilities where "everything is possible" [tudo ali pode ser (19)]. In the sea, "there are no words, and no one exacts an account from the truth" [no mar não há palavra, nem ninguém pede contas à verdade (20)]. In other words, the sea represents a zone of fantasies, the unconscious realm restored to the protagonists as the plot evolves. Furthermore, teardrops, a saline metonym for the sea, become a metaphor for a desired return to the universal uterus, "that little bit of water is us returning to our first womb" [essa aguinha somos nós regressando ao primeiro ventre (50)]. In this assertion, Couto echoes Sandor Ferenczi's notion of a "thalassal regressive trend," humankind's desire to return to the prototype womb, the sea.[40] Ferenczi, one of Freud's disciples, built on his teacher's association of the sea with maternity. According to Freud, water's link to birth was commonplace in dreams, and can be explained by two "evolutionary" truths. The first is that "all terrestrial mammals, including man's ancestors, descended from aquatic creatures." The second is that "every individual mammal, every human being, spent the first phase of its existence in water—namely as an embryo in the amniotic fluid in its mother's uterus, and came out of the water when it was born."[41] The symbolism of water as birth thus depends for its coherence on both evolution and gestation. Humankind was born of the sea and our first nine months in the womb parallel this historical fact; water represents our phylogenetic and our individual origin. An oneiric desire to enter the sea is therefore a desire for the restitution of the maternal.

In Couto's *Mar Me Quer*, both the protagonists have lost their mothers, and the sea functions as a substitute for that maternal loss. Looking out to the oceans, the backdrop to the narrative, constantly calms them. To paraphrase Bachelard, the sea "gives [them] back [their] mother." Luarmina's mother died from jealousy about her daughter's beauty, having gone mad and tried to destroy her offspring's perfect features. Zeca's mother appears to commit suicide by slitting her wrists and placing them in a tank of water. Her husband, Zeca's father Agualberto, whose name contains the Portuguese word for water [água], was a fisherman who would spend afternoons with his mistress in his boat. One day the mistress falls into the sea, and Agualberto plunges into the deep to try and rescue her. Many hours later, he resurfaces alone, but with his eyes changed. Like Tchuvisco, in *Vinte e Zinco*, Agualberto's eyes become the color of the oceans, marking a significant alteration in his perspective on life. He becomes insane and abandons his wife and child, Zeca. However, his wife never admits that her husband has gone, and goes insane herself, insisting that her son write letters to Agualberto. Once again, Couto plays with absence and presence through epistles. Zeca's mother "clothed absence with tissues of lies" [vestia ausência com panos de mentira (30)], fabricated through her son's never-written missives. When Zeca tells Luarmina the story of his parents' insanity, she cries without explaining why. The reason becomes obvious at the end of the story when Luarmina's identity is revealed: she was his father's mistress, and she saves Zeca by furnishing him with this information as he lies moribund. He is convinced that his father is punishing him for failing to provide food and solace to his drowned mistress, as Zeca had promised. By revealing her identity, Luarmina demonstrates that Zeca has kept his promise to his father, keeping her company over the years.

There is a second strand to the story which, like the first involving Agualberto's mistress, is intricately linked to the sea. Zeca had a wife, Henriquinha, who possessed incredible feminine beauty. She also appeared to be devoted to God, seemingly attending church religiously every Sunday. In fact, she would really leave the house to perform a striptease in public, an act of infidelity discovered by Zeca. In order to confront her *flagrante delicto*, he tricked her into thinking it was Sunday one weekday so that she left to perform her erotic Sabbath ritual on the sea-cliff. Without her usual audience, Zeca, unseen, pushed her over the edge. Like Joaquim de Castro in *Vinte e Zinco*, no splash was audible as Henriquinha fell toward the sea. Instead, the squawks of seagulls were heard, and this association led Zeca to detest the marine bird, harming it at every available opportunity. One night, he sets fire to a cage full of seagulls that Luarmina owns, and the remorse that his act causes leads him to reveal the secret about how his wife disappeared. After she has heard the tale, Luarmina forces Zeca to go and inspect the damage he has done. To his amazement, one bird has survived the inferno he caused and, as that strand of the story draws to a close, the assumption may be drawn that the seagull left in the cage whose fate Luarmina leaves Zeca to determine contains the spirit of his wife.

Both strands of *Mar Me Quer* involve objects of love being lost to the sea. In both strands, the sea does not kill those it consumes but rather transforms them. If we accept that the sea represents the unconscious realm of dreams and desires, the moral of Couto's story is that the unconscious has the power to transform the reality of those who enter it. Furthermore, within the unconscious lie the specters of our past. Entering such a recess is not an easy process for anyone, least of all a nation that has suffered like Mozambique. But it is a necessary aspect of the healing process, and in *Mar Me Quer,* both protagonists come to terms with their painful histories by talking through what they have endured. As in *Vinte e Zinco,* one aspect of the unconscious as represented by the sea is the colonial past. On one occasion, Zeca accidentally cuts his finger while on his boat. His father makes him suck his own blood, and asks him what it tastes like. Zeca's only response is to look at the sea, realizing the answer but failing to understand its significance: "What was my father really telling me? That we carry oceans that circulate within us? That we have to make journeys alone in our innermost beings? I will never know" [Meu pai, afinal, me estava a dizer o quê? Que trazemos oceanos circulando dentro de nós? Que há viagens que temos de fazer só no íntimo de nós? Ficarei sempre sem saber (59)]. The oceans within are, in part, the syncretistic result of years of colonization, a colonization that metaphorically marked the sea with blood, and psychologically scarred the Mozambican nation. By delving into the deep, Couto ventures a coming-to-terms with the past that permits prospects in the future. The sea's uterine aspect for the characters also symbolizes birth, and the restoration of the maternal, an association that parallels the birth of a new nation.

Vozes Anoitecidas:
RESTORING THE RIGHT TO DREAM

Mar Me Quer and *Vinte e Zinco* were both published after peace was firmly established in Mozambique. For Couto, the time had arrived to confront the colonial past and culturally to build on its legacy. These two works use the sea as both a symbol of that past and as a metaphor for dealing with an often-painful heritage through interaction with the unconscious. Couto's work has consistently demanded that his readers and his characters interact with the unconscious and, from his earliest short stories, that interaction has always been symbolized by water. However, there has been a marked shift in the motivations behind Couto's call to interact with the unconscious. While recently, in the safe space of a nation relatively at peace with itself, Couto uses the unconscious to come to terms with the colonial past, during the painful period of the civil war, when the country was torn apart by a conflict that aggravated its people's poverty, Couto deployed the unconscious as a means to imagine a future. This was at a time when there appeared to be no hope, and the loss of the ability to dream was Couto's greatest cause for concern. His first collection of short stories, *Vozes Anoitecidas* [Voices Made Night], begins with the following author's foreword:

> The most harrowing thing about poverty is the ignorance it has of itself. Faced by an absence of everything, men abstain from dreams, depriving themselves of the desire to be others. There exists in nothingness that illusion of plenitude which causes life to stop and voices to become night. (*VMN*, author's foreword).

The desire for personal transcendence, one of the preoccupations of Couto's early poems, is still present. However, it manifests itself in a more collective form and stresses the fading of that desire. It is no longer just the Self which needs to—but cannot—dream of being other than it is; it is the community as a whole. Dreaming is presented as more than a way to escape an unpalatable present; it is viewed as a mode of effecting change. Chesca Long-Innes reads the author's foreword as an allusion to a complex "psychic disturbance which inevitably follows upon lives grounded in extreme poverty."[42] She deems Couto's project in his first collection to be an effort to give voice to that disturbance and disputes Brenda Cooper's contention that "the voice of the people" is "ironically undercut even as they speak, given what is ultimately portrayed as the inadequacy of their resources."[43] Cooper repeats the arguments of those critics who position Couto as a spokesperson for the oral culture of Mozambique, in order to critique his posture. Her basic premise that Couto speaks for others is not beyond dispute, as Long-Innes highlights. Long-Innes offers a more satisfying reading of what Couto does in *Vozes Anoitecidas*, particularly given the subtlety of the work. As well as pointing to the psychological trauma inflicted on the nation, Couto offers recuperation through the restitution of the right to dream and, as we shall see, he always links the restoration of the link with the unconscious to water.

The geography of a substantial segment of Mozambican territory is such that it has historically suffered from a cycle of severe droughts, followed by flooding.[44] Indeed, the floods of 2000 brought the nation to the attention of the world.[45] Clearly, in such an environment, water is a preoccupation, while culturally serving to recuperate the nation by reminding the outside world of its existence. For Couto, in this collection, water is often deployed as a means of altering reality, a way in which the conscious world can give way to unconscious desire. As will be discussed later in this chapter, *Terra Sonâmbula* can be read to equate water to the unconscious world and drought to the conscious world. But before discussing that novel in detail, we turn our attention to those short stories in *Vozes Anoitecidas* that assign a central role to water.

"O Dia em que Explodiu Mabata-bata" and "Os Pássaros de Deus": Rivers of Primordiality and Faith

Rivers feature prominently in two of the short stories in *Vozes Anoitecidas*. The first is "O Dia em que Explodiu Mabata-bata" [The Day Mabata-bata Exploded], the tale of Azarias, a young boy, whose dreams are crushed by an uncaring and exploitative uncle. Unlike "other people's children," he is not allowed to attend school because, as an orphan, "he was nobody's son" (*VMN*, 18). He has no one to protect his interests and, instead of being able to enjoy the pleasures of childhood, he is made to work looking after his uncle's herd. Azarias's form of escape from the misery of his existence involves playing with the animals—substitutes for friends of his own age—and swimming in the river. The latter activity could be read as a manifestation of his desire for the restitution of a mother: entering water, he returns to the symbolic equivalent of the womb. Additionally, the river is more than the medium through which he swims. The Portuguese phrase Couto uses is "nadar o rio" (*VA*, 49)—"to swim the river." The river becomes the syntactical object of his action since the verb "nadar" is used transitively. It turns Azarias from an erased being whose significance is near naught into a fuller subject operating on a compliant object. As a result, the river serves both grammatically to restore to Azarias a partial degree of agency, and to furnish him with a source of maternal comfort. The waters act as an amniotic protection for the orphan.

His uncle cruelly mocks his loneliness, and everybody laughs at him, "without a care for his tiny soul, his mistreated dreams" (*VMN*, 19). One day, Mabata-bata, the prize bull in the herd, steps on a mine and explodes. The child does not realize what has happened. He assumes that the *ndlati*, the "bird of lightning," must have been responsible, as he looks toward the mountains: "it was there that the ndlati dwelt, there where all the rivers are one, born from the same desire to be water" (17–18). The bird, thus described, is both a symbol of fire and water: when it strikes as lightning, it offers a return to the womb, to the primordial space where the rivers are born. For the orphan Azarias, the bird of fire will offer him an escape into the aquatic dream world of the unconscious.

The child fears the reaction of his uncle at the loss of the bull and resolves to flee. The river is the place where he feels safest and is also the only thing left over which he exercises some degree of control since even the animals in his care have started to explode without his consent, reducing him to the role of a passive observer. As he reaches the river, the driving force behind his journey changes: "he felt that he was not running away: he was merely starting out along his road" (19). The need to flee his uncle's wrath, which had compelled him to leave initially, fades, and the journey itself becomes his purpose rather than his means of evading agnatic ire. But his journey is linked to the river, so that what replaces his fear of unjust retribution from his uncle is an unconscious desire to enter the realm of unknown possibilities, which the water represents. Having crossed the water, he waits but "without even knowing what he was waiting for" (19). He no longer knows why he is where he is. His motivation has ceased to be explicable by reference to the conscious realm alone. Once again, water provides comfort and protection for him. In fact, water will be his destiny. His fate will be the same as the bull's since the story will end with the child embracing the ndlati. In the real world, a sphere far from privileged in Couto's texts, Azarias is destroyed by a mine. In the parallel world of oneiric possibility, he will be carried away by the "bird of fire" to the place where it resides. The child dies falsely believing that his dream of being able to go to school will be granted to him by his uncle and never suffers the disillusionment of discovering that his relative has lied to him. At the moment of death, he clings to a false truth, and undergoes a sublimation that draws him into the cultural unconscious world of myth, depositing him safely in the primordial medium and womb of all life. The ndlati takes the child, at the moment of death, to the waters of the unconscious.

Couto draws on a variety of cultural sources in this particularly poignant tale that, in essence, seeks to restore Azarias's right to dream in the midst of the horrific civil war that victimized children and peasants long after the cessation of hostilities through a proliferation of landmines. The African myth of the ndlati is combined with the uterine resonance of water to restore agency to the seemingly helpless child. His demise may be read as a fusion with the unconscious, and seems to suggest that, for Couto, the only way to cope with Mozambique's national trauma in the 1980s was to dream once again.

Ernesto Timba's fate in "Os Pássaros de Deus" [The Birds of God] is one in which he too becomes part of a river, and thus is able to realize his dreams. His destiny is as ambiguous as that of Azarias. Both cling to beliefs that, as such, are beyond verification. Both also appear to achieve their desires by being physically destroyed. Timba is effectively a prophet and, like his biblical counterparts, he suffers for his convictions. His words are ignored and his actions are deemed to be signs of madness in the conscious world around him, where faith has been forfeited against the backdrop of a severe drought. Like Jeremiah, Timba cannot even rely on his family to stand by him.[46] Yet he remains true to his god and eventually will appear to be rewarded by an entry into the unconscious world represented by water, where his dreams will come true. The closing lines of the tale anthropomorphize the river but, in contrast to Azarias's river, Timba's assumes the position of a sentient subject: "the river flowed on into the distance, laughing at the ignorance of men. Ernesto Timba, gently lulled by the current, was carried downstream, and shown the by-ways he had only glimpsed in dreams" (*VMN*, 28). The river is both a tomb and womb, rocking him gently and leading him childlike to a place beyond the skepticism of his neighbors.

There are indications from the beginning of the story that Timba will end up as part of the river. His fate is sealed as he speculates that "one day they'll fish me out of the water, swallowed up by the river" (23). Everything in his life points to its end since all he has ever lived is "water, water, just nothing else" (23). His existence follows a teleological trajectory in which the concept of a god is intricately and continuously entwined, along with the ebbs and flows of water in the tale. His final resting place, his heaven at the end of the story, is the river. Yet water is also where it all starts, both narratively and in terms of the birth of his belief. The opening lines of the tale point to the fluvial association of the journey of faith that Timba will undertake: "I don't know anything more like a pilgrim than the river. The waves pass by on a journey that has no end" (23). The real pilgrim of the story is in fact Timba, who will enter the infinite riverine (dis)course, both physically—when he dies—and metaphysically—when he believes. His capacity to believe in something he cannot see stems from his childhood choice of a profession based on the neutral element. In the words of his father, "the fisherman believes in something he can't see" (24). Couto uses the phrase "credita uma coisa" (*VA*, 58) which is paradoxically what Timba will both do and not do as the story unfolds because, although the phrase implies the concept behind the English translation "believes in something," that is not exactly what it says. "Credita uma coisa," devoid of any context, would usually connote "he credits" or "guarantees" something. To credit or guarantee something—such as a sum of money—is to quantify it, to set limits to its scope, to know it absolutely, qualitatively different from believing in a god, which presupposes an element of doubt and depends on the infinity of his, her, or its reach.

The river conceals the fish from the fisherman in the same way as the unconscious is masked from the conscious realm. But it is also the means by which the fisherman reaches the fish. If gods are deemed to belong to the collective unconscious, to that space where rational proof and conscious logic fail, the water of the river becomes an outward sign of the means, faith, through which Timba reaches the unconscious where his god resides.

The world around Timba has lost all faith and he alone understands the symbolism of the bird that one day lands in his boat: it is sent by God. His wife logically demands that, hungry as they are, they eat the fowl that he brings home. But he prohibits such a fate, and makes his wife progressively more irate as he tends to the animal and a companion that he also comes across, while his family goes hungry. When the birds are desecrated, he begs to be allowed to expiate the sin of the community, in the face of divine fury. At this point in the story, "pescador"—the Portuguese word for fisherman—is effectively overwritten by "pecador"—the word for sinner. He seeks to atone for the guilt of others. It is only after his death, once he has become "stuck to the surface of the river" (*VMN*, 27), that those in the conscious world around him begin to doubt their own skepticism. The storm clouds gather and, rather than rejoicing at the impending rainfall that will break the drought, the community fears the retribution of a deluge for their lack of faith: "for the first time, their faiths joined together pleading that it might not rain" (28). This reaction is a curious irony because, before they went beyond the point of no return by destroying the birds, the rain would have been the solution to the drought that had triggered all their problems. Beyond a certain point, logic is reversed and the solution, water, becomes the problem. Timba's world appears to triumph at the end of the story, at two levels. An impending flood will sweep through the area so that the symbol of the unconscious, most associated with Timba, will drown the conscious realm. And, in an effort to halt the inevitable flood, that conscious world of rational thought and radical doubt appeals to the powers of the unconscious, uniting in their beliefs.

Both "O Dia em que Explodiu Mabata-bata" and "Os Pássaros de Deus" have morally ambiguous endings. Their protagonists die in the real, conscious realm after lives of intense hardship. Yet, at the same time, Ernesto

Timba and Azarias are given what they desire at the end of the stories. A troubling aspect of this narrative strategy, which prevails in Couto's early work, is its Christian, self-flagellating resonance: the concept that suffering in this world somehow leads to reward in the next and, consequently, this justifies suffering. In Couto's defense, he does not institutionalize suffering as a means to an end, but instead describes it as a reality and then foregrounds dreams as a means of conceptualizing a different reality.

"A Fogueira" and "De Como O Velho Jossias Foi Salvo das Águas": Flooding the Conscious

The first story in *Vozes Anoitecidas*, "A Fogueira" [The Fire], like "O Dia em que Explodiu Mabata-bata" and "Os Pássaros de Deus," places an emphasis on the need to retain the right to dream, even when destitute. It also characterizes water as the symbolic lubricant facilitating an entry into the unconscious world of dreams. The narrative is centered on an old woman who lives in a world of "nothingness" (*VMN,* 1). Her existence is summed up by the hollowness of the bowls and baskets that surround her. Her children are no longer with her and her husband is becoming less and less of a presence. In her own words, "my husband is shrinking . . . he is a shadow" (1). One day, he announces that he will begin to dig a grave for her; like everything else in her life, the last thing she will have will be a hollow. The reader learns that "for two weeks the old man busied himself with the hole. The nearer he got to completing it, the longer he took" (3). His purpose in life becomes the creation of another hollow space for his wife but, as he continues to dig, it begins to rain and water fills the void he has created for her. His project is threatened by the invasion of water as the rains continue for days. The old man carries on regardless. The more he tries to create a void, the more the waters fill it, gradually defeating the old man, and leading to his death. But, as the downpour causes his decline, it fills the old woman's life with meaning. For, as the rains overwhelm her husband and occupy the hollow he has created for her, she acquires the ability to dream of being other than she is. The waters have stirred her unconscious into action: "She dreamed of times far away from there: her children were present, the dead ones and those still alive, the machamba [small plot of land for cultivation] was full of crops, her eyes slid over the green of it all" (5). In this parallel world of the unconscious, life progresses "pregnant with promise" (5), a clear association with birth and new beginnings. However, the story ends with the old woman's involuntary return to the conscious world, "she begged night to stay so that her dream might linger" (5) and, on awakening, she discovers that her husband has died. At one level, the story is very pessimistic. The old woman begins with nothing and will end with nothing. At another level, however, it bestows on her a capacity to dream, to imagine a world different from the one she inhabits. Once again, Couto's message is that the first stage of effecting a change is the ability to conceptualize a different reality, which is why he privileges the dream world to such an extent. It is through her unconscious, to which she gains access through the intervention of water, that the old woman takes this first step.

Another story in which flooding features is "De Como O Velho Jossias Foi Salvo das Águas" [How Old Jossias Was Saved from the Water]. The story is split into three sections, and water pervades them all. In the first part, it serves to stimulate Jossias's memory and allows him to envisage a better future. His forecasts about the impending rainfall are a point of entry into the world of dreams: "While he made these prophecies, his eyes softened with promises, a procession of green taking charge of his dreams" (*VMN*, 63). His first statement is that "the water is going to go and read the ground" (63). As will briefly be considered later in this chapter, Couto makes several connections in some of his work between water and writing. In Jossias's world, however, water becomes the reader who is able to understand the troubles of the world and to provide succor. He says that the water is "going to lick the wounds of the earth" (63). The healing properties of water are linked with its ability to read the earth's situation and to respond to it. If water is seen to represent a flow from the unconscious realm, then what Jossias describes is tantamount to psychoanalytic therapy for those who occupy the land. The ailments of the earth's conscious sphere are understood and tackled through a channeling into and out of the unconscious.

This process of attempted healing by reading in the light of what cannot be seen in the conscious realm alone is paralleled in Jossias's own experience since, for him, water acts as a memory aid, reconnecting him to the traumas of his past. The impending waters transport him back to a previous existence, reminding him of what he has lost, the love of Armanda. He is assailed by the memory of a previous drought and the methods that had been used to try and break it. Libations were to be served to the dead, the permanent residents of the collective unconscious who, as such, "control the rain's pleasure" (64), controlling the flow between the two realms. The prolonged nature of the water shortage is explained in terms of a breakdown in communications between the living and the dead. The prayers of the elders had become empty signifiers, "words with no beyond" (64), as if they no longer believed in the traditions and rituals they enacted. By offering alcohol to the ancestors, it was hoped that contact could be reestablished. Jossias volunteered to carry the *ngovo,* and then proceeded to betray the trust of the community, due to the relentless temptation of the drink in his possession. In order to conceal the fact that he had consumed all the alcohol, he resolved to fill the pots in which it had been stored with stagnant water from the bottom of a well. At this point as he fell into the well, his fate foretokened a future entrapment in a South African mine, from which he would also be physically saved only to be immediately ignored and forgotten. That is the scar that mars his psyche: he has repeatedly been abandoned. As the rains descend in the present day, the land becomes flooded, and a rescue crew is sent to collect Jossias, but this time, he does not want to be saved. The memories restored to him of his previous experiences of deliverance from pending death make him unwilling to consent to yet another hollow salvation. The waters in which he is steeped are where he wishes to remain, as he tells his rescuers, "it's not cold in the water. Why don't you leave me there?" (68).

There are several motifs running through the story that make the waters appealing to Jossias. They are involved in the restitution of his memories. His sojourn in them also rejuvenates him since, at the end of the tale, he sees the twilight "with the eyes of a child" (69). Passing through the waters has been a rebirth for him; they have provided him with a second womb. Another characteristic of water's appeal is its infinity. Jossias initially declines the offer of a rescue, saying, "beyond the water all there is is water" (67). Water is everywhere, without beginning or end. After he is rescued and taken away in a boat, "he wished that his journey would have no end, as if they were saving him from time rather than the waters, as if they had freed him not from death but from his terrible and solitary waiting" (69). Jossias wants the guarantee of infinity; he wishes to step outside the flow of time. Yet what he desires is paradoxical. Water has served to remind him of his solitude and of his lost roots. In the first instance, water caused his exile, for it was his actions during a rain-requesting ceremony that led to his banishment. This exile has led to his solitary wait for the return of Armanda. His desire for water is a desire for a greater infinity that will drown the pain of his never-ending tarriance. Simultaneously, the waters restore the memory of the loss which instigates that wait. Without the waters, there is no memory. But without the waters, there is also no escape from the memory. Water acts as both the cause and the cure for Jossias's pain.

There are several points to be drawn from the two stories. Both use Mozambique's propensity to flooding to reveal the cyclical nature of existence within the poverty of Mozambique. It is a case of nature writing the nation; the geographical tendencies of the area metaphorize Mozambique's social problems. In the case of the old woman, in "A Fogueira," her husband wants to repeat the cycle of hollowness for her. At the heart of Couto's critique is an assault on sexual inequality and a desire to release the old woman from a patriarchal realm in which her dreams have been denied. In Jossias's case, Couto's critique is directed at a number of groups—the African traditions that divided Armanda from Jossias, those under the lure of alcohol whose lives are ruined and, most acutely, against the international aid community that enters the nation to save the people and dehumanizes individuals in the process. Once the rescue mission is over, the rescuers depart and the rescued are forgotten. The crux of the problem is the culture of dependency that such missions foster; a corollary of their good intentions is often the denial of agency to those supposedly assisted. Couto's solution is to retain agency at least in the dreams of the destitute so that when the crisis is over there is something on which to build.

"As Baleias de Quissico": Dreaming beyond Neocolonialism

As in "De Como O Velho Jossias Foi Salvo das Águas," "As Baleias de Quissico" [The Whales of Quissico] critiques, at some levels, the neocolonial role of international aid agencies in Mozambique. Couto deploys the association of the sea with the colonization process to make the critique more pointed, in a manner that echoes Manuel Rui's depiction of the sea's contents in *Memória de Mar*. Additionally, the sea in the tale functions as a store of dreams. Once again, water facilitates an interaction between the conscious and unconscious realms but with the additional colonial connotation of the sea as a thoroughfare used by foreign intruders.

    The main character of the story is Bento João Mussavele who decides he is going to search for some mystery whales that, according to rumors, have appeared on the beach of Quissico, loaded with consumer goods. His uncle tries to convince him that "it's all pie in the sky," little more than the desperate inventions of hungry people (*VMN*, 56). But, like Ernesto Timba in "Os Pássaros de Deus," Bento has faith in the midst of rational doubters and he believes in something that he has not seen. As he tells Agostinho, "I believe in the whale; I have to believe in it" (57), for, without his belief, he has nothing. Yet his faith is centered on a creature that is fundamentally duplicitous, a mammal that looks like a fish. As Agostinho explains to him, "the whale is not what it seems at first sight. Whales are prone to deceive" (57). Regardless of the advice he receives, Bento resolves to go to Quissico. When he reaches his destination, "it all seemed familiar to him," as if the waters already form part of his memory (58). Bento's first impression of that familiar space is that "the blue which melted away before one's eyes was beautiful" (58). The phrase Couto uses in Portuguese is "aquele azul a dissolver-se nos olhos" (*VMN*, 113), implying that the blue actually dissolves in and into one's eyes, so that the sea is both in Bento's field of vision and becomes his vision, turning into the medium through which he views the world. If the sea represents the unconscious, then Bento's perspective becomes one that is mediated through that realm.

Bento keeps faith, as others try to explain the whales away in terms of the neocolonial exploits of South Africa, who militarily supported Renamo for part of the civil war, or as the manipulation of imperialists intent on maintaining Mozambique's dependency on foreign aid. Furthermore, his faith is rewarded, like Timba's, by his union with water. He will be reborn into the waters of the unconscious, "stark naked" like a baby in the womb (61) as one night, during a storm, he disappears into the sea. But, as he enters the waters, doubt assails him: "there is no whale, these waters are going to be your tomb and punish you for the dream you nourished" (61). The fatal aspect of water is acknowledged at that point in the narrative; the bringer of life can kill too. Despite this momentary doubt, always a necessary component of belief, Bento's faith appears to be rewarded in the end as he enters the unconscious. Leaving behind a world which can only see the "relics of a dream" (61) in the form of his bag and clothes, and which has dismissed him as a madman beyond the realm of reason, Bento "waded on into the sea, and into his dream" (61).

"As Baleias de Quissico" operates at two levels, differentiated by the perspectives of the characters. Clearly, the sea symbolizes the unconscious for Bento; it is the repository of his dreams, and his union with the oceans is the culmination of his desire for personal transcendence. The whales act as an emblem of hope for him, while simultaneously representing the processes of neocolonization through the eyes of the secondary characters. Couto's critique of foreign aid as a nurturer of dependency culture is as powerful in this story as in "De Como O Velho Jossias Foi Salvo das Águas." At the same time, his sympathetic portrayal of the dreamer Bento once again reveals his message that however dire living conditions become, no one should ever relinquish his or her right to dream.

The stories from *Vozes Anoitecidas* hitherto discussed all use water as the symbolic tool through which access to the unconscious is granted. At the heart of Couto's portrayals is an underlying message that whoever we are, wherever we are, and no matter how bad things become, we are always capable of imagining a different reality. Asserting his characters' right to dream never causes Couto to shy away from a description of their misery, or of laying bare the causes of their poverty. This aspect of Couto's work differentiates his message from that of Christianity. He wants his characters and, by extension, his nation to dream so that a better reality can be achieved. There are clearly problems with this message, not least of which is the privileged position from which it is delivered. Additionally, it does not deliver very swiftly. At the same time, it is a message, which offered some hope, fashioned at a very pessimistic moment in Mozambique's history, as the nation plunged deeper and deeper into a civil war. We should view it from that perspective, and understand that Couto is not offering an apologetic for poverty, but rather an empowerment from poverty that challenges the status quo.

"Pingo e Vírgula" and "Natural da Água": Water and Writing

As discussed in the previous chapter, Couto presents writing as a fluid, denying it the total rigidity Western tradition has often sought to attribute to it. It is therefore not surprising that Couto compares writing with water, and interchanges the characteristics of each metaphorically. Water and writing interact in several of Couto's short stories. As has already been discussed, an attribute belonging to one is deployed in the service of the other in "De Como O Velho Jossias Foi Salvo das Águas" when water is described as reading. A similar instance of one borrowing from/being infected by the other is the title of one of Couto's chronicles, "Pingo e Vírgula." The Portuguese word for semicolon, a figure of writing, is corrupted and partially replaced with an alliterating term—"ponto" becomes "pingo"—which usually denotes a fluid drop. A semicolon, by its nature, fixes a boundary, but it is a boundary that is far from definitive. The content on either side of the demarcation flows into the other side. A semicolon is a compromise between a discontinuity and a continuity; it links and it separates. By mixing the term with water, Couto highlights the fluidity of the boundary.

In the chronicle itself, raindrops are described as leaving no trace. They are entirely transient, existing ephemerally. "Born prematurely from a cloud, rain neither nurtures a puddle, nor leaves descendants. It becomes extinct, swallowed up without trace." [Parto prematuro da nuvem, a chuva não cria poça, nem deixa descendência. Extingue-se, sorvida sem vestígio (*C*, 87)].

Water is an "uncertain lover" [amante incerta] whose "eternal indecision wavers between two abodes: the ground and the sky." [vagueia sua eterna indecisão entre duas residências: o chão e o céu (87)]. This renders water the link between the two spheres, between heaven and earth. If the home of the gods belongs to the unconscious realm, then water thus described once again represents a flow between the conscious and the unconscious.

Writing and water are also mixed together in "Natural da Água" [Native of Water]. A river is equated to the "calligraphy of water" [caligrafia da água (C, 81)], so that, in a manner analogous to the rain's ability to read the ground in "De Como O Velho Jossias Foi Salvo das Águas," rivers can write on it in "Natural da Água." In contrast to a land easily hurt by the actions of humankind, "up until now no one has been able to wound the river and leave a scar written on it" [até agora nenhum foi capaz de ferir o rio e deixar cicatriz nele escrita (82)]. Additionally, in Couto's universe, rivers write but cannot be written on. In an echo of Derrida's thesis in *Of Grammatology*, Couto situates writing's birth at the inception of the language system, since he links writing to water and water to primordiality: "Water's birth has no witness: we always appear afterwards" [o parto da água não tem testemunha: aparecemos sempre depois (81)]. The narrative trope of reducing writing to a liquid state thus draws on two aspects of water to make a statement about the script. Once again, writing is deemed to be fluid. But additionally, Couto moves it away from its Hegelian association with distance from primordiality and strongly implies that writing creates new beginnings. In Couto's world, its power derives from its ability to tell an infinitely inflected story.

"A MENINA SEM PALAVRA":
WATER AND SPEECH

The telling of a story is a crucial element to the plot of "A Menina Sem Palavra" [The Girl Without Words], a tale that designates the sea as an infinite reserve of myths and fables, an unconscious capable of returning a voice to the silenced. Like the young boy in "O Coração do Menino e o Menino do Coração" discussed in the previous chapter, the girl in this story speaks a language unintelligible to the rest of humanity, suffering from an inability to link the signifier and the signified into a coherent sign: "When she remembered the word, she would forget the thought. When she constructed her reasoning, she would lose her language. It wasn't that she was a mute. Rather, she spoke in a language that doesn't currently exist in humanity" [Quando lembrava as palavras ela esquecia o pensamento. Quando construía o raciocínio perdia o idioma. Não é que fosse muda. Falava em língua que nem há nesta actual humanidade (*CDNT*, 87)]. Her difficulty in connecting concept to word means that she cannot display reasoned thought and consequently lives outside the confines of human logic. Her parents represent the conscious realm in which the linguistic sign must function coherently. They are desperate for her to speak and thereby to join their realm.

Language is the sine qua non for the expression of conscious thought. Once unconscious elements are drawn into the linguistic discourse, they cease to be entirely of the unconscious realm and stray into the territory of consciousness. As the young girl is unable to express herself linguistically, her world is beyond the understanding of the conscious minds of her parents. At the same time, she is the center of their lives, particularly when she (non)articulates since "her voice was enchantingly beautiful. Even without understanding anything, people were captivated by her intonation" [sua voz era bela de encantar. Mesmo sem entender nada as pessoas ficavam presas na entonação (87)]. She possesses the complex paralinguistic cues of language, but not the basic vowel structure.

Her father becomes increasingly anxious and begins to weep. As the child kisses the salt water of his tear, she utters her first intelligible word, "mar"— the Portuguese for sea. Her consumption of the fluid seeping from her father—a metonym for the sea that represents the unconscious realm she inhabits—finally connects her with the paternal, conscious order. The taste of a tiny drop of her father's unconscious entices her to utter a monosyllabic element that is seized upon as evidence of her capacity to enter the conscious realm, the Lacanian realm of the linguistic and of the father.[47]

Immediately her father takes her to the sea, reasoning that, if the only word she has ever spoken is "mar," therein lies the key to unlocking the unconscious block that prevents her from communicating. On arriving at a place where "there was sea and sea and more sea," the child is disappointed, "the world which she held to be infinite, was it, after all, small?" [havia mar e mar depois do mar; o mundo que ela pretendera infinito era, afinal, pequeno? (88)] and she begins to cry too. If she leaves the unconscious realm, if she consents to speak, she will immediately set limits. She will enter the world of the possible, which presupposes the banishment of the impossible to a distant recess beyond the reach of the conscious order. She refuses to move, rooting herself to the sand as the tide rises threateningly, and ignores her father's pleas to see reason. Finally, he has an inspiration, "his daughter could only be saved by a story!" [sua filha só podia ser salva por uma história! (88)]. He at last understands the problem: she does not want to leave the unconscious realm. The telling of a story provides a suitable compromise, allowing the imagination to remain rooted in the unconscious where the impossible is not yet exiled. There, anything can happen. Through the story he tells, her father demonstrates that he can still enter the world of myths—the collective unconscious—the sphere to which his daughter belongs. But he loses the thread of his story as the cold water covers his feet and his consciousness prevents him from surrendering himself totally to the unconscious realm. As the sea rises, they appear doomed when, suddenly, his daughter rushes into the sea and acts out an end to the story. Once the tale is completed, the child consents to speak, in the knowledge that the story can be told again and again, that reality can be suspended and other worlds can be imagined and reached.

This story, dedicated to Couto's daughter Rita, repeats the message of so many of his other tales: everyone has the right to dream—to enter the unconscious—and should exercise it. Additionally, the telling of stories is an important aspect of the transmission of knowledge between generations, and teaches the listener to imagine worlds beyond his or her immediate reality. In that way, entering the unconscious forms a link between past and future and helps to cope with the present, conscious order, a space that is far from easy in the Mozambique Rita will inherit.

Terra Sonâmbula:
A Journey into the Unconscious

Difficulty in, and mechanisms for, coping with the present is one of the central concerns of Couto's first novel, *Terra Sonâmbula*. Here, we will focus on the manner in which Couto depicts the interplay between the conscious and unconscious, and consider how Couto incites his characters and, by extension, his readers and nation to restore the link between the two realms. Crucial to this particular reading of *Terra Sonâmbula* is an understanding of the symbolic importance Couto assigns to water, as a lubricant between psychic spheres. In the story, the conscious realm constitutes the chapters, and is initially particularly dry, while the notebooks portray the unconscious in suitably moist terms. As the story progresses, the two worlds become increasingly entwined.

One of the themes of the novel, as discussed previously, is the restitution of Muidinga's memory through Kindzu's notebooks, a process that fuses the oral and written realms. Here, it will be argued that Kindzu inhabits a wet world, which gradually moistens Muidinga's environment. If, as Jung suggests, the unconscious can be represented by water, then the process of moistening symbolizes the unconscious acting on the conscious. This reading is further strengthened by Muidinga's initial lack of memory; he has no contact with his unconscious because of the trauma he has suffered, living in the harsh reality of a country torn by war. Kindzu, on the other hand, inhabits the world of dreams where anything can and does happen.

At first, Tuahir and Muidinga's world is extremely arid. The area in which they are traveling has been suffering from a drought and they come across a burnt-out bus, another symbol of dryness, which becomes their home. In contrast, Kindzu's world is extremely wet. His father was a fisherman, who was put out to sea when he died, and Kindzu himself will journey through the sea throughout the novel. The interplay between the two worlds is a constant process of desiccation and dampening. Tuahir, of all the characters, represents consciousness to the greatest degree, for he knows the reality of the war situation. His first reaction on the discovery of the notebooks in an abandoned suitcase is to tell Muidinga to take the papers out of the case, and use them to light a fire. He wants to consign the first symbol of the unconscious—notebooks written by Kindzu—to flames. Muidinga's reaction is inexplicably to begin to cry. His tears, the first sign of moisture in the dry environment, herald his first entry into the unconscious world of Kindzu.

As the novel develops, there are more examples of moisture seeping into Muidinga's space. In the second chapter, Muidinga imagines himself to be Junhito, Kindzu's brother. In the preceding notebook, it was discovered that Junhito had once almost drowned and the water had penetrated his ears to such a degree that it could be heard sloshing in his head from then on. His brain, the seat of the unconscious, has literally become water. Muidinga's pretense signals a desire to enter that wet mind.

In the third chapter, the reader learns that "Muidinga begins to notice the countryside around changing its features. The land continues to be dry but leftovers of the dusk mist now appear in the sparse reeds." [Muidinga repara que a paisagem, em redor, está mudando suas feições. A terra continua seca mas já existem nos ralos capins sobras de cacimbo (*TS*, 53)]. The drought, which characterizes Muidinga's dry world, starts to be affected by Muidinga's interaction with the unconscious—Kindzu's notebooks. "Cacimbo"—the word used to connote dusk mist in Mozambican Portuguese—makes another appearance in the fourth chapter. This time it is strongly linked to the unconscious realm of dreams. At the beginning of the chapter, Muidinga has been thinking about Farida who, as will be discussed shortly, is the character most associated with water and dreams. When Tuahir discovers this, he smiles and then divides the world of women into two moist parts: "there are women who are rain, and others who are *cacimbo*" [há mulheres que são chuva, outras cacimbo (70)]. For Tuahir, women inhabit the unconscious and, as such, are always wet. As discussed earlier, Couto characterizes femininity as moist in *Vinte e Zinco,* in part as a critique of the patriarchal binary-ridden colonial order. *Terra Sonâmbula* is set in a different historical moment in Mozambique, toward the end of the civil war, but one in which the population lived under a similar degree of violence. By setting women apart from the realities causing the conflicts, Couto performs a gesture toward a feminism that holds traditional masculinist values, associated with inflexibility and rigid demarcation, primarily responsible for the moments of suffering in Mozambique.

Having received Tuahir's advice, Muidinga falls asleep and has a dream, his first personal entry into the unconscious. In it, he sees himself as a child leaving a school and perceives his name being called out but cannot hear it properly. All he can hear are unfocused sounds echoing in the "cacimbo" (*TS,* 71) and the secret of his identity remains locked in his unconscious. As he comes round, he is surrounded by "cacimbo" (71) so that a vestige of his journey into the unconscious temporarily remains. But the conscious order quickly predominates once more and, with the threatening arrival of the violent Siqueleto, the "cacimbo" vanishes in a gust of wind (71), symbolizing the reassertion of consciousness and violence through the desiccation of the dream world.

The fifth chapter has an even greater invasion of moisture. Initially, there is a heavy humidity in the air before Tuahir and Muidinga encounter Nhamataca who has undertaken the seemingly futile endeavor of digging a river. Nhamataca names his river "Mãe-água"—Mother-Water (*TS,* 95)—highlighting his desire to return to the womb. This same maternal water leads him to his death, depositing him, as all rivers do, in the prototype womb, the sea. Nhamataca, like Ernesto Timba and Bento João Mussavele from *Vozes Anoitecidas,* has faith in his project, even if nobody else does. He is another of Couto's many characters whose belief is rewarded: a torrential downpour gives birth to his desired river. As in the other cases, his prize comes at the cost of his own physical destruction. The river washes him away, as the wet world temporarily invades the dry. Then suddenly, "in an unbelievable change of scenery, the drought rules once again. Where water had reigned but a few hours before, dust now clouds the air." [no inacreditável mudar de cenário, a seca volta a imperar. Onde a água imperara há escassas horas, a poeira agora esfuma os ares (98)]. The conscious order, where violence reigns and dreams are crushed, is symbolically reestablished as the drought returns. Muidinga ponders what has happened: "a man who dreamed has died." [morreu um homem que sonhava (98)]. Nhamataca, as a dreamer, belonged to the realm of the unconscious to which he was taken by the flooding waters. At times, the cost of dreaming seems inordinately high in Couto's fiction, particularly in his texts written during the conflict. Yet his characters embrace their fates willingly for no other option is available to them.

Muidinga begins to realize that his perception of the world is altering through his interaction with Kindzu's unconscious world of notebooks. His new way of seeing things affects the environment around him. By the sixth chapter, the dry world is giving way to a Mozambique moist with greenery. At the same time, the child is reborn, or rather, his perspective is renewed. Couto uses the phrase "os olhos de Muidinga se meninam," which can be translated as "Muidinga's eyes became children" (109). The process of rejuvenating his perspective is achieved for Muidinga through an interaction with the wet world of the unconscious. By the beginning of the seventh chapter, "the rain chimed on the bus roof" [a chuva timbilava no tecto do machimbombo (133)]. From this point onward, Muidinga and Tuahir's world is inundated with moisture, culminating in their environment becoming an immense swamp. Tuahir, who had been the guardian of consciousness, will insist on being pushed out into the sea to die, out of sight of land. His desire is that articulated by what Bachelard designates the Ophelia complex: the sea as a final resting place represents a union with infinity.[48] Through that union, Tuahir is, at last, able to enter the unconscious realm where he can dream once more: "so begins Tuahir's journey into a sea full of infinite fantasies. On the waves a thousand stories are written, part of those used to lull children the world over" [começa então a viagem de Tuahir para um mar cheio de infinitas fantasias. Nas ondas estão escritas mil estórias, dessas de embalar as crianças do inteiro mundo (209)]. Like so many other characters in Couto's stories, Tuahir ends his life as a part of water. The many associations of water—fluidity, infinity, maternity and rebirth, the unconscious—come into play and expunge the barren scene of the novel's beginning. Ana Mafalda Leite reads the sea's allure as a final resting place in *Terra Sonâmbula* as the only option left for the inhabitants of a land so laden with death.[49] Tuahir's demise, though as poignant as any loss, is pregnant with hope since he is the character with the greatest degree of knowledge of the horrors of Mozambique's reality, and yet he is finally able to enter the realm of dreams, and to imagine an alternative.

In *Terra Sonâmbula,* shadows operate as an endeictic aspect of the unconscious. They represent unconscious counterparts within the psyche. As such,

Muidinga's whole purpose in the novel is to find the shadow he has lost and thus reestablish a link with his unconscious. Jung terms the unconscious counterpart of the conscious persona, the shadow, a concept with which Couto plays. The persona is the image that every person enacts to the world.[50] Muidinga is a child who has been traumatized by his experiences of the war, and consequently blots out his memory of what has happened. Shortly after Tuahir first discovers him, Muidinga is only able to consume water. Besides being the means through which his life is sustained, the ingestion of water represents the incipient restitution of a flow between the child's conscious and his unconscious—a connection which has been severed by his trauma. In fact, Muidinga has completely lost touch with his unconscious, to the extent that however much the child moves around "he produced no shadow." [não produzia nenhuma sombra (56)]. Tuahir explains this absence as "mantakassa," a disease caused by eating poisonous mandioca, the consumption of which is directly linked to the drought, since lack of water led to lack of food and to the ingestion of what would ordinarily be classified as inedible. Lack of water also symbolically and literally leads to a loss of touch with the realm of the unconscious. As the already cited foreword in *Vozes Anoitecidas* points out, "faced by an absence of everything, men abstain from dreams." Couto once again seems to be arguing that destitution curtails the ability to dream. Drought impedes the relationship with the unconscious and leads to the loss of contact with the shadow.

A number of relationships operate between characters within the novel, which reflect a process of circulation between the conscious and unconscious realms. Kindzu, for example, although predominantly associated with the unconscious by the reading above, is haunted by his deceased father and spends the novel trying to accommodate him in his own conscious space. Taímo, Kindzu's father, like Tuahir, is "buried in the waves" [sepultado nas ondas (20)], a significant parallel since each reflects the other in apposite realms. Tuahir represents extreme consciousness, Taímo, in turn, the deepest part of the unconscious. On his death, Taímo temporarily takes the entire realm of the unconscious with him: "the whole sea dried up, all the water vanished in a fraction of a second" [o mar todo secou, a água inteira desapareceu na porção de um instante (20)]. This power over the sea strengthens Taímo's symbolic association with the unconscious order. Furthermore, a witchdoctor instructs Kindzu to build a house for his father and put a boat in it, so that "[his] father could return, and come out of the sea" [meu pai poderia regressar, vindo do mar (22)]. While the other characters are drawn toward the unconscious, Taímo's trajectory is out of the unconscious, as he makes visits to Kindzu's conscious world. He represents the desire of the unconscious to restore a dialogue with the conscious world—a dialogue breached by the war. The other breach that Taímo's trajectory seeks to heal is the loss of respect for tradition the war has caused. As Kindzu's ancestor, who speaks from beyond his maritime grave, Couto uses Taímo to peddle another of his favorite messages: a loss of respect for elders and traditions has cost Mozambique dear. Like the old people in *A Varanda do Frangipani,* Taímo reasserts his right to be considered and heard as his nation steers a runaway course toward free-market globalization.

Farida is the character in *Terra Sonâmbula* most associated with water since her home is a shipwreck and Kindzu discovers her off the coast of Matimati, "the land of water" [a terra da água (59)]. In her youth, her fellow villagers required her only when they needed to perform rain-calling ceremonies, and for both Kindzu and Muidinga she is reached through water since Muidinga dreams of her through water, while Kindzu literally travels on his boat to her. In a sense, she operates as Kindzu's shadow, explaining to him, "we are shadows in your world" [nós somos sombras no teu mundo (91)]. As such, she is something internal to him, residing in the recesses of his mind, "like a bug which lives inside the fruit" [como o bicho que mora dentro do fruto (91)]. He, in turn, is "from the other side of the peel" [do lado de fora da casca (91)]—her projection to the conscious world, her persona. The two will fuse, bringing together aspects of the conscious and unconscious realms, as Kindzu and Farida make love, and her "fingers seemed to be water" [os dedos dela parecia eram de água] while "waves crashed up [their] bodies, ebbing and flowing" [as vagas ondeavam nossos corpos, indo e vindo (107)]. Kindzu explains in his notebook, "the two of us were now just one, emerging like an island in an immense void" [os dois éramos já só um, emergindo como uma ilha num imenso nada (107)]. The love scene between the two of them is heavy with aquatic metaphors and represents Kindzu's union with the shadow of his unconscious. In that way, Farida restores Kindzu's ability to dream, in the same way that Kindzu restores Muidinga's unconscious. Like the female characters in *Vinte e Zinco,* Couto chooses to portray the principal female protagonist in *Terra Sonâmbula* as inextricably associated with moisture. Once again, feminine fluidity becomes a powerful antidote to the male world of conflict.

As Patrick Chabal has pointed out, the process is at least as important as the result in *Terra Sonâmbula*; the journey matters as much as the destination.[51] Indeed, the novel is the tale of two parallel journeys that fuse into one. Kindzu, whose journey is through the sea, is told by a soothsayer, "it isn't the destination that matters but the route taken" [não é o destino que conta mas o caminho (32)]. The soothsayer "spoke of a journey whose only destination was the desire to start again. That journey, however, would have to be in line with his advice: I ought to go by sea" [falava de uma viagem cujo único destino era o desejo de partir novamente. Essa viagem, porém, teria que seguir o respeito de seu conselho: eu deveria ir pelo mar (32)]. The sea will be his cure, the way in which he can come to terms with his deceased father. Kindzu's journey through the sea represents a delving into the unconscious, and a means of tackling the destructive experience of a nation at war. His trek through the sea also symbolizes the restitution of a link with the past since the collective unconscious metaphorically resides there and, furthermore, it was a forum where key moments of Mozambican history took place. It brought the colonizers, and took the slaves and those condemned to forced labor on the plantations of São Tomé e Príncipe, Portugal's archipelago colony off the coast of West Africa, away. Mozambican blood as well as dreams flows through the sea. The reasons for the struggle for liberation the sea represents were occluded by a civil war in which Mozambicans fought against Mozambicans, and forgot their traditions. As Taímo explains to his son, his dreams cannot be realized as long as there is a "divorce from the ancestors" [divórcio com os antepassados (46)]. Couto's message is that an appreciation of the past must be a part of the present in order for there to be a future. Both Tuahir and Muidinga in the conscious realm of the chapters will come to understand this and seek the repose of "the sea with its infinities" [o mar, com seus infinitos (187)], the symbolic store of traditions and myths.

In *Terra Sonâmbula,* Couto calls for a recuperation of the ideals underpinning an imagined past and simultaneously deconstructs the myths behind Portugal's maritime dominance. Tuahir's lamentation of the rupture of the link with ancestors effectively forms part of Couto's critique of ideologies that have been grafted onto the nation from outside. Foreign dogmas demanded a disassociation from the nation's traditional roots. At the same time, the author debunks the official colonial discourses that asserted a particular role for the Portuguese as linkers of the world and lords of a transoceanic empire. The jewel, prior to its loss, in the lusophone imperial crown had been India, the imagination of which had impelled Portugal to explore in the fifteenth and sixteenth centuries, and open up sea routes for the European world. In Couto's novel, Surendra Valá, an Indian storekeeper, forms a friendship with Kindzu based on a shared "homeland: the Indian Ocean" [pátria: o Índico (26)]. Kindzu explains, "it was as if in that immense sea threads of history unfolded, old reels where our blood had been mixed" [era como se naquele imenso mar se desenrolassem os fios da história, novelos antigos onde nossos sangues se haviam misturado (26)]. He continues, "that's the reason why we lingered in our adoration of the sea: our mutual ancestors were there, fluctuating without frontiers" [eis a razão por que demorávamos na adoração do mar: estavam ali nossos comuns antepassados, flutuando sem fronteiras (26)]. Marie-Françoise Bidault reads the friendship between the Indian and the African, based on a common maritime heritage, as a fusion of their two cultures.[52] However, Bidault and Kindzu's reasoning perpetuates the myth of a lusotropical identity, an ideology propounded by the Brazilian anthropologist Gilberto Freyre from the 1940s and later used by the Salazar regime to justify its continued colonialism.[53] This ideology claimed that the Portuguese created a multiracial, transcontinental paradise, in which no color bar existed. The reality of the Portuguese colonial experience, as Gerald Bender points out, was far removed from this myth that infected every level of officially sanctioned discourse during the dying days of Portuguese colonialism.[54] Kindzu unwittingly ascribes to that lusotropical myth, and views the sea as the emblem of a common lusophone identity, and a shared history. However, the history it represents is one soaked in blood and the separation of families through slavery, the opposite of Kindzu's perception of thalassic harmony. In contrast, Surendra, the Indian with whom he supposedly shares that identity, has no illusion about the true meaning of the sea and crushes the child's naivety. For Surendra, the sea always designates a separation from his homeland, the India where he was born. He destroys Kindzu's oversimplified notion of a shared lusotropical heritage when he abandons him following a fire, motivated by racial hatred, that incinerates his store. Kindzu confesses, "I did not want to understand the shopkeeper. Because his words killed my illusion that one ocean had united us in the past" [eu não queria entender o lojeiro. Porque suas palavras matavam a miragem de um oceano que nos unira no passado (28–29)]. The sea had provided Kindzu with the myth of a shared identity. The tough reality of Surendra's world is that he now belongs nowhere. All he can do is to dream of a return to what he has never had.

At the level of self-definition, Surendra epitomizes one of the messages of *Terra Sonâmbula*. His yearning for an identity parallels Muidinga's need to know who he is which, in turn, reflects the Mozambican nation's moment of identity crisis. During the struggle for liberation from Portuguese colonialism, it was easy to define Mozambicaness in contrast to a European imperialism. The presence of a clearly identifiable enemy made cultural definition a relatively simple task, grounded in the othering of an opponent. However, the civil war that erupted soon after independence complicated the consolidation of that identity. How does one culturally define a nation at war with itself, where no consensus about the national sense of self can exist? One possibility is an appeal to the values of a by-gone era that predates the colonial period. The atavistic strand that appears in the novel through Taímo's assertions regarding a restitution of links with the past appears to be such a strategy and forms part of what Maria Manuel Lisboa identifies as a "neo-Romantic preoccupation with myth-revival" in Couto's work.[55] Lisboa, who provides an extremely perceptive critique of the ambiguities inherent in Couto's political stance as a national author who writes in a linguistic style that borders on impenetrable for the vast majority of a barely literate nation, draws a valid link with Romanticism because that was a period of national inscription in Europe in which heritages were reclaimed and reinvented. The parallels with Mozambique of the 1990s are plain to see: the country was in a phase of cultural inscription and national myths were rediscovered. However, Couto's work does not merely rest in the past, particularly in *Terra Sonâmbula*. He aims to project a future that is able to cope with, and build on, a past that has led to an unsavory present. The civil war did not break out ahistorically: it was, in part, the result of the colonial legacy and of political systems developed outside the country and then imposed intransigently on a whole nation. In that context, Couto's recourse to ancestral authenticity is a critique of the damage foreign systems dumped on the nation caused. More than a desire to recapture a lost past, throughout his work, Couto is concerned with imagining a different future. Even in work published after the end of hostilities, like *Mar Me Quer* and *Vinte e Zinco,* Couto uses a coming to terms with the past as a way of projecting a better reality into the future. In both those books, the sea represents aspects of the colonial legacy as well as the imagination of a tomorrow where the nation's right to dream is restored. The right to dream has been a constant throughout Couto's literary production, especially in the short stories written during the darkest moments of the civil war. Dreaming rejuvenates and creates. It also removes borders and allows for other realities. Water's association with rebirth and its repeated link in the discourses of psychoanalysis with the unconscious make it an appropriate metaphor deployed by Couto for an entry into the world of dreams. Its fluidity challenges clear demarcations and is another marker of Couto's alliance with postmodernism through which he fashions a world without frontiers. One of the most interesting aspects of Couto's portrayal of moisture is the manner in which he genders his characterization of it. Irene, Jessumina, Farida, Luarmina, Nãozinha, the old woman in "A Fogueira," and the young girl in "A Menina Sem Palavra" all have a particular association with water. At the same time, they all transgress the boundaries, floating be-

tween possibilities, between the conscious and the unconscious. Couto's depiction of the distinction between the genders reflects the fluidity he ascribes
to femininity. As we shall discuss in the next chapter, being a man in Couto's
world does not make one masculine, nor vice versa. The game he plays with
the delineation between the sexes constitutes his profoundest attack on the
logic of binary orders, and firmly grounds him as a postmodern writer in a
postcolonial space.

6

Playing Gam(et)es with Gender:
Subverting Orthodoxy
Through Sexual Confusion

IN HIS INTRODUCTION TO *Cronicando,* FERNANDO DACOSTA DESCRIBES MIA
Couto as "a young man despite having a woman's name" [um jovem apesar
de ter nome feminino (*C,* 8)]. In fact, it is not unreasonable for someone who
has never heard of the Mozambican writer to assume that the name by which
António Emílio Leite Couto is more commonly known designates a female.
A common syntactical constraint on the Portuguese language is that proper
nouns ending with an "a" are feminine. Couto actually claims that the origin
of his sobriquet is feline rather than feminine, supposedly acquired as a child
due to his passion for cats.[1] Regardless of myth around its provenance, it is
rather appropriate that the name Mia should sow the seed of gender confusion before the reader tackles the text written under that signature.

Gender, in Western tradition, is one of the fundamentals of identity. It is
often linked to the sex of an individual, even in the cases where the expectations of that link are subverted, and is regularly deemed by binary orthodoxy
to depict a natural order of things. In colonial discourse, policing the racial
divide was often intricately associated with the imposition of gender normativity. As Ann Laura Stoler demonstrates, racial categories were often secured
through forms of sexual control that prescribed the heterosexual and patriarchal domestic arrangements of European settlers.[2] The arrival of white
women in the colonies, who were often deemed to be the bearers of colonial
morality and jealous of any interracial sexual liaisons, led to a more rigorous
imposition of racial hierarchies. However, Stoler points out the fallacy of
blaming women for colonial racism. White women experienced colonialism
differently from their male counterparts, since they simultaneously occupied

an official and ambiguous position of patriarchal subalternity and racial superiority. They arrived in European colonies at a time when male colonizers needed to use their wives as the bearers of a redefined colonial morality. By attacking the rigid adherence to Western expectations of gender, Couto undermines the patriarchal premises supporting the colonial enterprise in Mozambique. As I shall show, he relates the crossing of the gender frontier explicitly with the dissolution of racial boundaries.

Postindependence Mozambique inherited many of the gender prejudices of the colonial order it replaced. In particular, a limited view of masculinity—characterized by sexual prowess, strength, and conquest—prevailed in popular culture and restricted the officially sanctioned image of what it meant to be a Mozambican man. Samora Machel repeatedly condemned homosexuality in the same tone of moral probity that informed Salazar's protection of family values. Campaigns were launched to encourage heterosexual monogamy, and to obliterate vice from public view. Of course, beneath the façade, a diverse range of gender and sexual practices continued, as Mia Couto highlights in an interview with Anabela Mota Ribeiro. He describes the practice among Mozambican miners in the Rand of taking a male wife for the duration of their stay in South Africa. On their return to Mozambique, they resume their married lives with their female wives, and are "not converted into homosexuals" [não se convertem em homossexuais].[3] The transitory nature of this sexual practice challenges the predominant Western mindset, which often conspires to oblige individuals to assume a label they must forever bear. In reality, sexual orientation is a much more complex phenomenon that shifts and develops and does not necessarily culminate. Underpinning the concept of a sexual orientation is, of course, the highly problematic construct of gender. Joan Wallach Scott tracks the evolution of the term in Western discourse from a grammatical category that imposed order on language systems to a term that sought to render patent the "social quality of distinctions based on sex."[4] Scott proceeds to argue that the rewriting of women into the discourses of history often goes hand-in-hand with a reassessment of the role of race and class, and such strategies demonstrate a "scholarly understanding that inequalities of power are organized along at least three axes."[5] In his fiction, Couto constantly plays with and subverts the expectations of the Western gender system—a system that many in the early years of the Frelimo government sought to perpetuate. His disavowal of a fixed gender order runs in parallel with his dissolution of other frontiers, most noticeably those of race and class. Through his treatment of gender, Couto reinforces his commitment to an identity in flux, and to a healthy, unstable multiplicity in the cultural inscription of his nation. Interestingly, the only word he claims is sacred and therefore immune from his linguistic iconoclasm is "mulher"—the Portuguese for "woman."[6] However, that does not impede his distortion of the traditional concept underpinning the word, as we will discuss in this chapter. Gender assignment stereotypically impinges on the realm of attire, behavior, religious practice, and sexual desire. It is a cultural artifice that penetrates deeply into the unconscious of each individual. Disruptions of orthodox gender paradigms can both destabilize and reinforce gender expectations, as Couto's use of cross-dressing will demonstrate. Couto often aligns a fading of the gender frontier with the loss of authority in correlatable binary relationships. The resulting identity is one that eschews racial apartheid, rigorous taxonomy, or defined hierarchies.

Many commentators adhere to Robert Stoller's distinction between "sex" and "gender." He claims that, for reasons of clarity, it is important to state that "*sex* (maleness and femaleness) refers to a biological realm" while "*gender* (gender identity) is a psychological state—masculinity and femininity."[7] In essence, he is arguing that sex is a naturally demarcated binary and gender is a culturally specific one. His assertion that the two are "by no means necessarily related" is curiously qualified by the statement that "postnatal experiences can modify and sometimes overpower already present biologic tendencies."[8] He implies that sex naturally predetermines gender and only the heavy-handed intervention of some wayward ordeal confuses the isomorphism between two rigidly defined binaries.

In contrast, theorists such as Terrell Carver and Martine Rothblatt question the extent to which either sex or gender can adequately, even if independently, be described in binary terms. Carver claims that "a one-to-one mapping of gender onto a commonplace categorization of sex as male/female is overly simple, even with respect to biology and medicine," adducing as evidence the fact that "there are chromosomal variations and syndromes, not to mention morphological ones, that create genuinely ambiguous individuals."[9] Rothblatt highlights the research of Anne Fausto-Sterling, a geneticist based at Brown University, who claims to have shown that as many as one in twenty-five births are "to some extent 'intersexed,' meaning that the infants have portions of both male and female sex organs."[10] Both Rothblatt and Carver are questioning the validity of the less contentious of Stoller's binaries. Rothblatt goes so far as to proclaim "five billion sexes," which may be read as a call to see the individual and not the category.[11] As we shall see, Couto heeds Rothblatt's call, and individualizes the genders of many of his characters, in a series of processes that undermines the very concept of a category.

"Lenda de Namarói":
Subverting the Creation Myth

If we define transsexuals as a group who feel that their gender is not compatible with their sex identity, then transsexualism is very much a culturally specific phenomenon. In Western cultures, gender is often perceived to be a binary, and transsexuals are, in Judith Shapiro's words, "simply conforming to their culture's criteria for gender assignment."[12] For transsexualism and also transvestism to be transgressive, that one-to-one mapping between two binary systems has to be the perceived orthodoxy. There are, however, many cultures that have more than two genders. In these, gender assignment is more complex than in Western culture, and gender reversal is not, strictly speaking, possible. The Xanith, for example, would be considered to be male homosexuals in Western culture but are defined as a third gender in Oman.[13] There are women who acquire wives among the Lovedu of South Africa and the Nandi of Kenya; the dominant partner is perceived to have a different gender, becoming a female husband.[14]

Third genders are often linked to religious rites. Hijras in India, for example, are considered to be neither male nor female but something in-between. Their role, as Kate Bornstein points out, has historically been "a spiritual one, presiding over marriages and births."[15] In many North American Indian tribes, there are more than two genders, the term "berdache" often being applied to what Western culture would consider to be a man behaving as a woman. Judith Lorber states that berdaches are assigned a "sacred role" in the communities in which they live.[16] Like the hijras, the berdaches perform specific rituals for their tribes, over which only their gender has authority.

An argument can be constructed in which Western culture is deemed to have a parallel for third-gendered persons with ritual roles, their manifestation being the priests of the Catholic Church. In general terms, their obligatory celibacy emasculates them, their robes during religious services are, under a contemporary Western reading of sartorial semiotics, more symbolic of femininity. Within Portuguese literary tradition, there is a very pertinent example of this sacerdotal third-genderedness, embodied in a sexually frustrated man of the cloth who is dressed in woman's clothes, namely Amaro Vieira.

In *O Crime do Padre Amaro* [The Sin of Father Amaro], the nineteenth-century Portuguese author, Eça de Queirós, continually conflates the "batina" and "sotaina"—items of priestly garb—with the priesthood itself. The novel is a humorous attack on the hypocrisy of the Catholic Church, and portrays the clergy in a less than flattering light. The protagonist, Amaro Vieira, seduces, impregnates, and effectively destroys the life of a young woman, Amélia. Eça's depiction of the priesthood in this novel is marked by gender ambiguity. Amaro and his colleagues become defined in terms of their peculiar attire, by themselves and by those who hate them. Amaro, for example, wants "the clerks and the Amelias to tremble at the shadow of his cassock."[17] His cassock becomes the symbol of his difference and his power. Dr Godinho, whose liver illness leads him to associate the Church and the cemetery, "detested the cassock."[18] Borges, a secular clerk, "hated the cassock."[19] An infamous diatribe against the clergy published in a liberal newspaper ends with the words: "Take care, black cassocks!"[20] In all these examples, the gender-ambiguous garb of the clergy, a symbol of power and distinction, displaces the priesthood, becoming the embodiment of those it cloaks. Eça plays further with the constraints of gender as he describes the soirées held at the Rua da Misericórdia, at which Amaro begins his seduction of Amélia, as "those reunions of cassocks and skirts."[21] During these, real men, that is youths unencumbered by vows of chastity such as João Eduardo, Amélia's suitor, are made to feel excluded. There is a bonding between the priesthood and the feminine, metonymically represented through a union of their attires. In all these examples, the cassock becomes the priest, distinguishing the accoutered from other men. At the same time, Eça fuses stereotypical attributes of the polaric genders in ecclesiastics who delight "femininely" in gossip while "masculinely" seducing vulnerable females. Additionally, Eça destines Amaro to a transvestite's life from his early childhood, spent in the house of the Marqueza d'Alegros, where the women servants "made him girlish": when the Marqueza was out, "they dressed him in their clothes."[22] These childhood cross-dressing experiences portend his future emasculation under the constraints of his profession's attire. As an adult, sexually frustrated priest, he comes to realize that he is neither masculine nor feminine but "neutral."[23] The Portuguese word used by Eça—"neutro"—, more explicitly than the term used in the English translation, connotes a third gender.[24]

Amaro provides a very interest precedent through which to read one of Couto's short stories, narrated through the optic of a man of the cloth. The tale, "Lenda de Namarói" [The Legend of Namarói] is, according to its epigraph, "inspired in the account of the wife of the Chief of the Namarói, in Zambézia, collected by Father Elia Ciscato" [inspirado no relato da mulher do régulo de Namarói, Zambézia, recolhido pelo padre Elia Ciscato (*EA*, 139)]. Elia Ciscato is, in real life, a Catholic priest who has spent many years studying the traditions of northern Mozambican tribes.[25] As a literary trope, he serves to complicate the story Couto purposefully attributes to him as a religious. Before reading the short story, a network of perspectives is established. The myth of how the two genders came into existence will be distilled through Mia, the gender-ambiguous writer. He draws on the knowledge of Elia Ciscato, the male Christian priest who, as such, may be read potentially to occupy that third-gendered space—the de-sexed celibate who dons a frock to celebrate the Eucharist and who is simultaneously the guardian of Christian orthodoxy. This orthodoxy is rooted in the myth of Adam and Eve. Ciscato, in turn, draws on the narrative of a woman defined in relation to a man. She is nothing but a wife. The man is defined in terms of a region, Zambézia, which has a peculiar heritage with regard to gender politics.

A concept often associated with Zambézia in histories of Mozambique is the prazo. Discussion of precisely what the prazos were is rendered complex by the fact that they meant different things to different people. Indeed, Malyn Newitt compares them to "holograms, presenting a different image according to the angle of vision."[26] The Portuguese legal system viewed them as emphyteutic contracts while many Africans who fell under their jurisdiction saw them as chieftaincies. Technically, they were tracts of land rented out by the Portuguese Crown for three generations. A fascinating aspect of the law governing prazos was that they were inherited from mother to daughter—a means by which the colonial power hoped to foster European settlement in the Zambesi region, and a perfect example of male colonizers using women to enforce a redefined notion of colonial morality based on a stable, racist domesticity. However, the institution became a peculiar hybrid that was "neither wholly Portuguese nor African."[27] The *prazeiros* "were essentially the converted rather than the converters," being assimilated into, rather than assimilating, African society.[28] One social pattern that existed in most of the region covered by the prazos, prior to their official introduction, was matriliny. The tribes of the Maravi Empire, the Tonga, the Yao, and the Makua are all matrilineal. Newitt argues that, as a consequence, the power wielded by what became known as the Zambesi *donas*—those women in whose name the prazos were held—must be viewed in light of an African heritage. "It is clear," he claims, "that among the Afro-Portuguese a dual system of inheritance had emerged in which traditional Portuguese patrilineal succession was grafted on to local notions of the primacy of the mother's clan."[29] Prior to this assertion, Newitt argues that matriliny frequently prevents the establishment of patriarchal societies. The power of the mother's lineage "is often translated into power for the female members of that lineage."[30] However, there is another way of viewing the effect of and motivations behind matrilineal succession in some African societies. It is seen as a means of protecting the bloodline. Chieftaincy does not transfer from mother to daughter, but rather from a man to his eldest sister's first-born son.[31] Men are still in charge. Insistence on this indirect inheritance route tacitly demonstrates a lack of confidence in the wife or wives' fidelity. This is because the only way a man can be sure that he shares a bloodline with someone of the next generation is if the descendant is seen to have emerged from the womb of a woman with whom the man shares a mother. The prazo inheritance law is interesting because it did not fully conform to either patrilineal or matrilineal practice, and it was in that space between the two paradigms that dominant women were able to emerge.

In practice, as Newitt points out, the prazos were often controlled by fathers or husbands. They became an asset that made women a more marketable commodity.[32] By the nineteenth century, the prazo system was collapsing, and a practice that could have significantly altered—and in a minority of cases did alter—the male-female power relationship gave way to mini-empires headed by men. These challenged the colonial state and were a significant factor that led to the Zambesi wars.[33]

Zambézia as a region is marked by this gender history. In "Lenda de Namarói," the region, which historically assigned a particularly idiosyncratic and ambiguous status to its women, is one of the first things that comes into play before reaching the main body of the text. The opening lines of the tale alert the reader to the fact that the spoken voice being read is that of a woman who, as such, is traditionally silenced. It is only because of an illness that she is permitted to digress into articulation: "I took advantage of the illness to receive this wisdom: what I am about to tell was passed to me by our ancestors through a dream. If this weren't the case, I would never be able to speak. I am a woman, I need permission to have a say" [Aproveitei a doença para receber esta sabedoria: o que vou contar me foi passado em sonho pelos antepassados. Não fosse isso nunca eu poderia falar. Sou mulher, preciso autorização para ter palavra (*EA*, 141)]. The woman, at this stage, claims not to understand the content of what she says. Her words are merely an effect of the fever from which she suffers and they come to her directly from what appear to be male ancestors. This masculine ancestral order not only commands the articulation of language—authorizing her speech—but also reigns supreme in the determination process of language, through the authority of naming. They "bring us into existence and give us and retake our names" [nos fazem existir e nos dão e retiram nossos nomes (141)]. All of this fits very comfortably alongside the Judeo-Christian Yahwistic version of the myth of Adam and Eve since Adam nominates everything prior to the creation of Eve, who will herself be fashioned by God with the assistance of one of his ribs. Ultimately, man, who arrived first, gets to name woman.[34] The woman in "Lenda de Namarói" appears to subjugate herself totally to a language framework controlled by men when she calls on the writer, presumably through the priest, to translate all that she says. There is immediacy to the female's state. She is allied to the voice and the now, and has no time to waste. Her ability to articulate is ephemeral and she needs men both to authorize it and to render it permanent through writing it down in an intelligible language. This process of translation adds a further perspective to the already multiply distilled tale because the language in which we read her words is not the language in which she spoke them.

Although there are gender ambiguities already simmering at the edge of the text through the associations linked to the writer, the priest, and the region, it appears by the end of the first paragraph that gender demarcations are in force which cast women as voiceless and secondary to men. The opening sentence of the second paragraph destroys this carefully crafted illusion through a strategic distortion of an intertextual allusion: "In the beginning, we were all women. There were no men" [No princípio, todos éramos mulheres. Os homens não haviam (141)]. The difference between this version of genesis and its biblical equivalent is that there is no need for a god because women have always already existed. God is necessary in order to secure male primacy, in order to explain how, on Earth, Adam preceded Eve. In Couto's version of the myth, that explanation is redundant since man can be born of the female womb. To compound man's relegation to the secondary, the reader quickly learns that the miracle of masculine creation is intricately linked to infertility. In fact, men appear to be the result of an abomination, infertile women who are immediately consumed by their fertile counterparts. After three days (di)gestation, men are born. Unlike Adam in the Priestly tradition of the creation myth, man is not created in the image of his god.[35] In fact, he is very different from her and this causes him shame. Quickly, the men descend into savagery and it becomes clear that they are responsible for the loss of Paradise, another distortion of the biblical story. Couto's myth continues with the men moving away from the women, and crossing a small stream, which then becomes an enormous river and separates them from their creators. This distancing over the water becomes a regression: the men become uncivilized, and are obliged to eat raw food since they do not possess the secret of fire. The women, in contrast, know how to harvest flames. This inability on the part of men becomes a desire for what they lack, foreshadowing the womb-envy that will serve as the spur to their masculine initiation rites. They cross the river and rejoin the women. The two genders become united once more and everything is fine until a woman gives birth. At that point, men feel another sense of lack, this time overcome by trying to copy the cutting of the umbilical cord: thus circumcision was born. The result of this castration by prox(imit)y in response to womb-envy is that the men feel consoled; they can at least give rise to a second birth. Through the ritual of circumcision, the men are seeking to erase the difference that separates them from their creators—the women. They want to believe that they can create too, that they are equal to their creators. But, as becomes clear through the voice of the woman speaker, the men live in a state of hollow if palliative self-deception, because only women can cut the cord that brings one life out of another. Furthermore, by this stage of the story it has become obvious that the most ancient and therefore the most primary of the ancestors were women. Therefore, the source of the speaker's authority is, in fact, female.

In his version of the creation myth, Couto plays with the notions of primacy and constructedness within gender assignment. Initially, the reader is led to believe that it is a man's world and that the realm of language is masculine and reigns supreme. The feminine initially appears to be defined by that realm. But it quickly becomes apparent that the sequence may be reversed. Men could come second; creation can be feminine. The masculine order then becomes a construct, fashioned out of the feminine rather than the other way around. Not only did women come first, men then sought to imitate them. But the birth that men reproduce is always secondary [um segundo parto], a deception in which the most essential preserve of women is arrogated in a performance of masculinity.

Couto's game with gender assignment has profoundly subversive implications on and beyond what Eve Sedgwick, Andrew Parker, and Judith Butler have discussed as the performative, that is the ways we are culturally programmed constantly to act out the expectations of our sex.[36] By putting woman before man, Couto avers Zarathustra's declaration concerning the mortality of the divine as He is conceived in Western tradition. The various distortions of the biblical story further undermine that tradition. The threat to patriarchal theology is matched by the menacing of psychoanalytical theory: in Couto's story, a sense of lack is not provoked by the phallus but by the womb. Humanity does not evolve to desire the emulation of what is masculine; rather men are reduced to the status of poor parodies of women.

"SAPATOS DE TACÃO ALTO" AND "A FILHA DA SOLIDÃO": THE HERMENEUTICS OF HIGH-HEELS, OR THE TRANSVESTITE AS A POSTMODERN TROPE

Couto's creation myth destabilizes the primacy of masculinity within the Judeo-Christian tradition. The more conservative elements of that tradition, embodied particularly in the Catholic and Evangelical Churches, have imposed rigid gender designations on their followers, in an effort to enforce a binary order and lend coherence to their belief in a Manichean duality (good/evil; man/woman). Ironically, only their priests are permitted to cross-dress during religious rites. However, the rites of other traditions have often blurred Western gender distinctions. Judith Ochshorn claims that in ancient Sumer, "that part of the world usually regarded as the cradle of Western religions," gender reversals were associated with cultic celebrations.[37] Sabrina Petra Ramet highlights similar customs in the Dionysian rites that continued into the seventeenth century.[38] Nicole Loraux points out that traits of transvestism were common in many Greek social rituals such as religious festivals and initiation ceremonies. She lists, as examples, the Argive festival of *Hubristika* in which men and women trade clothes, the initiation rites of the ephebe who on the eve of his accession into manhood "dramatizes his passage into full virility by momentarily playing the woman," and the Spartan marriage ceremony in which the bride masculinizes her appearance by shortening her hair length.[39] She argues that modern interpretations of these practices have placed them under the heading of inversions, as a means of preserving the binary structure assigned to gender.

> It will be observed that the notion of inversion satisfies the mind insofar as it does not introduce any breach in the binary division of Greek categories. Once applied to these always transitional practices, the canonical distribution is reformed, unblemished, and the regulated functioning of the civic order is fully capable of controlling provisional reversals, which are unable to shake its foundations.[40]

This echoes Judith Lorber's observation that, insofar as transvestism is recognized as a temporary transgression, it fails to remove the gender binary.[41] Like Bakhtin's notion of the parodic-travesty which, for the Romans, had to exist in order for a serious discourse to be conceptualized, cross-dressing parodies the "forms" of masculinity (and femininity), being the "comic *contre-partie*" that allows "the fullness of the whole" to be realized in the gender discourse.[42]

According to Bakhtin, the target of Roman parody was never the hero nor his exploits but rather the way in which the story was told.[43] Therefore, if attributes such as attire, make-up, hairstyle, and fragrance form part of the discourse of gender, cross-dressing may be read to parody but not to discredit the reasoning behind that semiotic system. The meaning of "masculine" and "feminine" remains and must remain the same before, during, and after the *image* of femininity has been reconsigned to the wardrobe. Yet, even if the intent behind the transvestite's frock is merely a temporary suspension of the culturally appropriate gender assignment, like any parody, this suspension leaves its mark on the serious discourse it mocked. The reason for this indelible trace is rooted in the "heteroglossia" that parody unleashes. Gender assignment becomes fundamentally relativized once the arbitrariness of its system of communication is revealed, once the transvestite has refracted sartorial semiotics in such a way that clothes become a "double-voiced discourse." If woman is a construct, then the transvestite is a copy of a construct. The cross-dresser, by being so obviously constructed, serves to highlight the very contructedness of gender itself. That is the permanent mark left by the transitoriness of the transvestite. Gender is revealed as "a performance that requires constant repetition: a daily performance that constitutes identity."[44]

The term "transvestite" was coined at the beginning of the twentieth century by the German sexologist, Magnus Hirschfeld. He was among the first to note that transvestism, among men at least, was generally a heterosexual phenomenon.[45] Stoller subsequently observed that the male transvestite "prefers sexual relationships only with women and is not effeminate when not dressed as a woman."[46] It is advisable to be wary of statistics used to generalize the practices of individuals. There is no way of knowing with much degree of certainty how many transvestites exist or how they define their sexual orientation. However, it is clear that there are those who refuse to countenance that transvestites could be anything other than gay. One reason for their reluctance to accept that most cross-dressers might be straight is, according to David Brez Carlisle, because of "the stereotype of the drag queen."[47] Moreover, all deviation from orthodox (heterosexual) culture is often assumed neatly to fit into the other side of the binary: unorthodox (homosexual) culture. In fact, transvestism is problematic within gay culture, and homosexuality is sometimes anathema to transvestites. Marjorie Garber highlights the hostility in the USA between straight transvestite groups and gay transvestites, stating that "the cultural effect of transvestism is to destabilize all such binaries: not only 'male' and 'female,' but also 'gay' and 'straight,' and 'sex' and 'gender.' This is the sense—the radical sense—in which transvestism is a 'third.'"[48]

Given transvestism's destabilizing effect on frontiers, it is not surprising that Couto includes cross-dressers in some of his narratives. Transvestites are the perfect literary device for signaling the postmodern age, and a rejection of the Manichean universe. In "Sapatos de Tacão Alto" [High-Heeled Shoes], a first-person narrator tells of his young-boy's passion for his next-door neighbor's secret lover whose existence is evidenced by the reverberation of her high-heeled shoes as she walks around his house. The neighbor, Zé Paulão, is physically characterized by extreme masculinity. But at the same time, there is something intangibly feminine about his mannerisms.

The first piece of information imparted by the narrator is that the occurrence took place in colonial times, when a patriarchal hierarchy, underscored by the Catholic Church, aggressively sought to define the world dualistically. Any assault in the tale on associated binaries will thus put in doubt the validity of that world. The narrator himself is at the point of entering adolescence—a continuum that acts as a boundary, marking the transition between infancy and manhood. He claims that he is not yet on that boundary but the plot of the story tends to suggest otherwise, resting as it does on his loss of innocence and a fantasized passion.

The neighborhood in which the story is set, which is full of ambitionless Portuguese, is called Esturro, a word which echoes "esturrar" and "esturrado," both of which connote scorching. Additionally, the past participle can be used to describe someone uncompromising or fanatical, someone who sees the world in black and white. The area's favorite topic of gossip is Zé Paulão whose virility metonymically extends to the crane on which he works. In fact, he is the only person who stands out in an otherwise homogenous vicinity. Despite his much-coveted masculinity, his wife abandoned him for an unknown reason, apparently leaving him alone, pitied by his fellow citizens. But the narrator's family know the truth or, at least, they think they do, jealously guarding and enjoying the secret of Zé Paulão's nocturnal activities. Every now and then, they see women's clothes drying in his yard. These garments in the daylight signal a nighttime female lover whose presence is further confirmed by the audible attribute associated with her feminine shoes.

Members of the narrator's family enjoy speculating about the lover's appearance and they use these empty signs of a woman's presence to reinforce their perception of Zé Paulão as particularly masculine. The young narrator himself dreams a woman of extraordinary beauty into existence, with whom he is besotted. Her attractiveness to the narrator is paralleled by the epigamic appeal of Zé Paulão to the local women.

One day, as the narrator plays a stereotypically boyish game of Cowboys and Indians, he accidentally finds himself in Zé Paulão's yard. He hides in the shadows until the presence of the mystery woman is suddenly signaled by the sound of her high-heeled shoes. His desire to lay eyes on the woman of his dreams overpowers his discretion, so that he steps out of the shadows to face the embodiment of his own shadow, the resident of his unconscious: "The fascinating lady had her back to me. She wasn't after all as tall or as fat as my family had speculated. Suddenly, she turned around." [A fascinável dama estava de costas. Não era afinal tão alta, nem tão gorda como as suposições da minha família. De repente, a mulher se virou (*EA,* 113)]. The narrator's world is turned into a void, as the structure upon which it rested is fundamentally challenged because, before him, "Zé Paulão's eyes, adorned with make-up, flashed." [os olhos de Zé Paulão, ornamentados de pinturas, me fitaram num relâmpago (113–14)]. The woman of his dreams stands there as a tangible presence that turns out to be a construct, doused in the excesses of Western female gender assignment: the dress, the shoes, and the make-up. The transvestite challenges what it means to be a woman and, at the same time, what it means to be a man. S/he is neither and both, rejecting and reinforcing the binary distinction between the two. In the context of this short story, the transvestite/woman/man flickers between absence and presence because the village as a whole remains sure of Zé Paulão's solitude while the narrator's family is still certain of the existence of a woman. The narrator himself discovers the uncomfortable veracity of both points of view—mutually exclusive possibilities that are simultaneously allowed to operate through the transvestite.

The narrator's reaction to the discovery of Zé Paulão's cross-dressing is remarkably similar to that of the transvestite's wife. She had been shocked and wept but was not prepared to explain what had happened. The two genders behave as one, once a transvestite enters the scene/seen. Both the wife and the narrator insist on retaining the secrecy surrounding the gender disruption. The world they represent depends on intransigent demarcations. Yet that world is never the same again. Zé Paulão's image may continue to be reinforced as excessively masculine with each outing of the high-heeled shoes, but the suspicion is sown that the secret of Zé Paulão's gender ambiguity is tacitly understood by the narrator's mother. As her son weeps over the "death" of a nondescript "girl"—who is "uncertain" [incerta] in every sense of the word (114)—the mother smiles knowingly, making arrangements for him never to hear the sound of the high-heeled shoes again. Whether she knows, or not, is never clarified, this uncertainty being an appropriate note on which to end a tale in which the most fundamental category of gender is revealed to be ambiguous.

Couto redeploys transvestism to similar ends in another short story, "A Filha da Solidão" [Daughter of Solitude], in which colonial society's binary certainties are shredded through cross-dressing. The blurring in the demarcation between genders is accompanied by an assault on the integrity of another spurious system of classification, in this case, race. In the tale, a white woman cross-dresses as a man and is then believed to have impregnated another white woman. Lurking behind this affront to the logic of gender categories is the possibility that the real father is black and, as such, despised by the girl's family. So blinding is their racial prejudice that a white female father is deemed to be more feasible than one of "those others, of a different color" who "were reduced to just one word, whispered between the jaw of fear and the jowl of contempt," the word itself being reduced to the masculine singular form of "black" [os outros, de outra cor; se reduziam a uma palavra, soprada entre a maxila do medo e a mandíbula do desprezo; o preto (*CDNT*, 46)].

The girl is called Meninita, a conceptually compounded diminutive. Her father, Pacheco, for dubious reasons known only to himself, chooses to live in a remote area of Sofala, "condemning his family to no longer live among people of an equal race" [condenando a família a não conviver mais com gente de igual raça (45–46)]. His decision means that there is no one with whom his daughter can fall in love because "around here there is only black scum" [aqui só há pretalhada (46)]. She becomes increasingly despondent because there are no white boys in the vicinity, and takes to her room where she indulges in unsatisfying onanistic orgies in the company of a photo magazine. The suggestion that his daughter will end up with a black is risible in Pacheco's eyes, certain, as he is, that "Meninita would comply with the teachings of her race" [cumpria os ensinamentos da raça (46)]. The only employee in the house is the young Massoco who "found amusing the contemptuous mannerisms of his little mistress" [achava graça aos modos desdenhosos da pequena patroa (46)]. He is Meninita's age and replaces her at the counter during her self-imposed solitary confinement. At the end of his working day, Massoco makes a curious request which remains unanswered in the tale: "I'd like to see the young mistress . . ." [peço licença ir lá ver a patroinha . . . (47)]. The three dots that follow this strange petition imply a continuation which is never satisfied. That thread of the story is left loose, tempting the reader to unravel the fabric of the text once its conclusion is reached. But before that, after the three dots that signal both an elision and the prospect of a resumption, a female vet arrives on the scene whose most notable characteristic is that she looks like a man. Initially, the vet's androgyny is a source of reassurance for Dona Esmeralda since her husband could not possibly be tempted into adultery. One night, their daughter takes a turn for the worse and they decide to call on the medical services of the vet. Their decision has implications beyond therapeutic necessity because, in using a vet to treat their daughter, they reduce her to the status of an animal. In their mindset, this correlates her with "the black." Their daughter manages to fall asleep but only after projecting her desire for a man onto the female visitor. She confuses her for a man, and kisses him/her passionately. Meninita's behavior causes her parents to become embarrassed as she crosses a tabooed frontier. Up until this point in the story, the masculine-looking vet has dressed as a woman. Her attire has emitted her gender assignment to the world, even if physically she resembles a man. After her initial contact with Meninita, however, the vet develops a plan of action designed to cure the girl, which involves reversing this paradigm of signification. She will disguise herself as a man. The Pachecos reluctantly agree. The vet proceeds to dress in Pacheco's old clothes and to visit his daughter over several nights. Her clothing now signals that she is a man, even if under it all she is a woman. Or so it appears. Neither of the parents is comfortable with the cure for their daughter's condition. Its only advantage is that it does not involve a black, and it appears to work. Shortly after the vet leaves the area, Meninita returns to work at the counter and is as abrasive as ever with the black customers. At this point, the absent Massoco resurfaces in the tale, smiling to himself and thinking how "life has got back to normal, as a plot which looks for a thread" [a vida se retomou, em novelo que procura o fio (48)]. However, the thread is still missing; the story still does not make sense. Then Dona Esmeralda discovers that Meninita is pregnant.

Pacheco's anger is directed toward the absent vet, as he smashes windows and declares: "I'll kill that lecherous brute of a woman doctor" [eu mato o cabrão da doutora! (48)]. The vet's role at this point is to cause Pacheco to defile the sanctity of gender classification because his illogical abuse of her/him fuses the masculine and the feminine. She/he also serves to obfuscate the obvious and to permit the continued crossing of the racial divide. As her parents leave Meninita unsupervised, determined to seek retribution for the defloration of their daughter, the girl "went up to her room, and opened up her magazine of old photos. Overcome by sleepiness, she made herself comfortable, snuggled up in the sheets. Before going to sleep, she squeezed the black hand which emerged from the white of the bedclothes" [subiu ao quarto, abriu a revista das velhas fotos. Vencida pelo sono se ajeitou no colchão em rodilha de lençóis. Antes de adormecer, apertou a mão negra que despontava no branco das roupas (49)]. Beneath those sheets, the construct of racial difference dissolves in a sexual union which is prefigured in the text by another coital act. This earlier act, between the vet and the girl, had signaled the collapse of the gender distinction.

In both "Sapatos de Tacão Alto" and "A Filha da Solidão," Couto uses the disruption of the gender binary embodied in the cross-dresser to rupture the premises of colonial society. Portuguese colonialism was a patriarchal construct, particularly under the leadership of Salazar. The Mozambique that emerged from the colonial era, under the presidency of Samora Machel, retained many of the dichotomized prejudices of the former epoch, and was intolerant of any deviation from the sexual norm. Couto's sympathetic portrayal of alternative gender possibilities reveals his unusually progressive attitudes for a man educated in Mozambique and goes hand-in-hand with his reassessment of the racial boundaries that scar Mozambican society. The complex issue of race appears entwined once more with gender in two short stories we will now discuss that involve Indians, a group often despised in East Africa for its dominance in the trade sector.

"De Como Se Vazou a Vida de Ascolino do Perpétuo Socorro" and "O Viúvo": Turning Your Manservant into Your Wife

The stories "De Como Se Vazou a Vida de Ascolino do Perpétuo Socorro" [How Ascolino do Perpetuo Socorro Lost His Spouse] and "O Viúvo" [The Widower] have a number of similarities. The protagonists in both stories were born in Goa, live in Mozambique and suffer from identity crises. Ascolino claims, "I am indeed an Indo-Portuguese, Catholic in my faith and in my customs" (*VMN*, 29). Jesuzinho, for his part, "called himself Indo-Portuguese. A practicing Lusitanian" [se chamava de Indo-Português. Lusitano praticante (*CDNT,* 79)]. Both lose their wives and drink too much and, at crucial moments, both confuse their faithful servants for their spouses, changing men into women and signaling the collapse of the categorized worlds to which they subscribed.

"De Como Se Vazou a Vida de Ascolino do Perpétuo Socorro" tells the story of how the eponymous antihero's world becomes progressively more devoid of any meaning, principally because the basis on which he grounds its meaning is fundamentally flawed. Ascolino wants to belong to the colonizer group—a desire which presumes exclusion because, in order for the belonging to be conceptualized, not-belonging must also be countenanced. Thus, for Ascolino, meaning rests on the fundamental binary of inclusion-exclusion. The world to which he stakes a claim is Gilberto Freyre's lusotropical paradise, whose common blood is a common language. His adopted *língua* —the Portuguese language—is his *pátria.* But it is also the first thing that excludes him; it marks him out as one of the "monhés" he disavows (*VA*, 75), because his negotiation of Portuguese is characterized by a voice that is audibly foreign.[49] He is not speaking his native language and, as he fumbles around, regurgitating random conjunctions tautologically, the listener can tell. The alienation implicit in his idiosyncratic phraseology is compounded by his accent. Despite the fact that he will never belong, he orientates everything in his life to replicating the colonizing group with which he wishes to identify. He lives in a colonial house, and compensates for his skin pigmentation by wearing a "suit of white linen, shoes of an identical whiteness, and a hat of the selfsame color" (*VMN*, 29). He also sings a genre of song associated with Portugal, namely *fado*.

The vulnerability of the inclusion-exclusion binary is reproduced in Ascolino's relationships with the other two main characters, Vasco and Epifânia. They function as two parallel poles in a patriarchal structure that attempts to cast Ascolino as Master-Husband to their respective roles as Servant and Wife. This complex relationship is analogous to the power dynamic between Hegel's Master and his Bondsman. Ascolino depends for his existence on the recognition afforded to him as Master and as Husband by his Servant and his Wife respectively.[50] The ethical edifice, which this triangular relationship mirrors, prohibits any confusion between the three component parts. That the Master-Husband must always be in charge for the system to be considered colonial is obvious. The reason why the Servant cannot be confused with the Wife is because the Master-Husband's authority is to a large extent derived from a clear demarcation between the genders. Once that distinction is lost, his imperium as both Master and Husband vanishes.

Applying Jung's theory, which is itself dependent on the crudest of binaries, to this structure, results in Epifânia and Vasco operating as complementary aspects of Ascolino's shadow. Epifânia is his wife who, as such, is supposed to "unhesitatingly receive the projection of his soul."[51] She is the manifestation of what he is within but, as the story progresses, that becomes more and more an absence. Even at the beginning of the tale, she is "so thin that one was not even aware she was approaching" (*VMN*, 30). By the end, as she disappears with all the furniture, she has no presence at all, leaving an empty house behind her. As her name suggests, she serves as a revelation pointing to Ascolino's inner emptiness.

The first description of Vasco João Joãoquino is that he is the "faithful and devoted servant" who "would emerge from the shadow" (30). He physically inhabits an umbral space. Also, like Hegel's Bondsman, he allows Ascolino to conceptualize himself as a Master. Ascolino drinks in the front part of the bar; Vasco, in dutiful contrast, in the back with the other blacks. The bar itself is called "Viriato," sharing its name with a Lusitanian chief who fought the Romans. The historical quintessence of Portugueseness is thus embodied in the name of the bar which the pair frequent daily.

Vasco, as the Servant, is supposed to be the polar opposite of Ascolino as the Master and, as the opposite, he also represents what Ascolino seeks to repress in his unconscious. The Goan tries to ally himself to the other masters, the group to whom he longs to belong—namely the Portuguese—echoing their insults against India. But the Master-Servant binary on which Ascolino depends for his desired status is extremely unstable. Firstly, Vasco's name marks him as a symbol of Portuguese greatness—Vasco da Gama was one of the nation's maritime pioneers—whereas Ascolino is burdened with perpetual supplication [Perpétuo Socorro], so that the soubriquets are really the wrong way round. Secondly, despite his efforts, Ascolino can never pass himself off as truly Portuguese because of his marked language and the color of his skin. Thirdly, the Servant on whom he depends for his recognition mimics his Master's voice menacingly for the amusement of his fellow blacks, a strategy Homi Bhabha identifies as subversive.[52] Fourthly, and most importantly, Ascolino's hegemonic pretension crumbles as he confuses the categories on which it is founded. "I'm a pale-arsed little darkie," he proclaims, proceeding to shout, "Long live Nehru!" (37). Immediately after this inebriated allegiance switch from Lusitanian to Indian nationalist, the tabooed boundary between Wife and Servant disappears in Ascolino's mind, as he "exchanged his servant for his wife and began to call him Epifânia" (37). Having rechristened Vasco, Ascolino begins to project his longings for the conjugal recognition, which Epifânia had failed to fulfil, onto the Servant whose role is to recognize him as Master. Initially, Vasco continues to act as the Servant, complying with his Master's instruction to move to the front of the bicycle on which they are both riding. For that one instant, Servant and Wife fuse, as Vasco occupies the spouse's place in order to obey his Master's command. Immediately, however, both binaries disintegrate, as "the Goan, excited, grabbed his servant round the waist" (37). Ascolino has confused a man for a woman. As he tries to kiss her/him, he elicits rebellion from his Servant who knocks his Master over, declaring "I'm not your woman" (37). Things can never be the same again. Normality may appear to be restored, as Vasco's masculinity is reinstated by the man he once again calls "boss," but it remains a masculinity that fluctuates, as Ascolino confuses him twice more for Epifânia. In any case, only one instance of gender confusion is needed to damage irretrievably the tenets of the patriarchal structure. Vasco's gender switch renders patent Ascolino's loss of authority in both the spheres he sought to control as a means of satisfying his ambition to belong. The pair cycle into the horizon after the now totally absent, third member of their power triangle. Concomitantly, the arbitrariness of the rigid categorizations governing the rules of the colonial group, which Ascolino had once aspired to join, is revealed by a breach in one of its most fundamental dichotomies: the distinction between man and woman.

In "O Viúvo," Jesuzinho da Graça's world also depends on order and clear-cut categories. A grotesquely long nail on his little finger represents this utilitarian design. Everything has its purpose and serves it, carefully fitting in its proper place, so that the whole structure operates efficiently. In fact, the nail itself turns the finger into a "mere accessory" [simples acessório (*CDNT*, 80)] because of its primary function in maintaining order, as it flips through papers methodically and noiselessly. His life is marked by routine, to the extent that his daily allocution in his native Indian language uttered on taking his leave from his colleagues, "ram-ram," is understood as a "ramerrão," the Portuguese word connoting a wearisome routine, which will be the death of him (79). In fact, from the opening lines of the short story, it is clear that Jesuzinho is not a viable entity, at least not in a well-ordered world, because he is associated with a shiver that "shows us how similar fever and cold are" [nos mostra como a febre se parece com o frio (79)]. Two opposites, which should be kept apart, are thus pathologically linked in his person.

The nail, which represents taxonomical reassurance, also alienates his wife. Like Ascolino, Jesuzinho loses his wife but the difference between the two is that the latter will be reunited with her once he relinquishes his passion for resolute categorization. After his wife dies, half his definition drains away because she was the shadow of his shadow: "If Jesuzinho was a shadow, his wife Vitória was the twilight of that shadow" [Se Jesuzinho era sombra, a esposa Vitória era crepúsculo dessa sombra (80)]. Vitória represents the part of Jesuzinho not fixated by categories. While she is alive, he can repress that aspect of his psyche because it is embodied in his shadow. After she is dead, "bit by bit, the Goan showed signs of the greatest disarray: time was lost on him" [aos poucos, o goês deu sinais de maior desarranjo: as horas se perdiam dele (81)]. Once an "enthusiastic bureaucrat, who complied with the letter of the law, he'd even stopped using blotting paper on the things he wrote" [funcionário do zelo, eterno cumpridor de regulamento, deixou de espremer o mata-borrão sobre os escritos de sua lavra (81)]. However, as his ordered life disintegrates, he keeps one routine: his Tuesday drinking sessions, the importance of which rests on the role-play that always follows them. Although this weekly activity by being rigidly periodic retains the vestigial semblance of order, the cross-dressing of his faithful servant, Piquinino, which is central to the routine, causes tabooed boundaries to be crossed and calls into question a number of fundamental categories. "Man" becomes "woman," as "the cute little servant struggled to tune his voice up an octave, imitating Vitorinha's shrillness" [o empregadito se esforçava em aflautinar a voz, copiando os esganiços de Vitorinha (82)]. His/her actions then go beyond mincing mimicry and enter the realm of affected/affectionate action, as "the servant copied his former mistress's mannerisms, and polished up his master's hair, adjusting the parting to be a diagonal on his head" [o empregado copiava os modos da antiga senhora e brilhantinava os cabelos do patrão, acertando a risca em diagonal no cabelo (82)]. As Piquinino restores order to his master's hair, he undermines it by operating from the wrong gender category.

Unlike Vasco, Piquinino does not feel any repulsion in role-playing a different gender. His uneasiness arises because the boundaries of another category are being blurred. As he pretends to be the deceased wife, he dangerously plays with the frontier between the living and dead, and it is on these grounds that he refuses to continue the charade. The next time that Jesuzinho asks him to act out Vitorinha, Piquinino remains silent. But by this stage of the story sufficient boundaries have already been relinquished by the Goan, so that he is now able to drop his aspiration to order and forfeit its ultimate totem, asking Piquinino to cut his nail. As the servant complies with the request, his master vanishes into thin air. At that moment, Jesuzinho and his belief that the world can be ordered and restricted to categories go up in smoke.

These two short stories share a common theme and a common trope. They both rupture gender classifications in order to undermine structures of power. Scott's assertion that gender has been "a persistent and recurrent way of enabling the signification of power in the West" renders Couto's strategy an assault on the tenets governing mainstream occidental society.[53] His play with gender also undermines the classification system of traditional African society, at least as it is constructed in Mozambique. Couto's humorous disturbance of gender roles troubles any reading of his work that seeks to position him as proposing a simplistic restoration of an African tradition. While it is true that in some of his work he appears to lament a loss of touch with an animistic past, an appreciation of roots and traditions does not imply in Couto's world an adherence to the fossilized constraints that such traditions are often deemed to impose. For Couto, gender is one of the most fluid boundaries we inherit. Playing with gender opens up possibilities, as we shall discuss in relation to two more of Couto's short stories, "Joãotónio, no Enquanto" and "Mulher de Mim."

"Joãotónio, no Enquanto" and "Mulher de Mim": Rupturing Roles

In "Joãotónio, no Enquanto" [Joãotónio, For the Time Being], gender is characterized as a flux, becoming something that is always transient rather than being a stable entity. The Portuguese title of this short story suggests that the protagonist inhabits an interstitial temporal space or, at least, that his name does. A conjunction that normally designates simultaneity (enquanto) slips syntactical category, functioning as an abstract noun and foreshadowing the concept behind the opening line of the story: "for the time being, I'm Joãotónio" [Por enquanto, sou Joãotónio (*EA*, 123)]. The phrase in the Portuguese original signals both temporariness and permanence. The verb "to be" Couto conjugates in this particular instance (ser) is most often used to indicate an innate, enduring quality. Couto himself, when interviewed, has exploited the distinction between "ser" and "estar," which both translate as "to be." The former generally designates a more permanent state of being. Couto, however, uses the latter to refer to himself as a writer on the grounds that being a writer is not a "genetic" or "definitive" state.[54] By a process of converse deduction, the reader may assume that the narrator self-identifies both "genetically" and "definitively" with Joãotónio. But, at the same time, his state is adverbially predefined in terms of transience since "por enquanto"—for the time being—is the first thing the reader learns about it. As the tale develops, it becomes apparent that the narrator's gender is the parameter subject to variation.

The narrator claims that every meeting with women is a battle, defining his interaction with females in militaristic terms that assume a conflict between opposites. The purpose of his battle is to reveal the inner nature of the woman's voice. Once again in this short story, Couto links the feminine and the moist. Furthermore, he conflates orality and women, and appears to fuse the writing and reading processes with masculinity since he consciously addresses his story to a male reader—"mano" (123)—and writes it, "still for the time being" [ainda e por enquanto], under a man's name, Joãotónio (124).

This male writer claims that men can never understand women because "their ideas are born in a place which is beyond thought" [as ideias delas nascem num lugar que está fora do pensamento (123)]. He situates masculinity in a rational framework and stereotypes femininity as beyond reason. But the demarcations he seeks to establish are already troubled since, as he writes, the voice of a woman resonates through his pen, dictating his thought, determining his reasons, and inspiring his script. As he consigns a certain Maria Zeitona's name to the page, her oral domain contaminates its written counterpart, becoming the embodiment of her flesh and, as such, something palpable.

Maria Zeitona was a woman of immense beauty whom Joãotónio married only to discover that she was frigid. Every tactic he tried failed to change her from her corpse-like state in bed. Finally, he sent her to a prostitute to learn the art of sex. On her return, she is a changed woman. In fact, she is almost a man. She is not, however, wholly a man but rather a creature who combines

the attributes of both the feminine and the masculine. She is "masculina"—
the feminine singular form of the adjective "masculine"—not "masculino,"
its masculine equivalent. She retains her link with moisture, Couto's marker
of femininity, but in the manner of a colossus, through the author's corruption of the Portuguese word "manda-chuvas" into "manda-bátegas." The former, which translates the concept of "boss" or "big cheese," is etymologically
rooted in the notion of "he who sends rain." Couto's corruption substitutes
the word for "downpour" in place of the morpheme for rain. Even Zeitona's
voice on her return, the incarnation of her femininity, has changed.

The result of Zeitona's metamorphosis is that Joãotónio begins to doubt
his own masculinity, to the extent that he has to scratch his crotch to reassure
himself. The narrator, who initially had sought a rigorous adherence to the
arbitrary limits of gender through his attribution of stereotypical qualities to
the two sexes, suddenly discovers that he enjoys the ambiguous state into
which he is plunged: it gives him access to a new truth. He proclaims, "In
sexual love, there is no male and female. The two lovers fuse into a single bi-
partite being" [nos amores sexuais não há macho nem fêmea. Os dois
amantes se fundem num único e bipartido ser (126)]. As the two sexes become one, they reveal qualities of one in the other. The two genders cease to
be contrastive and become complementary. The mutual exclusion of the
realm of binary logic gives way to a beneficial fusion, as the story ends with
the narrator's confession that he wants to become "un-rational." Every day he
longs for night when he is both Joãotónio, and the female, Joanantónia, in
the virile arms of his wife. He oxymoronically defines himself as "masculina"
and "feminino," rejecting the bipolar paradigm of reason. As one of the most
fundamental and controversial tools of human classification becomes un-
stuck, as "Joãotónio" flickers into "Joanantónia" in a process of erasure and
reinscription, the truth of the entire denominative edifice fades and, simultaneously, the definitive power of all categories begins to crumble.

"Mulher de Mim" [Woman of Me] is another of Couto's stories in which
the two genders appear to fuse into one. It is a particularly surreal narrative in
which boundaries that delineate opposites become blurred: the distinction
between the living and the dead, between existence and nonexistence, between the realm of dreams and reality, between past—those who have died—
and future—those who have yet to be born. The most fundamental binary
that permeates the text appears at first to be reinforced before it is undermined. Once again, Couto initially draws on gender stereotypes, seeming to
endorse them, before he craftily merges the opposites—a maneuver which
challenges the certainties that have been established.

The tale's epigraph posits the initial dichotomy: "The man is the axe, the woman is the hoe" (*EMIR*, 58). Men are associated with destruction—the axe chops the tree down—women are linked to fertility—the hoe tills the land. The narrator's reward, if he can resist the temptation of the mysterious woman who floats into his life, is that he will merit "the name of the warrior people" (59), another association between masculinity and destruction. Additionally, one of the possibilities that enter his mind as he considers how to defend himself from her influence is to kill her. In contrast, the mysterious woman is yet another example of Couto fusing femininity and moisture—the stuff of life—as the first description given of her demonstrates. "She was a woman whose soft eyes cast a moist film upon the room" (58). Her voice also "recalled the gentle murmur of a spring, the seduction of a return to times beyond, when there was no before" (59). As well as linking her to moisture, this phrase draws on the appeal of the primordial aspect of water and conceptually links the seductive power of women to a desired return to the womb. Her voice leads him to declare, "I was unfulfilling myself. And when I appealed to myself to return to reason, I could not even get as far as that austere judge, my brain" (59). Her effect on him is to contaminate with irrational fluidity his ordered world symbolized, in the tale, by a solid ice-cube. This world, however, has its end signposted from the beginning of the story since the narrator compares himself to a cube of ice melting in his glass: "Both of us were transitory, converting ourselves into the previous substance out of which we had been formed" (58). The comparison is significant because it communicates the temporariness of his wholly masculine state. The ice will become water again. Male solidity born of woman will reconvert to female moisture. It also signals a desired return to the primordial mass, to the water from which humankind emerged. If, as was argued in the last chapter, the uterus and water are oneirically interchangeable, then this sentiment prefigures a preoccupation that resurfaces later in the story, when the narrator describes each abode as a new edition of the maternal womb. Through the presence of the mystery woman, the narrator comes to realize that he never achieves a welcomed return to the womb. The rigid constraints of his world bar his access.

The mysterious woman operates as the narrator's shadow, ebbing and flowing in his conscious realm and serving to foist doubt onto him and the fixed order he represents through the solidity of the ice cube. He begins to lose the certainty of his own being: "Thanks to the intruder's arts, I was disappearing, intermittent from existence" (59). The woman, for her part, flickers in and out of the realm of shadows. Her purpose is to provoke the narrator's regression into childhood, to return him to the womb, and to start everything again. A vital component in her strategy reflects the tactics of so many of Couto's other characters since she "told her story, the episodes of her life. Variants of truth, they fed me the sweet taste of deceit" (59). Once again, a character's life is narrated in terms of a constant recreation, as a fiction which better serves access to the truth of truth, namely its relative and fluctuating nature. The story in flux, which the account of her life becomes, is seductive to the narrator because it is infinite, never reaching an end, constantly beginning again, and mirroring his own conclusion about the nature of life itself: "Life, the whole of it, is one extended birth" (60).

The tale's own conclusion is the description of a journey and, as such, signals that the process is always more important than the destination. Like those of Fortin in "A Princesa Russa," the narrator's footsteps bisexually walk the story to an end which, in fact, is a new beginning, or rather, the eternal continuation of a journey. Teleological constraint is sacrificed at the altar of constant recreation whose purpose is nothing other than itself. Temporal logic falls victim to this loss of "The End," as time loses all sense of time and drags on.

This loss of the category of the finite is foreshadowed by the woman's declaration of her purpose. She tells the narrator, "I have come to find a place in you" (62). She explains her reasons: "Only she harbored the eternal gestation of springs. Without me being her, I was incomplete, formed only in the arrogance of halves" (62). The binary order of gender is called into question by her presence. The sexual dichotomy had demanded replication across every aspect of human existence, but its foundations are themselves fraudulent, nothing more than a cultural artifice disguised as a natural order. The narrator finally realizes that "in her, I had found not a woman to be mine, but the woman of me" (62). Possession and hierarchy thus cede to mutual complementarity.

In both "Mulher de Mim" and "Joãtónio, no Enquanto," Couto at first appears to establish a gender stereotype and then proceeds to deconstruct it. This is a repetition of the pattern that he uses in "Lenda de Namarói," in which the standard patriarchal account of creation is endorsed prior to being undermined. Even in "Sapatos de Tacão Alto," Zé Paulão is portrayed as excessively masculine before his cross-dressing proclivities are revealed and the gender paradigm menacingly parodied. In his treatment of gender, Couto reveals his greatest affinity to the postmodern program. By liquefying the most sacred of frontiers, he disavows the innate legitimacy of all boundaries. The jurisdiction of categories is not a given in Couto's universe. On the contrary, any boundary that appears to be taken for granted inevitably becomes porous as his narratives unfold. A most interesting aspect of Couto's treatment of gender, as postmodern as it is as a diegetic strategy, is the manner in which he politicizes the abolition of clear gender demarcations. In stories like "De Como Se Vazou a Vida de Ascolino do Perpétuo Socorro" and "A Filha da Solidão," racial boundaries are crossed or racist aspirations exploded as the multiple possibilities of gender are unleashed. By linking the exposure of prejudices based on race with the deconstruction of those based on gender, Couto subverts discriminatory paradigms that are prevalent in contemporary Mozambique as much as he attacks the pillars of colonial society. Such a strategy is extremely astute because the argument against racism has, for the most part, been won in postindependence Mozambique. In contrast, a deep-held and irrational abhorrence of minority sexual orientations and gender practices, and a failure to promote meaningful equality between genders still cloud Mozambican society, where limited resources often lead families to choose to educate sons before daughters.[55] One profession to which many women turn in the midst of immense poverty, prostitution, surfaces in Couto's fourth novel where, as we shall discuss in the next chapter, he uses the marginalized voice of the prostitute to reveal "truths" to the mainstream.

7

Finding the Nation's Phallus:
Expelling the UN Specter
from Mozambique

IN THE EARLY 1990S, MOZAMBIQUE BECAME A FOCUS OF UNITED NATIONS' attention, as the international body desperately required a success story in Africa following a series of embarrassing failures on the continent. The Mission for the Referendum in Western Sahara, launched in 1991, had stalled before achieving anything other than its acronym, MINURSO. The UN operation in Somalia (UNOSOM), sanctioned in April 1992, disintegrated disastrously, and the verification mission to the Angolan peace process witnessed Jonas Savimbi's refusal to accept electoral defeat and the catastrophic return to a civil war that would only end with the death of the Unita leader in 2002. Against this backdrop, the Mozambican General Peace Agreement, or GPA as it became known, signed on 4 October 1992, offered the United Nations an opportunity to oversee successfully the resolution of an armed conflict that had marred the Mozambican nation for nearly two decades. On 16 December of the same year, Security Council Resolution 797 established ONU-MOZ, the peacekeeping operation that would cost the International Community over half a billion US dollars to maintain over the subsequent couple of years.[1]

ONUMOZ's mandate expired on 9 December 1994, the day Joaquim Alberto Chissano was sworn in as the first democratically elected president in the nation's history. The UN finally had its success story, and could point to the former Portuguese colony's newly tested but still fragile democracy as an example of the benefits of concerted action undertaken in the name of the International Community. The civil war was over; Afonso Dhlakhama had been transformed from the heinous leader of what Margaret Thatcher termed one of the "most brutal terrorist movements that there is" to the acceptable head of a parliamentary opposition that had performed surprisingly well in the nation's first multiparty elections.[2] The four million dollars in cash payments that he personally received were a small price to pay for his cooperation in the process.[3]

The two-year period between the signing of the GPA in Rome and Renamo's acceptance of Chissano's victory was fraught with brinkmanship, threats, boycotts, and breaches of agreements, but the ultimate result was a Mozambique at last free from conflict. Western-style democracy had its final victory over Soviet-inspired socialism, no longer viable after the fall of the Berlin Wall, and the would-be guardian of the new international order, the UN, oversaw the culmination of that transition. Of course, while the Frelimo government's rhetoric changed in order to accommodate international expectations, most of the faces in the government did not. Furthermore, in many respects, the United Nations' presence in Mozambique was a repetition of the paradigm of foreign interference that has scarred the country since Portugal's arrival at the end of the fifteenth century. Together with the plethora of international aid agencies that have poured into Mozambique in recent years, the United Nations' operation is symptomatic of the global shift toward "Empire" as defined by Michael Hardt and Antonio Negri. For them, "Empire" is the result of the latter stages of liberal capitalism, an era in which national boundaries yield sovereignty to the world economy, postmodern diversity is celebrated and cultural difference necessarily fetishized and, in the process, a paradoxically homogenous world order is firmly established.[4]

The international presence through NGOs and the United Nations in Mozambique operates as a continuation of the process of neocolonization, as Margaret Hall and Tom Young have pointed out. Even when they employ radical terminology, NGO discourse, like that of the UN, is fundamentally the same as that of the World Bank and Western States. All have "doubts about the capacities of Third World governments" and show "contempt for cultural traditions that do not square with Western notions of 'rights' and 'justice.'"[5] They are an intrinsic part of the "International Community," a misnomer that invariably points to exclusively Western interests, and finds its first historical manifestation with regard to Africa at the Berlin Conference of 1884–85, where the European colonial powers carved up the continent, amid a rhetoric of bringing order and civilization to the area. The shibboleths may have changed, as the UN and NGO alliance assumes the mantle of the International Community, for it is no longer permissible to talk of a civilizing mission. Unfortunately, the patronizing and ultimately self-interested mindset has not, a point made clear in Couto's fourth novel, *O Último Voo do Flamingo* (2000) [The Flamingo's Last Flight].

A common thread linking Couto's first three novels, *Terra Sonâmbula, A Varanda do Frangipani,* and *Vinte e Zinco,* is that external interference, first colonialism and then a civil war encouraged from abroad, had impeded the development of a Mozambican cultural identity. Couto's fourth novel breaks this cycle of blaming the outside for the problems involved in forging the nation's identity, while paradoxically foregrounding foreign interference in Mozambican territory. In fact, *O Último Voo do Flamingo* is a powerful and, at times, humorous critique of his nation's invasion by the United Nations and, by extension, aid agencies in general that places the responsibility for solving the country's problems squarely on the shoulders of Mozambicans.

The two-year-long mandate of ONUMOZ had a number of consequences beyond the supervision of the peace process, the most profound of which was the confirmation of donor-agency power and the diminution in the sovereignty of the Maputo government. The arrogance of the UN force, and the abuses associated with it, which we will discuss in relation to *O Último Voo do Flamingo,* was an acute manifestation of the ideology underpinning aid-agency culture. The Western aid agencies present in Mozambique are crossed by a central paradox, which they always refuse to address and which unavoidably renders them hypocritical within their own discourse. Development-speak privileges cultural difference and the sanctity of local mores while simultaneously pushing a very clear Western-biased agenda. While progressive Western thinkers may agree with the need to achieve, for example, gender equality, to what extent is such an agenda compatible with respecting the traditions of a patriarchal society? Like the Catholic colonizers before them, who used the sword to impose a creed based on turning the other cheek, the aid agencies of the postmodern age overlook the contradictions inherent in their activities.

The ONUMOZ presence in Mozambique was an exception to this rule. It never even pretended to be bothered with local customs. This was due, in part, to the time-limited nature of the operation, which could not, therefore, have a development agenda and, in part, to the arrogance of the personnel involved. Mozambique's experience of ONUMOZ was a clear manifestation of the new world paradigm, more discretely and contradictorily perpetrated by the aid agency community, in which the jurisdiction of governments is replaced by the will of the so-called International Community. As Richard Synge points out in relation to ONUMOZ's tenure in Mozambique, "the activities and operations of both the United Nations and the international community as a whole tended to be invasive and destabilizing to, rather than creative and supportive of, the shaky structures of the Mozambican state and society."[6] In fact, by the second year of its involvement in Mozambique, "the

United Nations came to be perceived as a parallel administration. At times it almost had the features of a colonial operation, fulfilling a foreign agenda rather than a domestic one."[7] After ONUMOZ withdrew at the end of its mandate, Mozambique continued to cede sovereignty to international aid agencies, which though subtler than the United Nations' operation, are equally representative of the postmodern paradigm shift to "Empire." Couto's critique of the activities of ONUMOZ spills over, by extension, into an interrogation of the rights of the International Community and its agents to dictate the agenda for Mozambique.

O Último Voo do Flamingo is a tale of exploding penises. Like the protagonist in A Varanda do Frangipani, Massimo Risi, who is charged with solving the mystery, will discover a variety of truths, not all of them comfortable. The story is set in Tizangara, an allegorical zone encapsulating the experiences of Mozambique in the 1990s, where UN soldiers keep disappearing leaving severed phalluses in their stead. A United Nations team is sent to investigate the alarming occurrences, headed by the Italian (Massimo Risi), whose name resonates with the Portuguese for "utmost laughter," as if his agency's presence in Mozambique was a complete farce. The town's prostitute, Ana Deusqueira, who is called upon by the investigation team to identify the owner of a stray member strewn across the national highway, puts a very pointed question to the Italian, highlighting the International Community's double-standards: "Thousands of Mozambicans have died, and not once have we seen you around here. Now, five foreigners go missing and that's the end of the world?" [Morreram milhares de moçambicanos, nunca vos vimos cá. Agora, desapareceram cinco estrangeiros e já é o fim do mundo? (UVF, 34)].

Couto did not choose Risi's nationality at random. Italy had a deep involvement in the Mozambican peace process, and its soldiers, the largest contingent of peacekeepers sent to police the terms of the General Peace Agreement, acquired a rather unsavory reputation for calling on the services of prostitutes and abusing young girls in the areas they administered. It is probably not a coincidence that the entire Italian battalion, Albatroz, was recalled to Italy following the acceptance of these allegations by a UN committee established to investigate them.[8] No one was ever prosecuted, but then, under the terms of the United Nations' presence in Mozambique, ONUMOZ personnel were granted diplomatic immunity as well as an exemption from all taxes. The disgraceful behavior of the Italian soldiers tarnished what had hitherto been a very positive involvement by Italy in the peace process. The peace deal had been negotiated under the auspices of an Italian Catholic organization, the community of Sant'Egidio. Founded in

1968, the community was able to exploit its links with the Mozambican Archbishop of Beira, Jaime Gonçalves, who is from the same ethnic group as a large proportion of Renamo's leadership and is related to Afonso Dhlakama by marriage.[9] These links helped to facilitate a long and ultimately fruitful dialogue between the government and the rebel movement.[10] The peace agreement was signed in Rome and, by sending peacekeepers to Mozambique, Italy sought to enhance its image on the international stage at a time when there was a debate surrounding Italian involvement in the UN operation in Somalia, given the previous colonial relationship between the two nations.[11] But Italy will be most remembered in the minds of most Mozambicans for providing Aldo Ajello, a colorful figure who dominated Mozambican television broadcasts for the two years he served as the UN secretary-general's special representative to Mozambique. A politician and diplomat, he was adept at manipulating the Mozambican media, and cajoling the two parties to the peace accords through difficult terrain.

Couto's character, Massimo Risi, bears more than a passing resemblance to Aldo Ajello. Ajello, who had a very difficult working relationship with Boutros Ghali, the UN secretary-general, was, prior to his appointment, one of the most senior-ranking Italians in the UN structure. An assistant secretary-general, he was seconded from his post in Geneva as director of the bureau of external relations of the United Nations Development Program to head the UN effort in Mozambique. Although he successfully completed his appointment, assessments of his work vary, and some of his own staff considered him to be "rough and rude," and prone to "many temperamental explosions."[12] He unashamedly interfered in the political process in Mozambique, severely compromising the sovereignty of the Maputo government, and was, at times, deemed to advocate Renamo's interests over those of Frelimo.[13] While many Mozambicans may be grateful for his interference, his use of the position of special representative highlighted the neocolonial undertones of the International Community's treatment of Mozambique. Many ONUMOZ personnel seemed to feel they were sent to impose order and to teach Mozambicans how to live together. They failed to understand how much they needed to and could learn from Mozambique. Ultimately, this is the lesson Couto inflicts on his literary voodoo-doll of Ajello, Massimo Risi.

The novel repeatedly critiques United Nation's arrogance. It is one of Couto's central concerns as he makes clear from the opening statement of Tizangara's translator, through whose perspective the narrative is distilled. In a manner analogous to the structure of "Lenda de Namarói," a fictionalized translator narrates and adds another level to the text, distancing the reader from what actually happened, and coloring the tale discretely with a subjectivity which is officially absent from the discourse but, in reality, totally dominates. The translator explains that the tale that follows is an account of what he witnessed in the first years of the postwar period. He feels compelled to write everything down as a means of "freeing himself from these memories" [livrar-me destas lembranças (*UVF*, 11)], a statement that mirrors Kindzu's declaration of purpose in *Terra Sonâmbula.* The parallel is unsettling since *Terra Sonâmbula* deals with the horrors of war, and the implication is that there is a continuity in horror characterizing Mozambique's peace. As we shall see, Couto makes explicit in *O Último Voo do Flamingo* his belief that Mozambique has failed in the postindependence and postwar period to break the paradigmatic cycle of social injustice and foreign interference that has governed the area since the first colonial moment. The soldiers of the United Nations, a force of occupation who arrived with "the insolence of any military" [com a insolência de qualquer militar (*UVF*, 12)], are merely symptomatic of a state of affairs in which the Mozambican nation has failed to jettison the mentality of the colonized and to assume responsibility for its own agency. This message is repeated as the story unfolds by Andorinho, the witchdoctor, and by the translator's father, Sulplício. The message will be inextricably linked to a play between orality and the written. Once again, Couto uses the blurring of the distinction between the two in order to destabilize the certainties of the prevalent orthodoxy. In his introduction, the translator claims to have been condemned for writing down the confessions he heard, and to have been accused of falsifying his account. Thus, any unitary truth underpinning his written text is immediately called into question and, once again, Couto propounds a multiplicity of interpretations and narrations in preference to a fixed version of events. The reader never really knows what actually happened in Tizangara, although, as in *A Varanda do Frangipani,* a range of characters claim responsibility for the disappearances under investigation. Massimo Risi's task, like Izidine Naíta's, is to discover the truth and write it down objectively in a report to be read in the UN citadel in New York. Risi views his entire project as a means to achieve promotion within the UN, a shrewd characterization on Couto's part of the careerism rife among UN and aid-agency personnel in Mozambique, who sanctimoniously lecture on the greater good while never losing sight of where their own self-interest lies. Yet, in Couto's relativistic universe, the only legitimate activity for someone seeking the truth is the telling of one's own story, a lesson that Massimo Risi will learn by the end of the novel.

As well as critiquing the UN, Couto is uncompromising in his attack on Frelimo corruption, and mirrors an argument outlined by Patrick Chabal and Jean-Pascal Daloz in their thought-provoking study on the use of disorder in Africa. They rightfully point out that the increasing NGO presence on the continent reflects an understanding on the part of African elites of the new world order, in which Cold War rivalries can no longer be exploited for profit. Instead, a commitment to the NGO agenda reaps rewards.[14] In Couto's novel, Estêvão Jonas, the corrupt administrator of Tizangara, who uses the hospital generator for his own comfort while constantly asserting his revolutionary credentials as someone who suffered the inconvenience and indignity of having to consume toothpaste during the armed struggle to free the people, is very conscious of the need to facilitate the viewing of poverty in order extract donor dollars and line his own pockets. His character is the central link in the narrative between the essence of Mozambique, which Couto constantly complicates, and foreign interference in the Mozambican domain. In the Marxist era of Operation Production, which sought to eliminate vice and poverty from public view, the government could not allow begging to gainsay its rhetoric about progress under scientific socialism. In contrast, the converted free-market Frelimo, dependent on "donations from the international community" [os donativos da comunidade internacional (*UVF,* 77)], needed to "bring together the debris, to facilitate the viewing of the disaster" [juntar os destroços, facilitar a visão do desastre (77)], ever mindful of the fact that "our misery is very lucrative" [a nossa miséria está render bem (77)]. Television pictures are of the essence in aid-agency culture, and Jonas sees personal advantage in staging multiple forms of destitution for easy consumption by Western consumers, whose angst at the televised sight of starving children leads to the cathartic ritual of donating money without questioning too profoundly their own privileges in the global economic system.

Through Jonas, who mediates Tizangara's image (i.e. Mozambique's image) to the outside, Couto savages the two extreme ideologies that were brought into Mozambique in the postindependence period. In *O Desejo de Kianda* [Kianda's Desire], the Angolan, Pepetela, performs a similar critique of the revolutionary elites of Marxist Angola who have become the nation's free-market entrepreneurs in recent years. Like Pepetela, Couto demonstrates that regardless of the system adopted, the same characters profit at the expense of the population they claim to serve. Couto distorts one of the verses from a famous Camões sonnet "mudam-se os tempos, mudam-se as vontades" [times change, wills change] into "mudam-se os tempos, desnudam-se as vontades" (*UVF,* 38), which can be translated as "times change, wills are laid bare." He places this pun shortly after revealing that the name of the hotel in which Massimo Risi lodges has been changed from the Proletarian Hammer [Martelo Proletário] into the Hammer Jonas [Martelo Jonas (38)]. A Soviet symbol from the nation's Marxist era is recodified for the late-capitalist ideology that the national elite recently embraced. Ownership can now be explicitly claimed; party apparatchiks no longer need conceal their privileges in the language of class struggle. Beneath the changed symbol, the same character (Jonas) benefits at the expense of others. By drawing on Camões's verse, and effectively reversing its meaning for it is no longer that wills are changed but rather that they become more apparent, Couto highlights the extent to which little has altered, except rhetorical packaging, and draws on the greatest cultural icon of the Portuguese expansion, to suggest that this stasis of injustice and inequality dates back five centuries. But, unlike *Vinte e Zinco, O Último Voo do Flamingo* is not an attack on Portuguese colonialism. It is far more daring, suggesting that Mozambique has, as yet, been unable to overcome the mentality of the colonized. The blame is very much laid in the internal sphere; interference from outside is no longer an acceptable, all-encompassing excuse for the state of the nation, although the continued desire of forces outside Mozambique to meddle in the country's affairs has not helped to overcome that mentality.

Sulplício, the narrator's father, understands the mental block that impedes the nation's development. Couto complicates the characterization of Sulplício by sowing the seed of doubt regarding his paternity of the narrator. It is not clear that the man the narrator has called his father is biologically related to him. At the same time, the narrator reveals that he was never completely born from his mother: "part of me remained there, stuck in my mother's inside" [parte de mim ficou lá, grudada nas entranhas de minha mãe (47)]. Following Lacan, the realm of the mother may be read as a prelinguistic phase in a child's development, where the distance between symbols and referents has not yet been understood. In contrast, the paternal sphere represents language, and the symbolic order.[15] As the novel progresses, the narrator finally individuates from his mother, and comes to believe in his father's paternity: "He had fabricated me as his descendent. He had immortalized himself, even if it was an illusion. However, I accepted it. After all, everything is just belief" [Me fabricava descendente. Se eternizava, fosse em ilusão. Porém, eu aceitava. Afinal, tudo é crença (167)]. This acquired belief in his father's paternity, premised on a Coutian understanding of falsehood as a different perspective on truth, represents a national maturation on the part of the narrator. His acceptance of his father is an acceptance of the nation in which his father believes.

Initially a marginalized character, condemned for his service to the colonial administration and for his refusal to indulge corrupt government officials, Sulplício, along with Zeca Andorinho, the witchdoctor, will bring to justice those who have been responsible for Mozambique's decline and who wish to flood Tizangara. The image of the potential flood that threatens to destroy Tizangara is rich in cultural significance. Beyond the mythological and theological resonance of inundations as a divine castigation that allows for new beginnings, the flooding of 2000, like the conflict of the preceding years, was another magnet that drew the attention of the International Community, and the world media circus to Mozambique. The natural disaster legitimized international interference in the former colony, and provided powerful television pictures to be consumed, and lamented, and quickly forgotten in Western homes. The actions of Mozambicans in Couto's novel will stop the flooding before it starts, and allegorically represent a desire from the inside to limit the nation's consumption by the outside. Furthermore, justice must be done by Mozambicans without the assistance or interference of the representative of the International Community. It is part of the process of overcoming "the slave that lives within us" [o escravo que vive dentro de nós (141)]. Sulplício remembered the promises made by the revolutionaries, who later tortured him: "we were going to be the owners and those in charge" [íamos ficar donos e mandantes (141)] but, in fact, "we just changed the boss" [só mudámos de patrão (141)]. The current governors of Mozambique are "colonizers at heart" [colonos de dentro (168)].

Andorinho, another figure that the Frelimo regime had marginalized for his belief in animism, an anathema to scientific socialism, repeats Sulplício's critique of the postindependence nation, asserting that colonialism had done more than occupy the land, it had occupied the people's minds. Interference from outside had changed the mindset of a people, rendering them dependent and childlike, a process that could only be overcome from the inside, by the people taking responsibility for their own lives and nation, and holding their leaders to account. In essence, Couto's very astute and controversial message in this novel is that the time has come for the nation, like the narrator of the story, to grow up.

Finding an explanation for the phallus, in the context of national maturation, is an essential part of the process of individuating the nation. The severed penises in the national highways are discovered next to blue berets, the emblematic uniform of the United Nation's soldiers, the latest force of occupation. This force also triggered the arrival of prostitution in Tizangara, where "until recently, there had been no prostitute . . . There was not even a word in the local language for such a creature" [até recentemente não existira uma prostituta . . . Nem palavra havia na língua local para nomear tal criatura (30)]. In fact, Ana Deusqueira is also a product of the previous foreign order to dominate Mozambique. She was transferred to Tizangara as part of the vice-clearing operation [Operação Produção (172)] that exiled to the countryside people deemed to be undesirable by the Marxist regime. As such, she is a character that represents a fusion of inside and outside, rather like Andorinho and Sulplício who were placed on the margins of society during the Marxist era. Also like Andorinho and Sulplício, Ana Deusqueira, whose surname pleads "God be willing," is adept at pointing out truths to which mainstream characters are blind. Ultimately, she reveals that Jonas is responsible for the deaths, by trafficking in mine-replacement as a means of accentuating need to the outside.

Couto's characterization of prostitutes, such Juliana Bastiana, the blind prostitute in *Terra Sonâmbula,* and Ana Deusqueira, is positive for the simple reason that they challenge the false morality of Judeo-Christian and Marxist ideologies, while being marginalized by society. He lets them speak truths as a way of centering what is deemed to be the periphery, in a maneuver that is analogous to his centering of his nation's peripheral national identity. Throughout its history as a political entity, Mozambique has been a margin to a distant center: first as a colony to a weak metropolis, then as an experiment in Eurocentric Marxism, then as a recipient of donor largesse. In order to become a nation, that mentality of a colonized periphery must be vanquished.

The severed phalluses of foreign occupation offer a means of claiming a national identity. Couto castrates the totem of foreign power and masculine violence, and uses the marginalized prostitute to make it clear that the phallus, or symbolic order, under which the nation lives is from the outside. After Deusqueira inspects the severed object, she declares "with the greatest and absolute certainty" [com a máxima e absoluta certeza (32)] that the phallus "does not belong to any of the men from around here" [não pertence a nenhum dos homens daqui (32)]. This disclosure, which occurs near the beginning of the narrative, is a challenge to Tizangara (i.e. Mozambique) to find its phallus, to assume its own symbolic order. The resolution of the narrator's paternity issue, and his belief in his father, parallels the discovery by the Tizangara community that they are capable of solving their own problems, and of fashioning their own distinct identity. In this process, respect for traditions will be restored, traditions despised by Mássimo Risi, who declares on arrival "I don't want any blah-blah, I'm sick of folklore" [não quero blá-blá, estou cansado de folclore (33)]. The representative of the International Community initially subscribes to the occidental prejudice that misunderstands African traditions as an impediment to progress. Indeed, he will proceed to kill a praying mantis, despite an injunction against so doing laid down by local custom that views the insect as a reincarnation of ancestors. Yet he is the character who changes most as the story unfolds. While the Tizangarans merely assume identities that have been suppressed by interference from the outside, Mássimo Risi discovers that he has more affinities with the inhabitants of Tizangara than his Western superiority initially would allow him to countenance. As he falls in love with Temporina, another of Couto's characters like Navaia Caetano in *A Varanda do Frangipani* who defies the logic of time and is simultaneously young and old (a "velha-moça"), he becomes less concerned with promoting his own career and more interested in benefiting from the alternative perspectives on reality that his experience in Africa bestows on him. His final report to the UN secretary-general attests to his new understanding of a national logic that has to distance the nation from the outside if it is to become a nation inside:

> The painful task of reporting the total disappearance of a country in strange and inexplicable circumstances falls on me. I am aware that this report will lead to my resignation from the ranks of UN consultants, but I have no alternative except to relate the reality with which I am confronted: this entire, huge country has vanished, as if by a flash of magic. There is no territory, no people, even the ground has evaporated into an immense abyss.

> [Cumpre-me o doloroso dever de reportar o desaparecimento total de um país em estranhas e pouco explicáveis circunstâncias. Tenho consciência que o presente relatório conduzirá à minha demissão dos quadros de consultores da ONU, mas não tenho alternativa senão relatar a realidade com que confronto: que todo este imenso país se eclipsou, como que por golpe de magia. Não há território, nem gente, o próprio chão se evaporou num imenso abismo. (223)]

Once Mozambique ceases to be an arena for foreign intervention, and asserts its own responsibility for a national development that builds on the past, respecting traditions but not being a hostage to them, the prospects for progress toward the more equitable and free society promised but never delivered by the Frelimo revolutionaries will have improved.

O Último Voo do Flamingo marks a radical break in Couto's literary trajectory. His prior work has used the techniques of postmodernity—the disruptive interrogation of Grand Narratives, a refusal to accept binary orders between the written and the spoken, or any natural demarcation between genders—as a mechanism to fashion a national identity that fissures the dichotomies foisted on the Mozambican nation from outside, first by colonialism, and then by scientific socialism. But the new creed to seep into the nation, ultraneoliberalism, embodied, for Mozambique, in the UN and donor-agency presence, is, by its very nature, a facet of a postmodern world.

We should not be surprised, therefore, that Couto, whose concern is to help develop an independent Mozambican identity, should begin a profound critique of the agents of "Empire," the postmodern world order so deftly described by Hardt and Negri, as they repeat the pattern of foreign interference that has characterized the Mozambican polity since its inception. There is, of course, no contradiction in this change of tact since postmodernism, the founding premises of which are a critique of Grand Narratives, has become the Grand Narrative of the turn of the twenty-first century. As we shall conclude, the techniques of postmodernism, as employed by Mia Couto, do not proscribe the creation of a national identity.

Conclusion:
Reaching Postcolonial Maturity?

LAURA PADILHA, IN A PAPER FIRST PUBLISHED IN 1998, ASKS WHETHER POST-modernism is a concept that may legitimately be applied to literature from Africa and, more particularly, from lusophone Africa.[1] As a critic who situates herself in the field of postcolonial studies, Padilha concludes by refusing to answer directly the point she raises. Instead, she argues that postcolonialism "brings us answers" [nos traz respostas] while postmodernism "obliges us to question" [obriga-nos a indagações].[2] In many respects the two theoretical trends have fed into each other in recent years, and the debate concerning the increasingly blurred distinction between the two schools of thought has been well rehearsed.[3] Nevertheless, if we accept Padilha's differentiation, to what extent is Mia Couto's work postmodern rather than postcolonial?

Alfred López's characterization of the postcolonial as a particular ontological moment in the evolution of nations doubly haunted by a memory-in-advance and by the specters of a colonial past manifests itself in the texts of Mia Couto. López's argument that "the postcolonial is both a past and a future inhabited" echoes through Couto's work, as the Mozambican author forges an identity-in-progress for his newly born nation, which is constantly haunted by the colonial past and dreams of the future.[4] Couto's use of dreams as a mechanism to imagine a better tomorrow and, simultaneously, to come to terms with the horrors of a previous era, is a strategy founded on the temporal fusion of past with future identified in López's definition of the postcolonial. Coutian characters such as Navaia Caetano from *A Varanda do Frangipani,* and Temporina from *O Último Voo do Flamingo,* who fuse infancy with old age and, by extension the future with the past, reflect the postcolonial moment in which Mozambique finds itself. The various epistemological shifts we discussed in relation to the sea, a discourse on which Couto

170

draws frequently, also point to the postcolonial in his texts. The sea's oneiric primordiality dialogues with a maritime colonial resonance and thalassic neo-colonial overtones. At the same time, it metaphorizes the cleansing of history, and a national rebirth. As a restorative marker of the flow between the realms of the conscious and the unconscious, the sea, and water in general, also embody Couto's obsession with the dissolution of frontiers, a primarily postmodern concern.

Throughout this study, I have highlighted Couto's desire to overcome boundaries and to subvert demarcations. His radical interrogation of the possibility of a unitary truth, read alongside his questioning of binary difference as a legitimate structure for gender, positions him as a postmodernist who challenges the Western dichotomized orthodoxies on which colonialism and then scientific socialism were based. Furthermore, because of their marked postmodernism, Couto's texts help to limit the power of the ghost of Portuguese colonialism as Mozambique defines itself as a nation. Portugal, as Boaventura de Sousa Santos points out, had a very limited experience of the technological boom of modernity and next to no experience of Marxism during the forty years of the *Estado Novo*.[5] As such, Couto's literary recourse to postmodernism, which was in part born in resistance to Marxism, as well as a reaction to modernity, does not exclusively, or even substantively, draw on or react to Portugal's five-century occupation of Africa. Instead, it critiques European interference in Mozambique, and extends to cover the eurocentric Marxist model that oppressed the nation from 1975 under Samora Machel. Understanding that nuance is vital if we are to recuperate Mia Couto as a Mozambican nationalist, since postmodernism becomes a strategy that severs him from the Portuguese cultural heritage he so expertly manipulates. The vast body of criticism about Couto's work has tended to focus on his role in the renovation of Portuguese, drawing him into Fernando Pessoa's neocolonially charged language-as-homeland. By focusing on Couto's postmodernism rather than the postcolonial and linguistic aspects of his texts, I block the trend that, in essence, reads Couto's Mozambique solely as a reaction to Portugal's presence in Africa.

Of course, the specter of Portugal lingers through Couto's work. His literary allusions to Camões in *O Último Voo do Flamingo* and his explicit treatment of the dying days of colonialism in *Vinte e Zinco* are examples that testify to this. However, Mozambique is not merely the creation of Portuguese colonialism. It has a syncretistic culture that draws on a range of origins, and simultaneously can claim no origin. That, at least, is the message Couto emits as much through his mulatto characters as through his disavowal of orthographic atavism. There is no return to tradition in his work, only the constant reinterpretation of traditions that parallels his injunction to retell history and recreate biography as a means of nurturing life. The perpetual refashioning of history performed by the writer assaults one of the central premises of the Hegelian Grand Narrative that commands history to be fixed. Couto, as we have discussed, not only disavows Hegel, but also his binary counterpart, Plato. As he ruptures their competing tendencies, most acutely in his depiction of writing as a mutable life source, Couto concocts a new identity that is, by necessity, subject to constant change. That identity, grounded on a repudiation of the demarcations privileged by Western traditional culture, becomes paradoxically national because of the way in which Couto is read by the outside world. Taken to represent the culture he inscribes, Couto uses the abolition of frontiers to help to create the heritage of his nation. Throughout most of his literary trajectory, the nation's need for a border has ceded to a postmodern culture of fluidity. In this postmodern flux, Mozambique is written not just in response to Portugal, but also to the political models of Europe in general, and in Couto's more recent work, to an International Community that tries to set the agenda for the country it seeks to render dependent.

Throughout Mozambique's history, foreign political systems have been imposed on the nation, and generally served the needs of the people badly. The advent of "Empire," the latter stages of neoliberalism described by Hardt and Negri, has led Couto to begin to interrogate more aggressively and explicitly the manner in which Mozambique has repeatedly been defined from outside. As we have discussed, in his fourth novel *O Último Voo do Flamingo*, his message has qualitatively altered. It is no longer acceptable to write the nation in response to outside influences. Mozambique has to resolve itself from within. It is the first time Couto demarcates a boundary, distinguishing the internal from the external. While fluidity is still present, a frontier is enforced. As such, *O Último Voo do Flamingo* marks a shift away from postmodernism. Furthermore, his prescription for resolving the dilemmas facing the nation positions him for the first time as a writer who provides answers rather than raising questions. Following Padilha, this veers Couto toward the postcolonial and away from the postmodern. His evolution as a writer has reached the point where it is no longer sufficient just to ask questions. The time has come for answers to be furnished. As a relatively young man with a prolific gift for the written word, it remains to be seen what further solutions he will postcolonially suggest for Mozambique in the years to come.

Notes

I. INTRODUCTION

1. See, for example, Michael Hardt and Antonio Negri, *Empire* (Cambridge: Harvard University Press, 2000), 150; or Gerry Smyth, "The Politics of Hybridity: Some Problems with Crossing the Border," in *Comparing Postcolonial Literatures,* eds Ashok Bery and Patricia Murray (New York: St Martin's Press, 2000), 51; or David Harvey, *The Condition of Postmodernity: An Inquiry into the Origins of Cultural Change* (Oxford: Blackwell, 1989).

2. See Madan Sarup, *An Introductory Guide to Post-Structuralism and Postmodernism,* 2nd ed (Athens: University of Georgia Press, 1993), pp. 131–32. The term originated as early as the 1930s, and seems to have been coined by the Latin American critic Federico de Onís. It has been reinvented and reapplied ever since. See Theo L. D'Haen, "Magical Realism and Postmodernism: Decentering Privileged Centers," in *Magical Realism: Theory, History, Community,* eds Lois Parkinson Zamora and Wendy B. Faris (Durham, N.C.: Duke University Press, 1995), 193.

3. Jean-François Lyotard, *The Postmodern Condition: A Report on Knowledge,* trans. Geoff Bennington and Brian Massumi (Minneapolis: University of Minnesota Press, 1984), 5.

4. Jean-François Lyotard, *Postmodern Fables,* trans. Georges Van Den Abbeele (Minneapolis: University of Minnesota Press, 1997), 200.

5. Ibid., 200.

6. Smyth, "Politics, Hybridity," 43–44.

7. Hardt and Negri, *Empire,* 138.

8. Ibid., 198.

9. Ibid.

10. David Brookshaw, *Voices From Lusophone Borderlands: The Angolan Identities of António Agostinho Neto, Jorge Arrimar and José Eduardo Agualusa* (Maynooth: National University of Ireland, 2002), 28.

11. Frelimo is an acronym for the "Frente de Libertação de Moçambique" [The Front for the Liberation of Mozambique], which will be discussed in more detail throughout this study. I have opted to standardize its name as "Frelimo," although I am aware that prior to the movement's Third Congress in 1977, which declared the movement a Marxist-Leninist vanguard party, it was common practice to denote the movement using capitals. See Mark

F. Chingono, *The State, Violence and Development: The Political Economy of War in Mozambique, 1975-1992* (Aldershot, England: Avebury, 1996), 20.

12. Mia Couto, *Raiz de Orvalho* (Maputo: Cadernos Tempo, 1983), revised and republished by Caminho in 1999.

13. Fernanda Angius and Matteo Angius, *O Desanoitecer da Palavra: Estudo, Selecção de Textos Inéditos e Bibliografia Anotada de um Autor Moçambicano* (Praia/Mindelo: Centro Cultural Português, 1998), 20.

14. Mia Couto, *Vozes Anoitecidas* (Maputo: AEMO, 1986); Mia Couto, *Vozes Anoitecidas* (Lisboa: Caminho, 1987); Mia Couto, *Voices Made Night,* trans. David Brookshaw (Oxford: Heinemann, 1990).

15. Mia Couto, *Cada Homem É Uma Raça* (Lisboa: Caminho, 1990); Mia Couto, *Cronicando* (Lisboa: Caminho, 1991). The latter was first published in Mozambique in 1988 as an anthology, by Notícias, and drew together texts already published in the local newspaper of the same name. Translations of a selection of stories from both collections were published by David Brookshaw in 1994: Mia Couto, *Every Man Is a Race,* trans. David Brookshaw (Oxford: Heinemann, 1994). Salmon Rushdie, "The Empire Writes Back With a Vengeance," in *The Times,* 3 July 1982: 8. Homi Bhabha, "Signs Taken for Wonders: Questions of Ambivalence and Authority Under a Tree Outside Delhi, May 1817," *Critical Inquiry,* 12 (1985): 144–65.

16. For examples of this tendency see Rodrigues da Silva, "Mia Couto: Um Escritor Abensonhado," *Jornal de Letras, Artes e Ideias,* 17 August 1994: 14–16; Nelson Saúte, "A Fatalidade da Ficção Moçambicana," *Jornal de Letras, Artes e Ideias,* 14 August 1990: 8; Nelson Saúte, "A Reinvenção da Língua Portuguesa," *Vértice,* 55 (1993): 75–76.

17. Fernando Pessoa, *Portugal, Sebastianismo e Quinto Império,* ed. António Quadros (Mem Martins: Europa-América, 1986), 171–82.

18. Mia Couto, *Terra Sonâmbula* (Lisboa: Caminho, 1992).

19. Michel de Certeau, *The Practice of Everyday Life,* trans. Steven Rendall (Berkeley: University of California Press, 1984), 131–53.

20. Mia Couto, *Estórias Abensonhadas* (Lisboa: Caminho, 1996).

21. See Judith Butler, *Gender Trouble: Feminism and the Subversion of Identity* (New York: Routledge, 1990).

22. Mia Couto, *A Varanda do Frangipani* (Lisboa: Caminho, 1996); Mia Couto, *Under the Frangipani,* trans. David Brookshaw (London: Serpent's Tail, 2001).

23. Mia Couto, *Contos do Nascer da Terra* (Lisboa: Caminho, 1997); Mia Couto, *Na Berma de Nenhuma Estrada e Outros Contos* (Lisboa: Caminho, 2001); Mia Couto, *Mar Me Quer* (Lisboa: Expo, 1998) republished by Caminho in 2000.

24. Mia Couto, "O Gato e O Novelo," *Jornal de Letras, Artes, e Ideias,* 8 October 1997: 59.

25. Mia Couto, *Vinte e Zinco* (Lisboa: Caminho, 1999).

26. Hardt and Negri, *Empire,* 142.

27. Mia Couto, *O Último Voo do Flamingo* (Lisboa: Caminho, 2000).

28. Christy Cannon Lorgen, "Villagisation in Ethiopia, Mozambique, and Tanzania," *Social Dynamics,* 26.2 (2000): 171.

29. Benedict Anderson, *Imagined Communities: Reflections on the Origin and Spread of Nationalism,* revised ed (London: Verso, 1991), 134; Russell Hamilton, "Language and Literature in Portuguese-Writing Africa," *Portuguese Studies,* 2 (1986): 196.

30. One of Couto's favorite mantras, quoted by Patrick Chabal in *Vozes Moçambicanas: Literatura e Nacionalidade* (Lisboa: Vega, 1994), 291.

31. Patrick Chabal, "Mozambique," in *The Postcolonial Literature of Lusophone Africa*, ed. Patrick Chabal (Evanston, Il.: Northwestern University Press, 1996), 31.

32. Ibid., 31.

33. See their respective interviews in Chabal, *Vozes Moçambicanas*, 81; 164–65.

34. Francisco Noa, *A Escrita Infinita* (Maputo: Universidade Eduardo Mondlane, 1998), 83.

35. Nelson Saúte, ed., *As Mãos dos Pretos* (Lisboa: Dom Quixote, 2000).

36. Ungulani Ba Ka Khosa, *Ualalapi* (Maputo: Associação dos Escritores Moçambicanos, 1987). For an example of Momplé's literary evolution, compare her *Ninguém Matou Suhura* (Maputo, Associação dos Escritores Moçambicanos, 1988) with her later *Os Olhos da Cobra Verde* (Maputo, Associação dos Escritores Moçambicanos, 1997).

37. For a more detailed survey of Mozambican literature over its various periods see Russell Hamilton, *Voices from an Empire* (Minneapolis: University of Minnesota Press, 1975); Patrick Chabal, *The Postcolonial Literature of Lusophone Africa*; Orlando de Albuquerque and José Ferraz Motta, *História da Literatura em Moçambique* (Braga: APPACDM, 1998).

2. Li(v)es, Li(v)es, Li(v)es

1. Fernando Pessoa, "Autopsicografia," in Fernando Pessoa, *Antologia Poética*, ed. Isabel Pascoal (Lisboa: Ulisseia, 1992), 82.

2. David Brookshaw, "Old Realisms and New Realities: African Literature in Portuguese since Independence and the Postmodernist Fiction of Germano Almeida," in *Portuguese at Leeds: A Selection of Essays from the Annual Semana Portuguesa*, ed. Lisa Jesse (Leeds: Trinity and All Saints College, 1995), 116.

3. Ibid., 117.

4. Friedrich Nietzsche, *Thus Spoke Zarathustra: A Book for Everyone and No One*, trans. R. J. Hollingdale (Harmondsworth: Penguin, 1961), 41.

5. Ibid., 110.

6. Ibid., 48.

7. Ibid., 139.

8. Ibid., 111.

9. Friedrich Nietzsche, "Beyond Good and Evil," in *Basic Writings of Nietzsche*, trans. and ed. Walter Kaufmann (New York: Modern Library, 1966), 202.

10. See Pietro Deandrea, "History Never Walks Here, It Runs in Any Direction: Carnival and Magic in the Fiction of Kojo Laing and Mia Couto," in *Coterminous Worlds: Magical Realism and Contemporary Post-Colonial Literature in English*, eds Elsa Linguanti, Francesco Casotti, and Carmen Concilio (Amsterdam: Rodopi, 1999), 209–25.

11. Wendy B. Faris, "Scheherazade's Children: Magical Realism and Postmodern Fiction," in *Magical Realism: Theory, History, Community*, eds Lois Parkinson Zamora and Wendy B. Faris (Durham, N.C.: Duke University Press, 1995), 163.

12. D'Haen, "Magical Realism," 193.

13. Carmen Lucia Tindó Secco, "De Mares, Exílios, Fronteiras," in *La Lusophonie: Voies/ Voix Oceaniques*, eds Anne Quataert and Maria Fernanda Afonso (Lisboa: Lidel, 2000), 289.

14. Examples include Mary L. Daniel, "Mia Couto: Guimarães Rosa's Newest Literary Heir in Africa," in *Luso-Brazilian Review*, 32.1 (1995): 1–16; Pires Laranjeira, *Literaturas*

Africanas de Expressão Portuguesa (Lisboa: Universidade Aberta, 1995), 309–19; Fernanda Cavacas, *Mia Couto, Brincriação Vocabular* (Lisboa: Mar Além, 1999); Perpétua Gonçalves, "Situação Linguística em Moçambique: Opções de Escrita," in *Colóquio Letras,* 110–11 (1989): 88–93; Perpétua Gonçalves, "Linguagem Literária e Linguagem Corrente no Português de Moçambique," in *Estudos Portugueses e Africanos,* 33–34 (1999): 113–21.

15. See Homi Bhabha, *The Location of Culture* (London: Routledge, 1994).

16. *Popular Encyclopedia of Plants,* ed. Vernon H. Heywood (Cambridge: Cambridge University Press, 1982), 269.

17. Ana Mafalda Leite, "Os Temas do Mar em Algumas Narrativas Africanas de Língua Portuguesa: Insularidade e Viagem," in *La Lusophonie: Voies/Voix Oceaniques,* eds Anne Quataert and Maria Fernanda Afonso (Lisboa: Lidel, 2000), 252.

18. See particularly Fanon's argument that the black man from the Antilles becomes proportionately whiter in relation to his mastery of the French language. Frantz Fanon, *Black Skin, White Masks,* trans. Charles Lam Markmann (London: Pluto Press, 1986), pp. 17-40.

3. Righting Wrongs for Writing Rongas

1. João M. Cabrito, *Mozambique: A Tortuous Road to Democracy* (Basingstoke, England: Palgrave, 2000), 22–23; Malyn Newitt, *A History of Mozambique* (Bloomington: Indiana University Press, 1995), 292.

2. Cabrito, *Mozambique,* 24.

3. Malyn Newitt, "Mozambique," in Patrick Chabal, et al., *A History of Postcolonial Lusophone Africa* (Bloomington: Indiana University Press, 2002), 206.

4. Cabrito, *Mozambique,* 102.

5. See Teresa Cruz e Silva, *Igrejas Protestantes e Consciência Política no Sul de Moçambique: O Caso da Missão Suíça, 1930–1974* (Maputo, Promédia, 2001), 141–65.

6. Ibid., 144.

7. Francisco Rodolfo, "Guitonga, Alfabetização e Números," in *Savana,* 13 October 1995: 9.

8. Patrick Harries, "Discovering Languages: The Historical Origins of Standard Tsonga in Southern Africa," in *Language and Social History: Studies in South African Sociolinguistics,* ed. Rajend Mesthrie (Johannesburg: David Philip, 1995), 164–65.

9. Hegel dismisses Africa as having no history because, according to him, it did not have a writing system. See Georg Wilhelm Friedrich Hegel, *The Philosophy of History,* trans. J. Sibree, ed. C. J. Friedrich (New York: Dover Publications, 1956), 61–93.

10. See José de Alencar *Iracema,* ed. M. Cavalcanti Proença, 31st ed (Rio: Ediouro, 1995).

11. Chantal Zabus, *The African Palimpsest: Indigenization of Language in the West African Europhone Novel* (Atlanta: Rodopi, 1991), 127.

12. Mário de Andrade, *Macunaíma: O Herói Sem Nenhum Caráter,* ed. Telê Porto Ancona Lopez, 30th ed (Rio: Villa Rica, 1997).

13. See as an example of his criticism of his peers, his "Carta a Pero de Andrade Caminha" reproduced in António Ferreira, *Poemas Lusitanas,* ed. Marques Braga, 2 vols (Lisboa: Sá da Costa, 1940), 2:47–48.

14. For more on Herder's role in changing the nationalist mindset in Europe see F. M. Barnard, *Herder's Social and Political Thought: From Enlightenment to Nationalism* (Oxford: Clarendon, 1965).

15. António Vieira, *História do Futuro,* ed. Maria Leonor Carvalhão Buescu (Lisboa: INCM, 1982), 54.

16. Fernando Pessoa, *Livro do Desassossego por Bernardo Soares,* ed. Jacinto do Prado Coelho, 2 vols (Lisboa: Ática, 1982), 1:17.

17. Ngugi wa Thiong'o, *Decolonising the Mind: The Politics of Language in African Literature* (London: James Currey, 1986).

18. Sousa Jamba, "Out of Lusophone Africa: The Situation of Writers in Angola and Mozambique," in *Times Literary Supplement,* 17 October 1997: 29.

19. Pepetela, one of Angola's foremost contemporary writers, commented on Sousa Jamba's reception within Angola, in an interview given to me in April 2002.

20. Jorge Bacelar Gouveia, "Moçambique sem Português?" in *Expresso,* 7 May 1994: 24.

21. I am grateful to Ouissena Alidou of Rutgers University Department of Africana Studies for this information.

4. De-Scribing the Text

1. David Diringer was a historian of writing systems.

2. Jacques Derrida, *Of Grammatology,* trans. Gayatri Chakravorty Spivak (Baltimore: John Hopkins University Press, 1974).

3. Walter J. Ong, *The Presence of the Word: Some Prolegomena for Cultural and Religious History* (New Haven: Yale University Press, 1967), 19.

4. Niyi Afolabi, *The Golden Cage: Regeneration in Lusophone African Literature and Culture* (Trenton, N.J.: Africa World Press, 2001), 160.

5. Benedict Anderson, *Imagined Communities: Reflections on the Origin and Spread of Nationalism* (London: Verso, 1991).

6. Michel de Certeau, *The Practice of Everyday Life,* trans. Steven Rendall (Berkeley: University of California Press, 1984), 132.

7. Ibid., 134.

8. Maria Lúcia Lepecki, "Mia Couto, *Vozes Anoitecidas,* O Acordar," in *Sobreimpressões: Estudos de Literatura Portuguesa e Africana* (Lisboa: Caminho, 1988), 177.

9. Jared Banks, "Mia Couto," in *Postcolonial African Writers: A Bio-bibliographical Critical Source Book,* eds Pushpa Naidu Parekh and Siga Fatima Jagne (Westport, CT: Greenwood Press, 1998), 113.

10. David Brookshaw, "Mia Couto: A New Voice from Mozambique," in *Portuguese Studies,* 5 (1989): 188.

11. João Louro, "Mia Couto: O Mito e a Realidade," in *Jornal de Letras, Artes e Ideias,* 11 February 1992: 6.

12. Orlando de Albuquerque and José Ferraz Motta, "Esboço de uma História da Literatura em Moçambique no Século Vinte," in *Luso-Brazilian Review,* 33.2 (Winter 1996): 34.

13. Gerald M. Moser, "A Daring Initiative: Starting a Periodical in Wartime Mozambique," in *Luso-Brazilian Review,* 34.2 (Winter 1997): 123.

14. "Um país, no fundo, é sempre uma coisa muito pequena: compõe-se dum grupo de homens de letras, homens de Estado, homens de negócio, e homens de clube, que vivem de frequentar o centro da capital. O resto é paisagem, que mal se distingue da configuração das vilas ou dos vales," from "O Francesismo," in Eça de Queiroz, *Obras de Eça de Queiroz*, 3 vols (Porto: Lello e Irmão, 1966), 2:819.

15. José N. Ornelas, "Mia Couto no Contexto da Literatura Pós-colonial de Moçambique," in *Luso-Brazilian Review*, 33.2 (Winter 1996): 48.

16. Couto quoted by Nelson Saúte, "Mia Couto: Disparar Contra o Tempo," in *Jornal de Letras, Artes e Ideias*, 12 January 1993: 9.

17. Patrick Chabal, "Mozambique," 79.

18. Ibid., 80.

19. Ibid., 82.

20. Ibid., 100.

21. Ibid., 102.

22. Walter J. Ong, *Orality and Literacy: The Technologizing of the Word* (London: Methuen, 1982), 67.

23. Plato, *Phaedrus*, trans. and ed. C. J. Rowe (Warminster: Aris and Phillips, 1986).

24. Ezekiel 3.25–27; 2.8–3.3.

25. Henry Louis Gates, Jr, "Writing 'Race' and the Difference It Makes," in *"Race," Writing and Difference*, ed. Henry Louis Gates, Jr (Chicago: University of Chicago Press, 1986), 11.

26. Georg Wilhelm Friedrich Hegel, *The Philosophy of History*, trans. J. Sibree, ed. C. J. Friedrich (New York: Dover Publications, 1956), 61.

27. David Diringer, *The Alphabet: A Key to the History of Mankind*, 3rd ed, 2 vols (London: Hutchinson, 1968), 1:1.

28. Claude Lévi-Strauss, *A World on the Wane*, trans. John Russell (London: Hutchinson, 1961), 290–93.

29. For more on Pombal, see Kenneth Maxwell, *Pombal: Paradox of the Enlightenment* (Cambridge: Cambridge University Press, 1995).

30. Malyn Newitt, *A History of Mozambique* (Bloomington: Indiana University Press, 1995), 384.

31. Malyn Newitt, *Portugal in Africa* (London: Hurst, 1981), 101, 139.

32. Gilberto Matusse, *A Construção da Imagem de Moçambicanidade em José Craveirinha, Mia Couto e Ungulani Ba Ka Khosa* (Maputo: Universidade Eduardo Mondlane, 1998), 61.

33. David Diringer, *The Story of Aleph Beth* (London: Thomas Yoseloff, 1960), 19.

34. Plato, *Phaedrus*, 125, [275 d].

35. For more details on the election results see Malyn Newitt, "Mozambique," in Patrick Chabal, et al., *A History of Postcolonial Africa* (Bloomington: Indiana University Press, 2002), 231–33; and Moisés Venâncio, "Can Peace-keeping Be Said to Have Worked in Mozambique? Bye Bye Onumoz," in *War and Peace in Mozambique*, eds Stephen Chan and Moisés Venâncio (New York: St Martin's Press, 1998), 105–06.

36. Paradigmatic examples of letters being intimately linked to adultery in the Western canon include Choderlos de Laclos's eighteenth-century *Les Liaisons Dangereuses* (Paris: Garnier, 1858); Edgar Allan Poe's nineteenth-century "The Purloined Letter," in his *Selected Prose, Poetry, and Eureka*, ed. W. H. Auden (New York: Holt, Reinhart and Winston, 1950), 95–115; and Eça de Queirós's nineteenth-century *Primo Bazilio* (Lisboa: Livros do

Brasil [n.d.]). Female culpability for adultery is paradigmatically signaled in Western tradition in the New Testament account in John's Gospel of the adulterous woman whom Jesus forgives with the injunction not to sin again (John 8.7). Her male accomplice is absent from the tale, and no one suggests that he bears any of the responsibility for the sin committed.

37. Lévi-Strauss, *World on the Wane,* 292–93.

38. Brookshaw translates this as "recording the words of the elders" (*UF,* 18).

39. See Roland Barthes, *Writing Degree Zero,* trans. Annette Lavers and Colin Smith (New York: Hill and Wang, 1968).

40. Robert Gersony, *Summary of Mozambican Refugee Accounts of Principally Conflict-Related Experience in Mozambique* (Washington DC: Department of State, April 1988).

41. Renamo received 37.78 percent of the popular vote, compared to Frelimo's 44.33 percent.

42. Chabal, *Postcolonial Literature of Lusophone Africa,* 77.

43. Ibid., 84.

44. David Mestre, *Lusografias Crioulas* (Évora: Pendor, 1997), 99.

45. Afolabi, *Golden Cage,* 143; Matusse, *Construção da Imagem,* 177.

46. Lévi-Strauss, *World on the Wane,* 293.

47. Saúte, "Disparar Contra o Tempo," 9.

48. Laura Cavalcante Padilha, *Novos Pactos, Outras Ficções: Ensaios Sobre Literaturas Afro-luso-brasileiras* (Porto Alegre: EDIPUCRS, 2002), 120.

49. Couto claimed this in an e-mail interview that I conducted with him in 1997.

50. Fionna Gonçalves, "Narrative Strategies in Mia Couto's *Terra Sonâmbula,*" in *Current Writing: Text and Reception in Southern Africa,* 7.1 (1995): 62.

51. Ferdinand de Saussure, *Course in General Linguistics,* trans. Wade Baskin, eds Charles Bally, Albert Sechehaye, and Albert Reidlinger (London: Peter Owen, 1960), 23.

52. Lévi-Strauss, *World on the Wane,* 291.

53. Jacques Derrida, "Plato's Pharmacy," in his *Dissemination,* trans. Barbara Johnson (London: Athlone Press, 1982), 61–172.

5. SEAING INTO THE UNCONSCIOUS

1. See Mia Couto, "Poema da minha alienação," in *No Reino de Caliban: Antologia Panorâmica da Poesia Africana de Expressão Portuguesa,* ed. Manuel Ferreira, 3 vols (Lisboa: Plátano Editora, 1985), 3:471.

2. Plato, *Timaeus,* trans. and ed. John Warrington (London: Dent, 1965), 137.

3. For more on the various incarnations of this myth see Clyde W. Ford, *The Hero with an African Face: Mythic Wisdom of Traditional Africa* (New York: Bantam, 1999), 180.

4. Alain Corbin, *The Lure of the Sea: The Discovery of the Seaside in the Western World, 1750-1840,* trans. Jocelyn Phelps (Cambridge: Polity Press, 1994), 1–2.

5. Ibid., 2.

6. W. H. Auden, *The Enchafèd Flood or the Romantic Iconography of the Sea* (London: Faber and Faber, 1985), 17.

7. Clyde Ford, *Hero,* 180.

8. Alev Lytle Croutier, *Taking the Waters: Spirit, Art, Sensuality* (New York: Abbeville Press, 1992), 14–15.

9. Timothy Gantz, *Early Greek Myth: A Guide to Literary and Artistic Sources* (Baltimore: The John Hopkins University Press, 1993), 10–11.

10. Sigmund Freud, *The Interpretation of Dreams,* trans. James Strachey, ed. Angela Richards (London: Penguin Books, 1991), 525.

11. Otto Rank, *The Myth of the Birth of the Hero: A Psychological Interpretation of Mythology,* trans. F. Robbins and Smith Ely Jelliffe (New York: The Journal of Nervous and Mental Diseases Publishing Company, 1914), pp. 12-16.

12. Ibid., 18.

13. Miguel de Unamuno, *Por Tierras de Portugal y de España* (Madrid: Biblioteca Renacimiento, 1911), pp. 67-68.

14. Gaston Bachelard, *Water and Dreams: An Essay on the Imagination of Matter,* trans. Edith R. Farrell (Dallas: The Dallas Institute of Humanities and Culture, 1983), 131.

15. Ibid., 74.

16. Luís de Camões, *Os Lusíadas,* ed. A. J. da Costa Pimpão (Lisboa: Instituto de Alta Cultura, 1972), 1:18; 1:19; 1:42; 4:76; 5:24; 5:37; 5:73; 7:70; 9:51, 10:144.

17. Ibid., 10:145.

18. António Quadros [Frei Ioannes Garabatus], *As Quybyrycas* (Porto: Afrontamento, 1991).

19. See Rodrigues Lapa, "Prefácio," in *Quadros da História Trágico-marítima,* ed. Rodrigues Lapa, 3rd ed (Lisboa: Bertrand Irmãos Lda, 1956), ix.

20. Almeida Garrett, *Frei Luis de Sousa* (Porto: Livraria Civilização Editora, 1987).

21. José de Alencar, *Iracema,* ed. M. Cavalcanti Proença, 31st ed (Rio: Ediouro, 1995).

22. Agostinho Neto, "Náusea," in *Contistas Angolanos,* ed. Fernando Mourão (Lisboa: Casa dos Estudantes do Império, 1960), 57.

23. José Luandino Vieira, *Nós, Os do Makulusu,* 3rd ed (Luanda: União dos Escritores Angolanos, 1989), 130.

24. Fernando Pessoa, *Mensagem e Outros Poemas Afins,* ed. António Quadros, 2nd ed (Mem Martins: Europa-América, n.d.), 114.

25. Pepetela, *A Geração da Utopia* (Lisboa: Dom Quixote, 1992), 85.

26. Pepetela, *Mayombe,* 3rd ed (Lisboa: Edições 70, 1988), 140.

27. Manuel Rui, *Memória de Mar* (Lisboa: Edições 70, 1980).

28. Phyllis Peres, *Transculturation and Resistance in Lusophone African Narrative* (Gainesville: University of Florida Press, 1997), 96.

29. Manuel Rui, *Quem Me Dera Ser Onda,* 5th ed (Lisboa: Cotovia, 1991), 66.

30. Carmen L. T. Secco, "O Mar e Os Marulhos da Memória na Ficção do Angolano Manuel Rui," in *Estudos Portugueses e Africanos,* 2:1 (1993): 59.

31. Ungulani Ba Ka Khosa, *Orgia dos Loucos* (Maputo: Associação dos Escritores Moçambicanos, 1990), 93.

32. Peres, *Transculturation,* 95.

33. Virgílio de Lemos, *Eroticus Moçambicanus* (Rio de Janeiro: Nova Fronteira, 1999), 37.

34. Ibid., 69.

35. Mia Couto, "Prefácio: O Pouco do Tudo," in Virgílio de Lemos, *Eroticos Moçambicanos,* 15.

36. Mia Couto quoted by Rodrigues da Silva, "Mia Couto: Antes de Tudo, A Vida," in *Jornal de Letras, Artes e Ideias,* 7 August 1994: 8.

37. C. G. Jung, *The Basic Writings of C. G. Jung,* trans. R. F. C. Hull, ed. Violet S. de Laszlo (Princeton: Princeton University Press, 1990), 373.

38. C. G. Jung, *Dream Analysis: Part I, Notes of the Seminar Given in 1928–1930 by C. G. Jung,* ed. William McGuire (London: Routledge, 1995), 126.

39. Martine Rothblatt, *The Apartheid of Sex: A Manifesto for the Freedom of Gender* (London: Harper Collins, 1995), 5.

40. Sandor Ferenczi, *Thalassa: A Theory of Genitality,* trans. Henry Alden Bunker (London: Karnac Books, 1989), 99.

41. Sigmund Freud, "Symbolism in Dreams," in Sigmund Freud, *Introductory Lectures on Psychoanalysis,* trans. James Strachey, eds James Strachey and Angela Richards (Harmondsworth: Penguin Books, 1987), 194.

42. Chesca Long-Innes, "The Psychopathology of Post-colonial Mozambique: Mia Couto's *Voices Made Night,*" in *American Imago,* 55.1 (1998): 157.

43. Brenda Cooper, "Book Reviews: *Voices Made Night,*" in *Social Dynamics,* 16.2 (1990): 91–92.

44. Julian Quan, *Mozambique: A Cry for Peace* (Oxford: Oxfam, 1987), 10.

45. For more on the floods, see Frances Christie and Joseph Hanlon, *Mozambique and the Great Flood of 2000* (Bloomington: Indiana University Press, 2001).

46. Jeremiah 12.6.

47. Jacques Lacan links the acquisition of language to an understanding of prohibitions imposed by the paternal order. See his *The Four Fundamental Concepts of Psycho-Analysis,* trans. Alan Sheridan, ed. Jacques-Alain Miller (London: Penguin Books, 1994).

48. Bachelard, *Water and Dreams,* 12.

49. Ana Mafalda Leite, "Os Temas do Mar em Algumas Narrativas Africanas de Língua Portuguesa: Insularidades e Viagem," in *La Lusophonie: Voies/Voix Oceaniques,* eds Anne Quataert and Maria Fernanda Afonso (Lisboa: Lidel, 2000), 255.

50. See Frieda Fordham, *An Introduction to Jung's Psychology* (London: Penguin Books, 1990), 47–49.

51. Chabal, *Postcolonial Literature of Lusophone Africa,* 84.

52. Marie-Françoise Bidault, "La Voie du Destin de Kindzu dans *Terra Sonâmbula* de Mia Couto," in *La Lusophonie: Voies/Voix Oceaniques,* eds Anne Quataert and Maria Fernanda Afonso (Lisboa: Lidel, 2000), 246–47.

53. Freyre begins his lusotropical mythology in *O Mundo que o Português Criou* [The World the Portuguese Created] published by José Olympio in Rio de Janeiro in 1940. His subsequent work continues the theme of a lusotropical paradise based on an assumed assimilative tendency among the Portuguese.

54. See Gerald Bender, *Angola under the Portuguese: The Myth and the Reality* (Berkeley: University of California Press, 1978).

55. Maria Manuel Lisboa, "Colonial Crosswords: (In)voicing the Gap in Mia Couto," in *Postcolonial Perspectives on the Cultures of Latin America and Lusophone Africa,* ed. Robin Fiddian (Liverpool: Liverpool University Press, 2000), 195.

6. Playing Gam(et)es with Gender

1. Anabela Mota Ribeiro, "Entrevista: Mia Couto," *Diário de Notícias,* (Suplemento), 15 May 1999: 15.

2. Ann Laura Stoler, "Carnal Knowledge and Imperial Power: Gender, Race, and Morality in Colonial Asia," in *Gender at the Crossroads of Knowledge: Feminist Anthropology*

in the Postmodern Era, ed. Micaela di Leonardo (Berkeley: University of California Press, 1991), 51–101.

3. Mota Ribeiro, "Entrevista," 12.

4. Joan Wallach Scott, *Gender and the Politics of History,* revised ed (New York: Columbia University Press, 1999), 28-29.

5. Ibid., 30.

6. Mota Ribeiro, 15.

7. Robert J. Stoller, *Presentations of Gender* (New Haven: Yale University Press, 1985), 6.

8. Ibid., 6.

9. Terrell Carver, *Gender Is Not a Synonym for Women* (London: Rienner, 1996), 5.

10. Martine Rothblatt, *The Apartheid of Sex: A Manifesto for the Freedom of Gender* (London: Harper Collins, 1995), 9.

11. Ibid., 1.

12. Judith Shapiro, "Transsexualism: Reflections on the Persistence of Gender and the Mutability of Sex," in *Body Guards: The Cultural Politics of Gender Ambiguity,* eds Julia Epstein and Kristina Straub (London: Routledge, 1991), 260.

13. Judith Lorber, *Paradoxes of Gender* (New Haven: Yale University Press, 1994), 94.

14. Shapiro, "Transsexualism," 266–67.

15. Kate Bornstein, *Gender Outlaw: On Men, Women and the Rest of Us* (London: Routledge, 1994), 131.

16. Lorber, *Paradoxes of Gender,* 90.

17. Eça de Queirós, *The Sin of Father Amaro,* trans. Nan Flanagan (Manchester: Carcanet, 1994), 80.

18. Ibid., 95.

19. Ibid., 126.

20. Ibid., 98.

21. Ibid., 110.

22. Ibid., 21–22.

23. Ibid., 87.

24. Eça de Queirós, *O Crime do Padre Amaro* (Lisboa: Livros do Brasil [n.d.]), 153.

25. See for an example of his work, Elia Ciscato, "A Dimensão Cosmológico do Político," in *Autoridade e Poder Tradicional,* eds I. B. Lundlin and F. J. Machava (Maputo: Ministério de Administração Estatal, 1995), vol. I. See also for comments on his importance, Signe Arnfred, "Ancestral Spirits, Land and Food: Gendered Power and Land Tenure in Ribáuè, Nampula Province," in *Strategic Women, Gainful Men: Gender, Land and Natural Resources in Different Rural Contexts in Mozambique,* eds Rachel Waterhouse and Cari Vijfhuizen (Maputo: Universidade Eduardo Mondlane, 2001), 156.

26. Newitt, *History of Mozambique,* 217.

27. Thomas H. Henriksen, *Mozambique: A History* (London: Rex Collings, 1978), 74.

28. Allen Isaacman, *Mozambique, the Africanization of a European Institution: The Zambesi Prazos, 1750–1902* (Madison: University of Winsconsin Press, 1972), 47.

29. Newitt, *History of Mozambique,* 231.

30. Ibid., 230.

31. Shubi Lugemalila Ishemo discusses the succession customs of the Yao, in *The Lower Zambezi Basin in Mozambique: A Study in Economy and Society, 1850–1920* (Aldershot, England: Avebury, 1995), 58.

32. Newitt, *History of Mozambique,* 229.

33. Ibid., 298–316.

34. Genesis 2.23.

35. Genesis 1:27.

36. See Eve Kosofsky Sedgwick and Andrew Parker, eds, *Perfomativity and Performance* (New York: Routledge, 1995); Eve Kosofsky Sedgwick, *The Epistemology of the Closet* (Berkeley: University of California Press, 1990); Judith Butler, *Gender Trouble: Feminism and the Subversion of Identity* (New York: Routledge, 1990).

37. Judith Ochshorn, "Sumer: Gender, Gender Roles, Gender Role Reversals," in *Gender Reversals and Gender Cultures: Anthropological and Historical Perspectives,* ed. Sabrina Petra Ramet (London: Routledge, 1996), 52.

38. Sabrina Petra Ramet, "Gender Reversals and Gender Cultures: An Introduction," in *Gender Reversals and Gender Cultures,* 4.

39. Nicole Loraux, *The Experiences of Tiresias: The Feminine and the Greek Man,* trans. Paula Wissing (Princeton: Princeton University Press, 1995), 8.

40. Ibid., 8.

41. Lorber, 21.

42. Bakhtin, M. M., *The Dialogic Imagination: Four Essays,* trans. Caryl Emerson and Michael Holquist, ed. Michael Holquist (Austin: University of Texas Press, 1981), 58.

43. Ibid., 55.

44. Julia Cream, "Re-Solving Riddles: The Sexed Body," in *Mapping Desire: Geographies of Sexualities,* eds, David Bell and Gill Valentine (London: Routledge, 1995), 38.

45. Marjorie Garber, *Vested Interests: Cross-Dressing and Cultural Anxiety* (London: Routledge, 1992), 131.

46. Robert J. Stoller, *Sex and Gender: On the Development of Masculinity and Femininity* (London: Hogarth Press, 1968), 177.

47. David Brez Carlisle, *Human Sex Change and Sex Reversal: Transvestism and Transsexualism* (Lewiston, Wales: Edwin Mellen Press, 1998), 57.

48. Garber, *Vested Interests,* 133.

49. A term of abuse applied to Indians in Mozambique.

50. G. W. F. Hegel, *The Phenomenology of Mind,* trans. J. B. Baillie, 2 vols (London: Swan Sonnenschein, 1910), 1:175–88.

51. Jung, *Basic Writings,* 163.

52. Bhabha, "Signs Taken for Wonders."

53. Scott, *Gender,* 45.

54. "Ninguém é escritor geneticamente. Ninguém adquire este estatuto definitivamente. Então prefiro o verbo estar ao verbo ser"; quoted in Silva, "Um Escritor Abensonhado," 16.

55. In 1994–95, when I worked for UNICEF in Mozambique, the disparity between the number of boys sent to school and the number of girls was one of the major concerns of the UN organization.

7. FINDING THE NATION'S PHALLUS

1. Chris Alden asserts that the total cost of ONUMOZ's presence in Mozambique was USD 503 million, while Richard Synge claims the cost was over USD 700 million. In either case, the expense was considerable and there was criticism at the time about the large

size of the operation. Synge uses the analogy of a "sledgehammer employed to crack a relatively small nut." See Chris Alden, *Mozambique and the Construction of the New African State* (New York: Palgrave, 2001), 65 and Richard Synge *Mozambique: UN Peacekeeping in Action, 1992–1994* (Washington DC: United States Institute of Peace Press, 1997), 12. I capitalize the term "International Community" because I consider it to be a proper noun pointing to a group of Western interests.

2. Thatcher quoted in Alex Vines, *Renamo: Terrorism in Mozambique* (London: James Currey, 1991), 1.

3. Synge, *Mozambique,* 60.

4. See Hardt and Negri, *Empire.*

5. Margaret Hall and Tom Young, *Confronting Leviathan: Mozambique since Independence* (Athens: Ohio University Press, 1997), 225.

6. Synge, *Mozambique,* 145.

7. Ibid., 148.

8. Ibid., 94.

9. Stephen Chan and Moisés Venâncio, *War and Peace in Mozambique* (New York: St Martin's Press, 1998), 21.

10. For more on the involvement of Sant'Egidio, see Cameron Hume, *Ending Mozambique's War: The Role of Mediation and Good Offices* (Washington DC: United States Institute of Peace Press, 1994).

11. Synge, *Mozambique,* 33.

12. Ibid., 153.

13. See Hall and Young, *Confronting Leviathan,* 232, and Alden, *Mozambique,* 50.

14. Patrick Chabal and Jean-Pascal Daloz, *Africa Works: Disorder as Political Instrument* (Bloomington: Indiana University Press, 1999), 22–23.

15. See Jacques Lacan, *Écrits: A Selection,* trans. Alan Sheridon (New York: Norton, 1977).

CONCLUSION: REACHING POSTCOLONIAL MATURITY?

1. Laura Padilha's paper, "Literaturas Africanas e Pós-modernismo: Uma Indagação," was first published in the acts of the fifth congress of the International Lusitanists Association, and is republished in her *Novos Pactos, Outras Ficções: Ensaios Sobre Literaturas Afro-luso-brasileiras* (Porto Alegre: EDIPUCRS, 2002), 317–29.

2. Ibid., 329.

3. See the articles in part 4 "Postmodernism and Post-colonialism" in Bill Ashcroft, Gareth Griffiths, and Helen Tiffin, *The Post-colonial Studies Reader* (New York: Routledge, 1995), 117–50.

4. Alfred J. López, *Posts and Pasts: A Theory of Postcolonialism* (Albany: State University of New York Press, 2001), 67.

5. See Boaventura de Sousa Santos, *Pela Mão de Alice: O Social e o Político na Pós-modernidade* (Porto: Afrontamento, 1994).

Bibliography

Afolabi, Niyi. *The Golden Cage: Regeneration in Lusophone African Literature and Culture.* Trenton, N.J.: Africa World Press, 2001.

"Africa em Português." *Colóquio Letras* 132–33 (1994): 286.

African European Institute. *1990 Constitution of Mozambique/Constituição de Moçambique.* Amsterdam: African European Institute, 1990.

Ager, Dennis. *"Francophonie" in the 1990s: Problems and Opportunities.* Clevedon, England: Multilingual Matters, 1996.

Agualusa, José Eduardo. "Literatura Moçambicana: Mia Couto, *Estórias Abensonhadas.*" *Colóquio Letras* 135/136 (1995): 279.

———. "So many Africas!" Translated by Chris Whitehouse. *European Bookseller* 22 (1997): 68–72.

Albuquerque, Orlando de, and José Ferraz Motta. "Esboço de uma História da Literatura em Moçambique no Século Vinte." *Luso-Brazilian Review* 33.2 (Winter 1996): 27–36.

———. *História da Literatura em Moçambique.* Braga: APPACDM, 1998.

Alden, Chris. *Mozambique and the Construction of the New African State.* New York: Palgrave, 2001.

Alencar, José de. *Iracema.* Edited by M. Cavalcanti Proença. 31st ed. Rio: Ediouro, 1995.

Almeida Garrett. *Frei Luis de Sousa.* Porto: Livraria Civilização Editora, 1987.

———. *Um Auto de Gil Vicente.* Edited by Francisco Lyon de Castro. 2nd ed. Mem Martins: Publicações Europa-América, 1995.

———. *Viagens na Minha Terra.* 2nd ed. Lisboa: Editorial Estampa, 1992.

Anderson, Benedict. *Imagined Communities: Reflections on the Origin and Spread of Nationalism.* London: Verso, 1991.

Andersson, Hilary. *Mozambique: A War against the People.* New York: St Martin's Press, 1972.

Andrade, Mário de. *Macunaíma: O Herói Sem Nenhum Caráter.* Edited by Telê Porto Ancona Lopez. 30th ed. Rio: Villa Rica, 1997.

Angius, Fernanda, and Matteo Angius. *O Desanoitecer da Palavra: Estudo, Selecção de Textos Inéditos e Bibliografia Anotada de um Autor Moçambicano.* Praia Mindelo: Centro Cultural Português, 1998.

185

Appiah, Kwame Anthony. *In my Father's House: Africa in the Philosophy of Culture.* London: Methuen, 1992.

Arnfred, Signe. "Ancestral Spirits, Land and Food: Gendered Power and Land Tenure in Ribáuè, Nampula Province." In *Strategic Women, Gainful Men: Gender, Land and Natural Resources in Different Rural Contexts in Mozambique,* edited by Rachel Waterhouse and Cari Vijfhuizen, 153–78. Maputo: Universidade Eduardo Mondlane, 2001.

Ashcroft, Bill, Gareth Griffiths, and Helen Tiffin. *The Empire Writes Back: Theory and Practice in Post-Colonial Literatures.* London: Routledge, 1989.

———. *The Post-Colonial Studies Reader.* New York: Routledge, 1995.

Auden, W. H. *The Enchafèd Flood, or the Romantic Iconography of the Sea.* London: Faber and Faber, 1985.

Ba Ka Khosa, Ungulani. *Orgia dos Loucos.* Maputo: Associação dos Escritores Moçambicanos, 1990.

———. *Ualalapi.* Maputo: Associação dos Escritores Moçambicanos, 1987.

Bachelard, Gaston. *Water and Dreams: An Essay on the Imagination of Matter.* Translated by Edith R. Farrell. Dallas: The Dallas Institute of Humanities and Culture, 1983.

Bakhtin, M. M. *The Dialogic Imagination: Four Essays.* Translated by Caryl Emerson and Michael Holquist. Edited by Michael Holquist. Austin: University of Texas Press, 1981.

Banks, Jared. "Mia Couto." In *Postcolonial African Writers: A Bio-bibliographical Critical Source Book,* edited by Pushpa Naidu Parekh and Siga Fatima Jagne, 111–17. Westport, CT: Greenwood Press, 1998.

Barnard, F. M. *Herder's Social and Political Thought: From Enlightenment to Nationalism.* Oxford: Clarendon Press, 1965.

Barthes, Roland. *Writing Degree Zero.* Translated by Annette Lavers and Colin Smith. New York: Hill and Wang, 1968.

Bell, David, and Gill Valentine. *Mapping Desire: Geographies of Sexualities.* London: Routledge, 1995.

Bender, Gerald. *Angola under the Portuguese: The Myth and the Reality.* Berkeley: University of California Press, 1978.

Bery, Ashok, and Patricia Murray. *Comparing Postcolonial Literatures.* New York: St Martin's Press, 2000.

Bhabha, Homi. *The Location of Culture.* London: Routledge, 1994.

———. "Signs Taken for Wonders: Questions of Ambivalence and Authority Under a Tree Outside Delhi, May 1817." *Critical Inquiry* 12 (1985): 144–65.

Bidault, Marie-Françoise. "La Voie du Destin de Kindzu dans *Terra Sonâmbula* de Mia Couto." In *La Lusophonie: Voies/Voix Oceaniques,* edited by Anne Quataert and Maria Fernanda Afonso, 245–50. Lisboa: Lidel, 2000.

Birmingham, David. *Frontline Nationalism in Angola and Mozambique.* London: James Currey, 1992.

Bornstein, Kate. *Gender Outlaw: On Men, Women and the Rest of Us.* London: Routledge, 1994.

Boxer, C. R. *A Great Luso-Brazilian Figure: Padre António Vieira, S. J., 1608–1697.* London: The Hispanic & Luso-Brazilian Councils, 1957.

———. *Race Relations in the Portuguese Colonial Empire: 1415–1825*. Oxford: Clarendon, 1963.

Brookshaw, David. "Four Mozambican Writers." *Wasafiri* 10 (1989): 2–4.

———. "Mia Couto," In *African Writers*, edited by C. Brian Cox, 2 vols, 1:185–97. New York: Charles Scribner, 1997.

———. "Mia Couto: A New Voice from Mozambique." *Portuguese Studies* 5 (1989): 188–89.

———. "Old Realisms and New Realities: African Literature in Portuguese since Independence and the Postmodernist Fiction of Germano Almeida." In *Portuguese at Leeds: A Selection of Essays from the Annual Semana Portuguesa*, edited by Lisa Jesse, 115–33. Leeds: Trinity and All Saints College, 1995.

———. *Voices from Lusophone Borderlands: The Angolan Identities of António Agostinho Neto, Jorge Arrimar and José Eduardo Agualusa*. Maynooth: National University of Ireland, 2002.

Burns, E. Bradford. *Nationalism in Brazil: A Historical Survey*. New York: Praeger, 1968.

Butler, Judith. *Gender Trouble: Feminism and the Subversion of Identity*. New York: Routledge, 1990.

Cabral, Amílcar. *Análise de Alguns Tipos de Resistência*. 2nd ed. Lisboa: Seara Nova, 1975.

Cabral, Filomena. "Xipalapala: Cada Homem É uma Raça." *Notícias* (6 July 1992): 7.

Cabrito, João M. *Mozambique: A Tortuous Road to Democracy*. Basingstoke, England: Palgrave, 2000.

Caetano, Marcello. *Progresso em Paz*. Lisboa: Verbo, 1972.

Camões, Luís de. *Os Lusíadas*. Edited by A. J. da Costa Pimpão. Lisboa: Instituto de Alta Cultura, 1972.

Cann, John P. *Counterinsurgency in Africa: The Portuguese Way of War, 1961–1974*. Westport, CT: Greenwood Press, 1997.

Cannon Lorgen, Christy. "Villagisation in Ethiopia, Mozambique, and Tanzania." *Social Dynamics* 26.2 (2000): 171–98.

Carlisle, David Brez. *Human Sex Change and Sex Reversal: Transvestism and Transsexualism*. Lewiston, Wales: Edwin Mellen Press, 1998.

Carneiro, Roberto. "A Língua É um Dom Gratuito." *Jornal de Letras, Artes e Ideias* (7 January 1992): 18.

Carver, Terrell. *Gender Is Not a Synonym for Women*. London: Rienner, 1996.

Cavacas, Fernanda. *Mia Couto, Brincriação Vocabular*. Lisboa: Mar Além, 1999.

Certeau, Michel de. *The Practice of Everyday Life*. Translated by Steven Rendall. Berkeley: University of California Press, 1984.

Chabal, Patrick. *Vozes Moçambicanas: Literatura e Nacionalidade*. Lisboa: Vega, 1994.

Chabal, Patrick, and Jean-Pascal Daloz. *Africa Works: Disorder as Political Instrument*. Bloomington: Indiana University Press, 1999.

Chabal, Patrick, et al. *A History of Postcolonial Lusophone Africa*. Bloomington: Indiana University Press, 2002.

———. *The Postcolonial Literature of Lusophone Africa*. Evanston, IL: Northwestern University Press, 1996.

Chagas, Pinheiro. "Literatura Brasileira: José de Alencar." In José de Alencar. *Iracema, Lenda do Ceará, e Cartas sobre "A Confederação dos Tamaios,"* 137–43. Coimbra: Livraria Almedina, 1994.

Chan, Stephen, and Moisés Venâncio, eds. *War and Peace in Mozambique.* New York: St. Martin's Press, 1998.

Chilcote, Ronald H. *Emerging Nationalism in Portuguese Africa: Documents.* Stanford, CA: Hoover Institution Press, 1972.

Chingono, Mark F. *The State, Violence and Development: The Political Economy of War in Mozambique, 1975–1992.* Aldershot, England: Avebury, 1996.

Christie, Frances, and Joseph Hanlon. *Mozambique and the Great Flood of 2000.* Bloomington: Indiana University Press, 2001.

Cidade, Hernâni. *Padre António Vieira.* Lisboa: Arcádia, [n.d.].

Ciscato, Elia. "A Dimensão Cosmológico do Político." In *Autoridade e Poder Tradicional,* edited by I. B. Lundlin and F. J. Machava, vol 1. Maputo: Ministério de Administração Estatal, 1995.

Cohen, Thomas M. *The Fire of Tongues: António Vieira and the Missionary Church in Brazil and Portugal.* Stanford, CA: Stanford University Press, 1998.

Coleman, Vernon. *Crossdressing: The Path to Male Emancipation.* Devon: European Medical Journal, 1996.

Commonwealth Secretariat. *Capacity-Building in Mozambique: The Commonwealth Contribution.* London: Commonwealth Fund for Technical Co-operation, 1991.

Cooper, Brenda. "Book Reviews: *Voices Made Night." Social Dynamics* 16.2 (1990): 91–95.

Corbin, Alain. *The Lure of the Sea: The Discovery of the Seaside in the Western World, 1750–1840.* Translated by Jocelyn Phelps. Cambridge: Polity Press, 1994.

Courteau, Joanna. "D'*A varanda do frangipani* à morte dos heterônimos." *Lusorama* 50 (June 2002): 73–84.

Couto, Mia. *A Varanda do Frangipani.* Lisboa: Caminho, 1996.

———. "Auto-Retratos: O Gato e o Novelo." *Jornal de Letras, Artes e Ideias* (8 October 1997): 59.

———. *Cada Homem É uma Raça: Estórias.* Lisboa: Caminho, 1990.

———. *Contos do Nascer da Terra.* Lisboa: Caminho, 1997.

———. *Cronicando.* Maputo: Notícias, 1988.

———. *Cronicando.* Lisboa: Caminho, 1991.

———. "Escrevoar." In *Poemas da Ciência de Voar e da Engenharia de Ser Ave,* by Eduardo White, 9–10. Lisboa: Caminho, 1992.

———. *Estórias Abensonhadas: Contos.* Lisboa: Caminho, 1994.

———. *Every Man Is a Race.* Translated by David Brookshaw. Oxford: Heinemann, 1994.

———. "From *A Sleepwalking Land.*" Translated by David Brookshaw. *The Literary Review* 38.4 (1995): 593–603.

———. "Gerar Futuro e Não Gerir Saudade." *Jornal de Letras, Artes e Ideias* (22 June 1994): xxiv.

———. *Mar Me Quer.* Lisboa: Expo 98, 1998.

———. *Mar Me Quer.* Lisboa: Caminho, 2000.

———. *Na Berma de Nenhuma Estrada e Outros Contos.* Lisboa: Caminho, 2001.

———. "O Perigo Existe." *Jornal de Letras, Artes e Ideias* (27 July 1993): 5.

———. *O Último Voo do Flamingo.* Lisboa: Caminho, 2000.

———. "Poema da Minha Alienação." In *No Reino de Caliban: Antologia Panorâmica da Poesia Africana de Expressão Portuguesa,* edited by Manuel Ferreira, 3 vols, 3:471. Lisboa: Plátano Editora, 1985.

———. *Raiz de Orvalho.* Maputo: Cadernos Tempo, 1983.

———. *Raiz de Orvalho e Outros Poemas.* Lisboa: Caminho, 1999.

———. *Terra Sonâmbula.* Lisboa: Caminho, 1992.

———. "Um Escritor-Escola." *Jornal de Letras, Artes e Ideias* (19 July 1995): 15.

———. *Under the Frangipani.* Translated by David Brookshaw. London: Serpent's Tail, 2001.

———. *Vinte e Zinco.* Lisboa: Caminho, 1999.

———. *Voices Made Night.* Translated by David Brookshaw. Oxford: Heinemann, 1990.

———. *Vozes Anoitecidas.* Maputo: AEMO, 1986.

———. *Vozes Anoitecidas: Contos.* Lisboa: Caminho, 1987.

Cranshaw, Steve. "Nigeria in the Dock: Welcome to 53rd Member of the Club." *Independent* (13 November 1995): 10.

Craveirinha, José. "O Português Pode Ser Substituído numa Geração." *Jornal de Letras, Artes e Ideias* (27 July 1993): 5.

Cream, Julia. "Re-Solving Riddles: The Sexed Body." In *Mapping Desire: Geographies of Sexualities,* edited by David Bell and Gill Valentine, 31–40. London: Routledge, 1995.

Cristóvão, Fernando. *Notícias e Problemas da Pátria da Língua.* 2nd ed. Lisboa: Instituto de Cultura e Língua Portuguesa, 1987.

Croutier, Alev Lytle. *Taking the Waters: Spirit, Art, Sensuality.* New York: Abbeville Press, 1992.

Crowley, Tony. "Bakhtin and the History of Language." In *Bakhtin and Cultural Theory,* edited by Ken Hirschkop and David Shepherd, 68–90. Manchester: Manchester University Press, 1989.

Cruz e Silva, Teresa. *Igrejas Protestantes e Consciência Política no Sul de Moçambique: O Caso da Missão Suíça, 1930–1974.* Maputo, Promédia, 2001.

Daniel, Mary L. "Mia Couto: Guimarães Rosa's Newest Literary Heir in Africa." *Luso-Brazilian Review* 32.1 (Summer 1995): 1–16.

Deandrea, Pietro. "History Never Walks Here, It Runs in Any Direction: Carnival and Magic in the Fiction of Kojo Laing and Mia Couto." In *Coterminous Worlds: Magical Realism and Contemporary Post-Colonial Literature in English,* edited by Elsa Linguanti, Francesco Casotti, and Carmen Concilio, 209–25. Amsterdam: Rodopi, 1999.

Deleuze, Gilles. *Nietzsche et la Philosophie.* Paris: Presses Universitaires de France, 1962.

Derrida, Jacques. *Dissemination.* Translated by Barbara Johnson. London: The Athlone Press, 1981.

———. *Margins of Philosophy.* Translated by Alan Bass. Brighton: The Harvester Press, 1982.

————. *Of Grammatology.* Translated by Gayatri Chakravorty Spivak. Baltimore: The John Hopkins University Press, 1974

————. *The Ear of the Other: Otobiography, Transference, Translation: Texts and Discussions with Jacques Derrida.* Translated by Peggy Kamuf. Edited by Christie McDonald. Lincoln: University of Nebraska Press, 1988.

D'Haen, Theo L. "Magical Realism and Postmodernism: Decentering Privileged Centers." In *Magical Realism: Theory, History, Community,* edited by Lois Parkinson Zamora and Wendy B. Faris, 191–208. Durham, N.C.: Duke University Press, 1995.

Diop, Cheikh Anta. *The African Origin of Civilization: Myth or Reality.* Translated and edited by Mercer Cook. Chicago: Lawrence Hill Books, 1974.

Diringer, David. *The Alphabet: A Key to the History of Mankind.* 3rd ed. 2 vols. London: Hutchinson, 1968.

————. *The Story of Aleph Beth.* London: Thomas Yoseloff, 1960.

————. *Writing.* London: Thames and Hudson, 1962.

Duffy, James. *Portugal in Africa.* Harmondsworth: Penguin Books, 1962.

————. *Portuguese Africa.* Cambridge: Harvard University Press, 1959.

Eça de Queirós. *O Crime do Padre Amaro.* Lisboa: Livros do Brasil, [n.d.].

————. "O Francesismo." In *Obras de Eça de Queiroz.* 3 vols. Porto: Lello e Irmão, 1966: 2:813–27.

————. *Primo Bazilio.* Lisboa: Livros do Brasil, [n.d.].

————. *The Sin of Father Amaro.* Translated by Nan Flanagan. Manchester: Carcanet, 1994.

Epstein, Julia, and Kristina Straub, eds. *Body Guards: The Cultural Politics of Gender Ambiguity.* London: Routledge, 1991.

Fanon, Frantz. *Black Skin, White Masks.* Translated by Charles Lam Markmann. London: Pluto Press, 1986.

————. *Studies in a Dying Colonialism.* Translated by Haakon Chevalier. London: Earthscan Publications, 1989.

Faris, Wendy B. "Scheherazade's Children: Magical Realism and Postmodern Fiction." In *Magical Realism: Theory, History, Community,* edited by Lois Parkinson Zamora and Wendy B. Faris, 163–90. Durham, N.C.: Duke University Press, 1995.

Ferenczi, Sandor. *Thalassa: A Theory of Genitality.* Translated by Henry Alden Bunker. London: Karnac Books, 1989.

Ferreira, António. *Poemas Lusitanos.* Edited by Marques Braga. 2 vols. Lisboa: Livraria Sá da Costa, 1940.

Ferreira, Eduardo de Sousa. *Portuguese Colonialism in Africa: The End of an Era.* Paris: UNESCO, 1974.

Ferreira, Manuel. "Ficção: Mia Couto, *Vozes Anoitecidas." Colóquio Letras* 101 (1988): 132–33.

————. *Que Futuro para a Língua Portuguesa em África: Uma Perspectiva Sociocultural.* Linda-a-Velha: ALAC, 1988.

————, ed. *No Reino de Caliban: Antologia Panorâmica da Poesia Africana de Expressão Portuguesa.* 3 vols. Lisboa: Plátano Editora, 1985.

Ferro, António. *Salazar: Portugal and Her Leader.* Translated by H. de Barros Gomes and John Gibbons. London: Faber and Faber, 1938.

Fiddian, Robin. *Postcolonial Perspectives on the Cultures of Latin America and Lusophone Africa.* Liverpool: Liverpool University Press, 2000.

Filho, Luís Viana. *A Vida de José de Alencar.* Rio: Livraria José Olympio, 1979.

Ford, Clyde W. *The Hero with an African Face: Mythic Wisdom of Traditional Africa.* New York: Bantam, 1999.

Fordham, Frieda. *An Introduction to Jung's Psychology.* London: Penguin Books, 1990.

Foucault, Michel. *The Order of Things: An Archaeology of the Human Sciences.* [n. translator]. London: Tavistock, 1970.

Freud, Sigmund. *Introductory Lectures on Psychoanalysis.* Translated by James Strachey. Edited by James Strachey and Angela Richards. Harmondsworth: Penguin Books, 1987.

————. *The Interpretation of Dreams.* Translated by James Strachey. Edited by Angela Richards. London: Penguin Books, 1991.

Freyre, Gilberto. *O Luso e o Trópico: Sugestões em Torno dos Métodos Portugueses de Integração de Povos Autóctones e de Culturas Diferentes da Europeia num Complexo Novo de Civilização, o Luso-Tropical.* Lisboa: Comissão Executiva das Comemorações do V Centenário da Morte do Infante D. Henrique, 1961.

————. *O Mundo que o Português Criou.* Rio: José Olympio, 1940.

Fry, Peter. *Cultures of Difference, Colonial Legacies in Zimbabwe and Mozambique: First Smuts Lecture to Mark the Entry of Mozambique into the Commonwealth.* Cambridge: African Studies Centre, 1998.

Fryer, Peter, and Patricia McGowan Pinheiro. *Oldest Ally: A Portrait of Salazar's Portugal.* London: Dennis Dobson, 1961.

Gantz, Timothy. *Early Greek Myth: A Guide to Literary and Artistic Sources.* Baltimore: The John Hopkins University Press, 1993.

Garber, Marjorie. *Vested Interests: Cross-Dressing and Cultural Anxiety.* London: Routledge, 1992.

Gates, Jr., Henry Louis. "Writing 'Race' and the Difference It Makes." In *"Race," Writing and Difference,* edited by Henry Louis Gates, Jr., 1–20. Chicago: University of Chicago Press, 1986.

Gersony, Robert. *Summary of Mozambican Refugee Accounts of Principally Conflict-Related Experience in Mozambique.* Washington DC: Department of State, April 1988.

Gonçalves, Fionna. "Narrative Strategies in Mia Couto's *Terra Sonâmbula." Current Writing: Text and Reception in Southern Africa* 7.1 (1995): 60–69.

Gonçalves, Perpétua. "Linguagem Literária e Linguagem Corrente no Português de Moçambique." *Estudos Portugueses e Africanos* 33–34 (1999): 113–21.

————. *Português de Moçambique: Uma Variedade em Formação.* Maputo: Universidade Eduardo Mondlane, 1996.

————. "Situação Linguística em Moçambique: Opções de Escrita." *Colóquio Letras* 110–11 (1989): 88–93.

Gouveia, Jorge Bacelar. "Moçambique Sem Português?" *Expresso* (7 May 1994): 24.

Hahn, Walter F., and Alvin J. Cottrell. *Soviet Shadow over Africa.* Miami: University of Miami, 1976.

Hall, Margaret, and Tom Young. *Confronting Leviathan: Mozambique since Independence.* Athens: Ohio University Press, 1997.

Hamilton, Russell. "Language and Literature in Portuguese-Writing Africa." *Portuguese Studies* 2 (1986): 196–207.

———. *Literatura Africana, Literatura Necessária.* 2 vols. Lisboa: Edições 70, 1981/1984.

———. *Voices from an Empire: A History of Afro-Portuguese Literature.* Minneapolis: University of Minnesota Press, 1975.

Hanlon, Joseph. *Mozambique: The Revolution Under Fire.* London: Zed Books, 1984.

Hardt, Michael and Antonio Negri. *Empire.* Cambridge: Harvard University Press, 2000.

Harries, Patrick. "Discovering Languages: The Historical Origins of Standard Tsonga in Southern Africa." In *Language and Social History: Studies in South African Sociolinguistics,* edited by Rajend Mesthrie, 154–75. Johannesburg: David Philip, 1995.

Harris, Anne Singer. *Living with Paradox: An Introduction to Jungian Psychology.* Pacific Grove, CA: Cole Publishing, 1996.

Harvey, David. *The Condition of Postmodernity: An Inquiry into the Origins of Cultural Change.* Oxford: Blackwell, 1989.

Hegel, G. W. F. *Hegel's Philosophy of Nature Being Part Two of the Encyclopaedia of the Philosophical Sciences (1830) Translated from Nicolin and Pöggeler's Edition (1959) and from the Zusätze in Michelet's Text (1847).* Translated by A. V. Miller. Oxford: Clarendon Press, 1970.

———. *The Phenomenology of Mind.* Translated by J. B. Baillie. 2 vols. London: Swan Sonnenschein, 1910.

———. *The Philosophy of History.* Translated by J. Sibree. Edited by C. J. Friedrich. New York: Dover Publications, 1956.

Henriksen, Thomas H. *Mozambique: A History.* London: Rex Collings, 1978.

Herculano, Alexandre. *Eurico, O Presbítero.* 5th ed. Mem Martins: Publicações Europa América, 1994.

Herder, I. G. von. *Treatise upon the Origin of Language, Translated from the German of I. G. von Herder.* [n. translator]. London: Messrs Longman, Rees, Orme, Brown and Green, 1827.

Herrick, Alison Butler, et al. *An Area Handbook for Mozambique.* Washington DC: American University, 1969.

Heywood, Vernon H., ed. *Popular Encyclopedia of Plants.* Cambridge: Cambridge University Press, 1982.

Hirschkop, Ken. "Introduction: Bakhtin and Cultural Theory." In *Bakhtin and Cultural Theory,* edited by Ken Hirschkop and David Shepherd, 1–38. Manchester: Manchester University Press, 1989.

Hume, Cameron. *Ending Mozambique's War: The Role of Mediation and Good Offices.* Washington DC: United States Institute of Peace Press, 1994.

Isaacman, Allen. *A Luta Continua: Creating a New Society in Mozambique.* Binghamton: SUNY, 1978.

————. *Cotton Is the Mother of Poverty: Peasants, Work, and Rural Struggle in Colonial Mozambique, 1938–1961.* London: James Currey, 1996.

————. *Mozambique, the Africanization of a European Institution: The Zambesi Prazos, 1750–1902.* Madison: University of Winsconsin Press, 1972.

Isaacman, Allen and Barbara Isaacman. *Mozambique: From Colonialism to Revolution, 1900–1982.* Boulder: Westview Press, 1983.

————. *The Tradition of Resistance in Mozambique: The Zambesi Valley, 1850–1921.* Berkeley: University of California Press, 1976.

Ishemo, Shubi Lugemalila. *The Lower Zambezi Basin in Mozambique: A Study in Economy and Society, 1850–1920.* Aldershot, England: Avebury, 1995.

Jamba, Sousa. "Out of Lusophone Africa: The Situation of Writers in Angola and Mozambique." *Times Literary Supplement* (17 October 1997): 29.

Jobim, José Luís, and Roberto Acízelo de Souza. *Iniciação à Literatura Brasileira.* Rio: AO Livro Técnico, 1987.

Jouanneau, Daniel. *Le Mozambique.* Paris: Éditions Karthala, 1995.

Jung, C. G. *Dream Analysis: Part I, Notes of the Seminar Given in 1928–1930 by C. G. Jung.* Edited by William McGuire. London: Routledge, 1995.

————. *The Basic Writings of C. G. Jung.* Translated by R. F. C. Hull. Edited by Violet S. de Laszlo. Princeton: Princeton University Press, 1990.

Kay, Hugh. *Salazar and Modern Portugal.* London: Eyre and Spottiswoode, 1970.

King, Bruce. *New National and Post-Colonial Literatures: An Introduction.* Oxford: Clarendon Press, 1996.

Knopfli, Rui. *A Ilha de Próspero: Roteiro Poético da Ilha de Moçambique.* 2nd ed. Lisboa: Edições 70, 1989.

Laban, Michel. *Moçambique: Encontro com Escritores.* 3 vols. Porto: Fundação Eng. António de Almeida, 1998.

Lacan, Jacques. *Écrits: A Selection.* Translated by Alan Sheridon. New York: Norton, 1977.

————. *The Four Fundamental Concepts of Psycho-Analysis.* Translated by Alan Sheridan. Edited by Jacques-Alain Miller. London: Penguin Books, 1994.

Laclos, Choderlos de. *Les Liaisons Dangereuses.* Paris: Garnier, 1858.

Lapa, Rodrigues, ed. *Quadros da História Trágico-marítima.* 3rd ed. Lisboa: Bertrand, 1956.

Laranjeira, Pires. *Literaturas Africanas de Expressão Portuguesa.* Lisboa: Universidade Aberta, 1995.

————. "Mia Couto: Sonhador de Lembranças, Inventor de Verdades." *Letras e Letras* 100 (1993): 43–45.

Leiste, Doris. "Aspekte der lexikalischen Entwicklung des Portugiesischen in Mosambik." In *Studien zum Portugiesischen in Afrika und Asien,* edited by Matthias Perl and Axel Schönberger, 39–48. Frankfurt: TFM, 1991.

Leite, Ana Mafalda. *Oralidades e Escritas nas Literaturas Africanas.* Lisboa: Edições Colibri, 1998.

————. "Os Temas do Mar em Algumas Narrativas Africanas de Língua Portuguesa: Insularidade e Viagem." In *La Lusophonie: Voies/Voix Oceaniques,* edited by Anne Quataert and Maria Fernanda Afonso, 251–56. Lisboa: Lidel, 2000.

Lemaire, Ria. "Re-reading *Iracema:* The Problem of the Representation of Women in the Construction of a National Brazilian Identity." *Luso-Brazilian Review* 26.2 (Winter 1989): 59–73.

Lemos, Virgílio de. *Eroticus Moçambicanus.* Rio de Janeiro: Nova Fronteira, 1999.

Leonardo, Micaela di, ed. *Gender at the Crossroads of Knowledge: Feminist Anthropology in the Postmodern Era.* Berkeley: University of California Press, 1991.

Lepecki, Maria Lúcia. "Mia Couto, *Vozes Anoitecidas,* O Acordar." In *Sobreimpressões: Estudos de Literatura Portuguesa e Africana,* 175–178. Lisboa: Caminho, 1988.

Lévi-Strauss, Claude. *Tristes Tropiques.* Paris: Plon, 1955.

———. *A World on the Wane.* Translated by John Russell. London: Hutchinson, 1961.

Linguanti, Elsa, Francesco Casotti, and Carmen Concilio, eds. *Coterminous Worlds: Magical Realism and Contemporary Post-Colonial Literature in English.* Amsterdam: Rodopi, 1999.

Lisboa, Eugénio. "Carta de Moçambique." *Colóquio Letras* 6 (1972): 67–70.

———. "Inquérito." *Colóquio Letras* 21 (1974): 9–10.

Lisboa, Maria Manuel. "Colonial Crosswords: (In)voicing the Gap in Mia Couto." In *Postcolonial Perspectives on the Cultures of Latin America and Lusophone Africa,* edited by Robin Fiddian, 190–212. Liverpool: Liverpool University Press, 2000.

Long-Innes, Chesca. "The Psychopathology of Post-colonial Mozambique: Mia Couto's *Voices Made Night.*" *American Imago* 55.1 (1998): 155–84.

López, Alfred J. *Posts and Pasts: A Theory of Postcolonialism.* Albany: State University of New York Press, 2001.

Loraux, Nicole. *The Experiences of Tiresias: The Feminine and the Greek Man.* Translated by Paula Wissing. Princeton: Princeton University Press, 1995.

Lorber, Judith. *Paradoxes of Gender.* New Haven: Yale University Press, 1994.

Louro, João. "Mia Couto: O Mito e a Realidade." *Jornal de Letras, Artes e Ideias* (11 February 1992): 6.

Luandino Vieira, José. *Nós, Os do Makulusu.* 3rd ed. Luanda: União dos Escritores Angolanos, 1989.

Lyotard, Jean-François. *Postmodern Fables.* Translated by Georges Van Den Abbeele. Minneapolis: University of Minnesota Press, 1997.

———. *The Postmodern Condition: A Report on Knowledge.* Translated by Geoff Bennington and Brian Massumi. Minneapolis: University of Minnesota Press, 1984.

Machel, Samora Moisés. *A Nossa Luta.* 2nd ed. Maputo: Imprensa Nacional de Moçambique, 1975.

Maja-Pearce, Adewale. "Mia Couto: Lack of Access Makes the Press More Bureaucratic." *Index on Censorship* 19.5 (May 1990): 28.

Martinho, Fernando J. B. "A América na Poesia de Rui Knopfli." In *Literaturas Africanas de Língua Portuguesa: Compilação das Comunicações Apresentadas durante o Colóquio sobre Literaturas dos Países Africanos de Língua Portuguesa Realizado na Sala Polivalente do Centro de Arte Moderno em Julho de 1985,* edited by Manuel Ferreira, 119–37. Lisboa: Fundação Calouste Gulbenkian, 1987.

Matusse, Gilberto. *A Construção da Imagem de Moçambicanidade em José Craveirinha, Mia Couto e Ungulani Ba Ka Khosa.* Maputo: Universidade Eduardo Mondlane, 1998.

Maxwell, Kenneth. *Pombal: Paradox of the Enlightenment.* Cambridge: Cambridge University Press, 1995.

Melo, João de. "Ualalapi e a Literatura Moçambicana." *Jornal de Letras, Artes e Ideias* (2 July 1991): 13.

Mendonça, Fátima. *Literatura Moçambicana: A História e as Escritas.* Maputo: Universidade Eduardo Mondlane, 1988.

Mestre, David. *Lusografias Crioulas.* Évora: Pendor, 1997.

Minter, William. *Portuguese Africa and the West.* Harmondsworth: Penguin Books, 1972.

Momplé, Lília. *Ninguém Matou Suhura.* Maputo, Associação dos Escritores Moçambicanos, 1988.

———. *Os Olhos da Cobra Verde.* Maputo, Associação dos Escritores Moçambicanos, 1997.

Mondlane, Eduardo. *The Struggle for Mozambique.* London: Zed Books, 1983.

Morozzo della Rocca, Roberto. *Moçambique da Guerra à Paz: História de uma Mediação Insólita.* Translated by Brazão Mazula. Maputo: Universidade Eduardo Mondlane, 1998.

Moser, Gerald. "A Daring Initiative: Starting a Periodical in Wartime Mozambique." *Luso-Brazilian Review* 34.2 (Winter 1997): 123–26.

———. *Essays in Portuguese-African Literature.* University Park: Pennsylvania State University Press, 1969.

Moser, Gerald, and Manuel Ferreira. *A New Bibliography of the Lusophone Literatures of Africa.* London: Hans Zell, 1993.

Mourão, Fernando. *Contistas Angolanos.* Lisboa: Casa dos Estudantes do Império, 1960.

Munslow, Barry. *Mozambique: The Revolution and Its Origins.* New York: Longman, 1983.

Neto, Agostinho. "Náusea." In *Contistas Angolanos,* edited by Fernando Mourão, 56–59. Lisboa: Casa dos Estudantes do Império, 1960.

Newitt, Malyn. *A History of Mozambique.* London: Hurst, 1995.

———. "Mozambique." In *A History of Postcolonial Lusophone Africa,* edited by Patrick Chabal, 185–235. Bloomington: Indiana University Press, 2002.

———. *Portugal in Africa: The Last Hundred Years.* Harlow: Longman, 1981.

Ngugi wa Thiong'o. *Decolonising the Mind: The Politics of Language in African Literature.* London: James Currey, 1986.

———. *Devil on the Cross, Translated from the Gikuyu by the Author.* London: Heinemann, 1982.

Nietzsche, Friedrich. *Basic Writings of Nietzsche.* Translated and edited by Walter Kaufmann. New York: Modern Library, 1966.

———. *Philosphy and Truth: Selections from Nietzsche's Notebooks of the Early 1870's.* Translated and edited by Daniel Breazeale. Sussex: Harvester Press, 1979.

———. *Thus Spoke Zarathustra: A Book for Everyone and No One.* Translated by R. J. Hollingdale. Harmondsworth: Penguin, 1961.

Noa, Francisco. *A Escrita Infinita.* Maputo: Universidade Eduardo Mondlane, 1998.

Nunes, Maria Luisa. *Becoming True to Ourselves: Cultural Decolonization and National Identity in the Literature of the Portuguese-Speaking World.* New York: Greenwood Press, 1987.

Ochshorn, Judith. "Sumer: Gender, Gender Roles, Gender Role Reversals." In *Gender Reversals and Gender Cultures: Anthropological and Historical Perspectives,* edited by Sabrina Petra Ramet, 52–65. London: Routledge, 1996.

Oliveira, Teresa Roza. "Mia Couto Entrevistado." *Letras e Letras* 90 (1993): 6.

Oliveira Martins. *Portugal nos Mares.* 2 vols. Lisboa: Guimarães & Ca Editores, 1954.

Ong, Walter J. *Orality and Literacy: The Technologizing of the Word.* London: Methuen, 1982.

————. *The Presence of the Word: Some Prolegomena for Cultural and Religious History.* New Haven: Yale University Press, 1967.

Onyewuenyi, Innocent Chilaka. *The African Origin of Greek Philosophy: An Exercise in Afrocentrism.* Nsukka: University of Nigeria Press, 1993.

Ornelas, José N. "Mia Couto no Contexto da Literatura Pós-colonial de Moçambique." *Luso-Brazilian Review* 33.2 (Winter 1996): 37–52.

Padilha, Laura Cavalcante. *Novos Pactos, Outras Ficções: Ensaios Sobre Literaturas Afro-luso-brasileiras.* Porto Alegre: EDIPUCRS, 2002.

Parekh, Pushpa Naidu, and Siga Fatima Jagne, eds. *Postcolonial African Writers: A Bio-bibliographical Critical Source Book.* Westport, CT: Greenwood Press, 1998.

Parker, Andrew, and Eve Kosofsky Sedgwick, eds. *Performativity and Performance.* New York: Routledge, 1995.

Payne, Stanley G. *A History of Spain and Portugal.* 2 vols. Madison: University of Winsconsin Press, 1973.

Pechey, Graham. "On the Borders of Bakhtin: Dialogisation, Decolonisation." In *Bakhtin and Cultural Theory,* edited by Ken Hirschkop and David Shepherd, 39–67. Manchester: Manchester University Press, 1989.

Pélessier, René. *Le Naufrage des Caravelles: Études sur la Fin de l'Empire Portugais, 1961– 1975.* Montamets: Editions Pelissier, 1979.

Pepetela. *A Geração da Utopia.* Lisboa: Dom Quixote, 1992.

————. *Mayombe.* 3rd ed. Lisboa: Edições 70, 1988.

————. *O Desejo de Kianda.* Lisboa: Dom Quixotes, 1995.

Peres, Phyllis. *Transculturation and Resistance in Lusophone African Narrative.* Gainesville: University of Florida Press, 1997.

Pessoa, Fernando. *Antologia Poética.* Edited by Isabel Pascoal. Lisboa: Ulisseia, 1992.

————. *Livro do Desassossego por Bernardo Soares.* Edited by Jacinto do Prado Coelho. 2 vols. Lisboa, Ática, 1982.

————. *Mensagem e Outros Poemas Afins.* Edited by António Quadros. 2nd ed. Mem Martins: Publicações Europa-América, [n.d.].

————. "O Marinheiro: Drama Estático em um Quadro." In *Orpheu: Edição Facsimilada,* 27–39. Lisboa: Contexto, 1989.

————. *Portugal, Sebastianismo e Quinto Império.* Edited by António Quadros. Mem Martins: Publicações Europa-América, 1986.

————. *Sobre Portugal: Introdução ao Problema Nacional.* Edited by Joel Serrão. Lisboa: Ática, 1978.

Plato. *Phaedrus.* Translated and edited by C. J. Rowe. Warminster: Aris and Phillips, 1986.

————. *Timaeus.* Translated and edited by John Warrington. London: Dent, 1965.

Poe, Edgar Allan. "The Purloined Letter." In his *Selected Prose, Poetry, and Eureka,* edited by W. H. Auden, 95–115. New York: Holt, Reinhart and Winston, 1950.

Pratas, Fernanda. "Ler o Mundo de Muito Perto." *Público* (2 June 2001): XIS 27.

Quadros António [Frei Ioannes Garabatus]. *As Quybyrycas.* Porto: Afrontamento, 1991.

Quan, Julian. *Mozambique: A Cry for Peace.* Oxford: Oxfam, 1987.

Quataert, Anne, and Maria Fernanda Afonso, eds. *La Lusophonie: Voies/Voix Oceaniques.* Lisboa: Lidel, 2000.

Ramet, Sabrina Petra. "Gender Reversals and Gender Cultures: An Introduction." In *Gender Reversals and Gender Cultures: Anthropological and Historical Perspectives,* edited by Sabrina Petra Ramet, 1–21. London: Routledge, 1996.

Ramos, Ricardo, ed. *Contos Moçambicanos.* São Paulo: Global, 1990.

Rank, Otto, *The Myth of the Birth of the Hero: A Psychological Interpretation of Mythology.* Translated by F. Robbins and Smith Ely Jelliffe. New York: The Journal of Nervous and Mental Diseases Publishing Company, 1914.

Ribeiro, Anabela Mota. "Entrevista: Mia Couto." *Diário de Notícias* [Suplemento] (15 May 1999): 10–15.

Ribeiro, Luis Filipe. *Mulheres de Papel: Um Estudo do Imaginário em José de Alencar e Machado de Assis.* Niterói: EDUFF, 1996.

Rocha, Ilídio. "Cronicando." *Jornal de Letras, Artes e Ideias* (22 August 1989): 12.

Rodolfo, Francisco. "Guitonga, Alfabetização e Números." *Savana* (13 October 1995): 9.

Rosário, Lourenço. "A Oralidade através da Escrita na Voz Africana." In *Literaturas Africanas de Língua Portuguesa: Compilação das Comunicações Apresentadas durante o Colóquio sobre Literaturas dos Países Africanos de Língua Portuguesa Realizado na Sala Polivalente do Centro de Arte Moderno em Julho de 1985,* edited by Manuel Ferreira, 181–89. Lisboa: Fundação Calouste Gulbenkian, 1987.

Rose, Gillian. *Dialectic of Nihilism: Post-Structuralism and Law.* Oxford: Blackwell, 1984.

Rothblatt, Martine. *The Apartheid of Sex: A Manifesto for the Freedom of Gender.* London: Harper Collins, 1995.

Rui, Manuel. *Memória de Mar.* Lisboa: Edições 70, 1980.

————. *Quem Me Dera Ser Onda.* 5th ed. Lisboa: Cotovia, 1991.

Rushdie, Salman. "The Empire Writes Back With a Vengeance." *The Times* (3 July 1982): 8.

Sachs, Albie. "Introduction." In *Short Stories from Mozambique,* edited by Richard Bartlett, 9–17. Johannesburg: Cosaw Publishing, 1995.

Sadler, Ted. *Nietzsche: Truth and Redemption, Critique of the Postmodernist Nietzsche.* London: Athlone, 1995.

Saraiva, José Hermano. *História de Portugal.* 3rd ed. Mem Martins: Publicações Europa América, 1993.

Sarney, José. "Carta de Amor à Língua Portuguesa." *Jornal de Letras, Artes e Ideias* (7 April 1999): 10.

Sarup, Madan. *An Introductory Guide to Post-Structuralism and Postmodernism.* 2nd ed. Athens: University of Georgia Press, 1993.

Saussure, Ferdinand de. *Course in General Linguistics.* Translated by Wade Baskin. Edited by Charles Bally, Albert Sechehaye and Albert Reidlinger. London: Peter Owen, 1960.

Saúte, Nelson. "A Fatalidade da Ficção Moçambicana." *Jornal de Letras, Artes e Ideias* (14 August 1990): 8.

————. "A Nova Geração de Escritores Moçambicanos." *Jornal de Letras, Artes e Ideias* (6 March 1990): 25.

————. "A Reinvenção da Língua Portuguesa." *Vértice* 55 (1993): 75–76.

————, ed. *As Mãos dos Pretos: Antologia do Conto Moçambicano.* Lisboa: Dom Quixote, 2000.

————. "Carta de Moçambique." *Colóquio Letras* 119 (1991): 209–211.

————. "Intelectuais Moçambicanos Preocupados: Língua Portuguesa em Perigo." *Jornal de Letras, Artes e Ideias* (27 July 1993): 4–5.

————. "Mia Couto: 'Escrevo por Mãos de Outros.'" *Jornal de Letras, Artes e Ideias* (13 August 1991): 10–11.

————. "Mia Couto: Disparar contra o Tempo." *Jornal de Letras, Artes e Ideias* (12 January 1993): 9–10. [The date on some of the inside pages of this issue, including pages 9 and 10, is misprinted as 12 January 1992].

————. "Moçambique: Prémios Nacionais de Poesia e Ficção." *Jornal de Letras, Artes e Ideias* (5 February 1991): 5.

————. "O Escritor Moçambicano e a Língua Portuguesa." *Jornal de Letras, Artes e Ideias* (9 January 1990): 16–17.

Scott, Joan Wallach. *Gender and the Politics of History.* Revised ed. New York: Columbia University Press, 1999.

Secco, Carmen L. T. "De Mares, Exílios, Fronteiras." In *La Lusophonie: Voies/Voix Oceaniques,* edited by Anne Quataert and Maria Fernanda Afonso, 288–94. Lisboa: Lidel, 2000.

————. "O Mar e Os Marulhos da Memória na Ficção do Angolano Manuel Rui." *Estudos Portugueses e Africanos* 2:1 (1993): 59–65.

Sedgwick, Eve Kosofsky. *Epistemology of the Closet.* Berkeley: University of California Press, 1990.

Seixo, Maria Alzira. "Mia Couto: Olhares sobre o Mundo." *Jornal de Letras, Artes e Ideias* (19 June 1996): 22–23.

Sena, Jorge de. *The Poetry of Jorge de Sena: A Bilingual Selection.* Edited by Frederick G. Williams. Santa Barbara, CA: Mudborn Press, 1980.

Shapiro, Judith. "Transsexualism: Reflections on the Persistence of Gender and the Mutability of Sex." In *Body Guards: The Cultural Politics of Gender Ambiguity,* edited by Julia Epstein and Kristina Straub, 248–79. London: Routledge, 1991.

Shore, Herbert. "Resistance and Revolution in the Life of Eduardo Mondlane." In *The Struggle for Mozambique,* Eduardo Mondlane, xiii–xxxi. London: Zed Books, 1983.

Silva, Rodrigues da. "Entrevista, Mia Couto: Antes de Tudo, a Vida." *Jornal de Letras, Artes e Ideias* (10 March 1999): 7–9.

———. "Mia Couto: Um Escritor Abensonhado." *Jornal de Letras, Artes e Ideias* (17 August 1994): 14–16.

Smyth, Gerry. "The Politics of Hybridity: Some Problems with Crossing the Border." In *Comparing Postcolonial Literatures,* edited by Ashok Bery and Patricia Murray, 43–55. New York: St Martin's Press, 2000.

Soares, Mário. "Português, Língua de Afecto e de Liberdade." *Jornal de Letras, Artes e Ideias* (6 March 1990): 28–29.

Soler, Isabel. "Narrativa Portuguesa." *Cuadernos Hispanoamericanos* (October 1998): 123–25.

Sousa Santos, Boaventura de. *Pela Mão de Alice: O Social e o Político na Pós-modernidade.* Porto: Afrontamento, 1994.

Southern African Development Community. *Mozambique in the Commonwealth.* Maputo: Southern African Research and Documentation Centre, 1997.

Stoler, Ann Laura. "Carnal Knowledge and Imperial Power: Gender, Race, and Morality in Colonial Asia." In *Gender at the Crossroads of Knowledge: Feminist Anthropology in the Postmodern Era,* edited by Micaela di Leonardo, 51–101. Berkeley: University of California Press, 1991.

Stoller, Robert J. *Presentations of Gender.* New Haven: Yale University Press, 1985.

———. *Sex and Gender: On the Development of Masculinity and Femininity.* London: Hogarth Press, 1968.

Subrahmanyam, Sanjay. *The Career and Legend of Vasco da Gama.* Cambridge: Cambridge University Press, 1997.

Synge, Richard. *Mozambique: UN Peacekeeping in Action, 1992–1994.* Washington DC: United States Institute of Peace Press, 1997.

Todorov, Tzvetan, *Mikhail Bakhtin: The Dialogic Principle.* Translated by Wlad Godzich. Manchester: Manchester University Press, 1984.

Unamuno, Miguel de. *Escritos de Unamuno sobre Portugal.* Edited by Angel Marcos de Dios. Paris: Fundação Calouste Gulbenkian, 1985.

———. *Por Tierras de Portugal y de España.* Madrid: Biblioteca Renacimiento, 1911.

Unicef Mozambique. *The Situation of Children and Women in Mozambique.* Maputo: Unicef, 1993.

Utéza, Francis. "Mia Couto: 'A Princesa Russa' ou au Nom de la Mère." *Quadrant* 11 (1994): 129–48.

Vail, Leroy, and Landeg White. *Capitalism and Colonialism in Mozambique: A Study of Quelimane District.* Minneapolis: University of Minnesota Press, 1980.

Venâncio, José Carlos. *Literatura e Poder na África Lusofona.* Lisboa: Imprensa Nacional, 1992.

Venâncio, Moisés. "Can Peace-keeping Be Said to Have Worked in Mozambique? Bye Bye Onumoz." In *War and Peace in Mozambique,* edited by Stephen Chan and Moisés Venâncio, 98–116. New York: St Martin's Press, 1998.

Vieira, António. *História do Futuro.* Edited by Maria Leonor Carvalhão Buescu. Lisboa: INCM, 1982.

Vines, Alex. *Renamo: Terrorism in Mozambique.* London: James Currey, 1991.

Waterhouse, Rachel, and Cari Vijfhuizen, eds. *Strategic Women, Gainful Men: Gender, Land and Natural Resources in Different Rural Contexts in Mozambique.* Maputo: Universidade Eduardo Mondlane, 2001.

White, Eduardo. *Poemas da Ciência de Voar e da Engenharia de Ser Ave.* Lisboa: Caminho, 1992.

Wield, David. "Mine Labour and Peasant Production in Southern Mozambique." In *Mozambique: Proceedings of a Seminar Held in the Centre of African Studies, University of Edinburgh, 1–2 December 1978,* [n. ed.], 78–85. Edinburgh: University of Edinburgh, 1978.

Zabus, Chantal. "Language, Orality, and Literature." In *New National and Post-Colonial Literatures: An Introduction,* edited by Bruce King, 29–44. Oxford: Clarendon Press, 1996.

———. *The African Palimpsest: Indigenization of Language in the West African Europhone Novel.* Atlanta: Rodopi, 1991.

Zamora, Lois Parkinson, and Wendy B. Faris. *Magical Realism: Theory, History, Community.* Durham, N.C.: Duke University Press, 1995.

Zand, Nicole. "D'Autre Mondes." *Le Monde* (9 December 1994): II.

Index